T0010942

# SONIC BOOM

### THE IMPOSSIBLE RISE OF WARNER BROS. RECORDS, FROM HENDRIX TO FLEETWOOD MAC TO MADONNA TO PRINCE

## Peter Ames Carlin

Henry Holt and Company  New York

Henry Holt and Company
*Publishers since 1866*
120 Broadway
New York, New York 10271
www.henryholt.com

Henry Holt® and ® are registered trademarks of Macmillan Publishing Group, LLC.

Library of Congress Cataloging-in-Publication Data

Names: Carlin, Peter Ames, author.
Title: Sonic boom : the impossible rise of Warner Bros Records, from
    Hendrix to Fleetwood Mac to Madonna to Prince / Peter Ames Carlin.
Description: First edition. | New York : Henry Holt and Company, 2021. |
    Includes bibliographical references and index.
Identifiers: LCCN 2020034793 (print) | LCCN 2020034794 (ebook) |
    ISBN 9781250301567 (hardcover) | ISBN 9781250301574 (ebook)
Subjects: LCSH: Warner Bros. Records—History. | Sound recording
    industry—History.
Classification: LCC ML3792.W37 C37 2021 (print) | LCC ML3792.W37
    (ebook) | DDC 338/.76178164—dc23
LC record available at https://lccn.loc.gov/2020034793
LC ebook record available at https://lccn.loc.gov/2020034794

Our books may be purchased in bulk for promotional, educational,
or business use. Please contact your local bookseller or the Macmillan
Corporate and Premium Sales Department at (800) 221-7945, extension
5442, or by e-mail at MacmillanSpecialMarkets@macmillan.com.

First Edition 2021

Designed by Meryl Sussman Levavi

Printed in the United States of America

1   3   5   7   9   10   8   6   4   2

*To my parents, Albert and Ellen Carlin*

*"I'm in love—what's that song?*
*I'm in love—with that song."*

—"Alex Chilton"
(Chris Mars/Paul Westerberg/Tommy Stinson)

# CONTENTS

1 ● *SONG CYCLE*　1

2 ● WELCOME TO THE CHALET　13

3 ● WARNER BROS. RECORDS:
TERRIBLY SOPHISTICATED SONGS　19

4 ● REPRISE RECORDS:
NEWER, HAPPIER, EMANCIPATED　39

5 ● WARNER/REPRISE:
A  QUITE UNLOSABLE GAME　53

6 ● CHRISTMAS AND NEW YEAR'S AND
YOUR BIRTHDAY ALL TOGETHER　67

7 ● ONCE YOU GET USED TO IT,
HIS VOICE IS REALLY SOMETHING　84

8 ● HOW CAN WE BREAK THE RULES TODAY?　109

9 ● THE GOLD DUST TWINS　125

10 ● THE ROCK MORALITY　146

11 ● IT AIN'T NOTHIN' BUT A WARNER BROS. PARTY   166

12 ● FUCK THE BUNNY   179

13 ● THE NAME OF THE GAME IS PERFORMANCE   195

14 ● JUST GO DO   209

15 ● COMING FOR THE COWBOYS   230

16 ● LOSING MY RELIGION   241

POSTLUDE: ON VINE STREET   247

Notes   251

Bibliography   255

Acknowledgments   257

Index   259

## *SONG CYCLE*

One recent afternoon, I padded upstairs to my bedroom, dug up some legal weed I had stashed in a drawer, and got stoned. It was just after lunch, usually the most productive part of my workday, and the late summer sun illuminated my midday indulgence in clear, withering light. Back in my basement office ten minutes later, I donned my fancy Bose headphones (noise-canceling, consciousness-consuming, sonically perfected to some canine ear degree) and crawled under my desk to escape all other stimuli. I had important work to do. I clicked the Play button on my iTunes, lay down on the floor, and closed my eyes, preparing to hear—I mean *really* hear—Van Dyke Parks's 1967 album, *Song Cycle*, for the first time.

Full disclosure: I've owned a copy of *Song Cycle* for at least twenty years and have listened to it, or tried to, dozens of times. I had known the record's legend for probably twenty years before I bought it, and had come to admire the music in its grooves even as I found it inscrutable and—how can I put this?—an experience that was something other than fun. And I *like* eccentric art. But *Song Cycle* threw me off time after time. It requires your full attention and a willingness to open your ears and your mind, cut loose every expectation of popular music you might possess and let it take you over.

So, I went under my desk. No one else was in the house. The lights were dark, and so was my cell phone. Cut off, I willed the modern world away: the Twitter rage, the sanctity of shareholder value, the desiccated dreams, the institutionalized fuckery, the fact that everything is worse than it's ever been—but when has that *not* been true?

In 1967, Van Dyke Parks, a twenty-four-year-old classically trained composer and pianist with his antennae tuned to the *avant*-most edge of the *garde*, came to his latest opportunity with wild ambitions. Given a multi-album contract with Warner Bros. Records (WBR), a deal that came with a big recording budget, creative control, and no deadline, Parks composed songs for an original album that would marry his intricately orchestrated music with Delphic lyrics invoking the dreams and disasters of America's past while also opening new horizons for musical and spiritual exploration. Like the Beatles' in-progress pop art masterpiece, *Sgt. Pepper's Lonely Hearts Club Band*, and the Beach Boys' unfinished psychedelic/symphonic *Smile*, on which Parks had served as Brian Wilson's collaborator in 1966, Parks's debut album would create its own curiously sparkling world. As Parks and his twenty-five-year-old WBR staff producer Lenny Waronker agreed, they would enter the studio each morning with no guidelines or boundaries. If Parks heard a sound in his head, he and Waronker would work for however long it took, using whatever tools they had or could invent, to capture it on tape.

None of this was normal—not in the popular music business of the mid-1960s, anyway. In 1967, when the top five singles of the year were, in descending order, Lulu's old-school pop hit "To Sir with Love," the Box Tops' straight-rocking "The Letter," Bobbie Gentry's gothic country ballad "Ode to Billie Joe," the Association's romantic "Windy," and the Monkees' pop-rock "I'm a Believer," the vast majority of pop songs could still be recorded, from basic track to vocals to overdubs, before lunch. But that's not what Parks and Waronker intended to do, and it wasn't what the visionary executive reinventing their record company wanted.

After I hit Play, I had time for a deep breath before the rising sound of a bluegrass band filled the emptiness: banjos, strummed guitars, a slide guitar, a string bass, and voices, all clattering through "Black Jack Davy," an ancient American folk song about a scalawag who seduces a proper lady into abandoning her family and taking up with him. The rattletrap fades in fifty seconds, revealing a song within another song. This is "Vine Street," an original tune Parks commissioned from fellow composer, pianist, and newly signed Warner Bros. artist Randy Newman. The scratchy opening vignette blooms into a string quartet and the winsome voice of Parks, as he describes what we've just heard: a tape of his old band, a folk combo of no repute whose members have long since vanished from his life.

Parks's strings leap and tumble, speeding up and slowing down, alluding to eighteenth-century Europe, nineteenth-century ragtime, and the sentimental movie soundtracks of twentieth-century Hollywood, that never-never land where "dreams are still born."

Or is that *stillborn*?

Hmm.

And here comes more, more, more: String sections collide with electronic keyboards, which keep their distance from the Russian violins and balalaikas. Steam locomotives rumble west in one song and then chug eastward through another. There are birds and single-cylinder motors; the dying blast of the *Titanic's basso magnifico* horn; then a tattered verse of "Nearer My God to Thee," artificially Dopplered to portray our movement past the doomed vessel. There are harps, chattering locust percussion, and electronic distortions of Parks's wispy vocals, his words and melodies cloaked in gossamer and subjected to the cardboard tape-yawing device he and Waronker jury-rigged onto the recorder's spindle and dubbed "the Farkle." Also, they sped up almost every song. "I used to speed up everything," Waronker says. "I was taking so much speed back then it just sounded better that way."[1]

Parks was just as keen on high-velocity consciousness, and sometimes the fellows would get so pilled up they'd have to run around the block to calm themselves down between takes. But even when they were high, they were not sloppy. Parks was one of the rare hippie musicians who brought unerring discipline to his galactic explorations. His lyrics—multi-*entendred* musings on life, liberty, and the inevitability of death and failure—are Joycean in their linguistic invention and their Farkled perspective of America and the outer limits of physical and metaphysical existence.

*Song Cycle* clocks in at less than thirty-three minutes, but it's such complicated listening that it can feel like hours. Just try to track the quirky harmonics written into the string charts or all the colliding time signatures, or the way a steam whistle cry jumps off the horn section's melody in the middle of "The All Golden" and is then quickly resolved by the horn's next note. Can you tell if the operatic shriek at the start of "By the People" belongs to a trained soprano or to a theremin wailing through the top of its range? I can't. Then come the church bells and claps of thunder and a fiddle that is part front porch sing-along, part German surrealist horror movie. "Strike up the band brother, hand me another bowl of your soul," Parks and his chorus chirp amid the bells and the light drumming of a rainstorm. "We now are near to the end / If you stay with the show say we all had to go . . ."

Later, I sat in my backyard blinking in the sunlight. Now it was *Song Cycle* that had me spinning. The inventiveness, the skirting of the impossible, the Farkling of reality by a pair of ambitious youngsters with more daring than common sense. So, what were they doing in the employ of a major American entertainment corporation?

To Mo Ostin, then the chief of the Reprise half of Warner/Reprise Records, *Song Cycle* was the living example of the albums he wanted his record label to be producing. This was in 1967 when Ostin was first in the position to put his imprimatur on the record company he'd been managing for nearly a decade. Forty years old and only just beyond the dark suits and skinny striped ties of the midcentury executive, Ostin had neither the look nor the spirit of a radical. He'd come up in the music business through the widely admired jazz label Verve Records in the 1950s and was tapped by Frank Sinatra to run his about-to-launch boutique label, Reprise, in 1960. When the singer sold his company to Warner Bros. Pictures tycoon Jack Warner in 1963, Reprise merged with Warner Bros. Records in a new company called Warner/Reprise. The conjoined labels ran mostly independently from one another, with Ostin at the fore of Reprise while WB's Joe Smith performed the same duty at Warner Bros. The pair of execs came from different backgrounds and had very different personalities, but in the mid-1960s both had been quick to recognize that society, and particularly popular music, was on the verge of a significant shift.

If you were listening in 1966, you could hear it growing: in the increasingly esoteric songs of the Beatles, in the literary nuance of Simon and Garfunkel's lyrics, in the Howlin' Wolf–meets–Ornette Coleman psychedelia of the Grateful Dead and so many other glitter-eyed bands lighting up the night in San Francisco. And you heard it not just in the music but also in all that other sixties business, in the don't-trust-anyone-over-thirty stuff; the smash-the-stateism; the tune in, turn on, drop outedness; the *everybody get together and try to love one another right now* of it all.

The New Youth, as music critic and cultural observer Ralph J. Gleason called them, wanted the world and they wanted it now. And it seemed like a reasonable demand. It wasn't like their parents were doing anything worthwhile with it.

In the circle of hip young artists in Los Angeles in the mid-1960s, Van Dyke Parks was always somewhere near the center. Most of the L.A. scenesters, the Roger McGuinns and David Crosbys, the Peter Fondas and so on, knew him best for being Brian Wilson's collaborator for the Beach Boys' mysteriously shelved psychedelic masterpiece *Smile* and for his contributions to the Byrds and Buffalo Springfield. He had charisma and could often be found delivering magnetic disquisitions on philosophy, history, and the pursuit of transcendent consciousness. Chicks dug that sort of thing, and Parks dug chicks, none more than his artist wife, Durrie. Parks was impish, five foot eight on a good day, with the paisley-and-tweed look of a stylish PhD candidate. Smart, talented, and handsome, the baby-faced post-collegiate Parks also had a life on him that you would not believe.

Born to a psychiatrist and English teacher and raised in Lake Charles, Louisiana, Van Dyke had spent his grade school years developing a crystalline falsetto perfect enough to earn him a slot as a soloist in the American Boychoir. Attending the group's boarding school in Princeton, New Jersey, Parks paid his tuition by taking jobs in New York City, first as the lead soloist in Arturo Toscanini's 1951 live television production of Gian Carlo Menotti's one-act opera *Amahl and the Night Visitors*. Parks's stage presence earned him a side career in acting, playing a young neighbor on Jackie Gleason's TV sitcom *The Honeymooners*, and then a child on opera singer Ezio Pinza's short-lived family TV show, *Bonino*. The boy spent a summer in Hollywood performing in *The Swan*, a costume drama starring Grace Kelly, Alec Guinness, and Louis Jourdan. No one intimidated him. He'd already met, and sung Christmas carols in the kitchen of the Boychoir's Princeton neighbor Albert Einstein; the genius accompanied the young singers on his fiddle.

After a year studying piano, composition, and arranging at Carnegie Tech (now Carnegie Mellon University), Parks dropped out and joined his older brother Carson in a folk duo they called the Steeltown Two. The brothers moved to Los Angeles in 1962, only to break up their act a year later. Set loose in the recording studios and salons frequented by the city's hippest young musicians, actors, and writers, Parks wrote and/or recorded a few clever singles for MGM, including "Number Nine," a pop interpretation of the central theme in Beethoven's Ninth Symphony, and "High Coin," a sparkling tune that describes the heights of his ambition. "I'm going for high coin baby," he declared.

"I'm fine, it's my time."

Parks never recorded "High Coin" himself, but a handful of other artists did, and when he first heard Skip Battin's version on his car radio, Lenny Waronker, a young record producer who had just taken an Artists and Repertoire (A&R) staff job with Warner/Reprise, lurched his car to the curb to listen closely. *No kid could have written that song*, he thought. But Parks was two years younger than Waronker, and when they met, the two musical adventurers became fast friends and recording studio collaborators.

On the day in late 1966 when Waronker brought Parks to meet Ostin in the Warner/Reprise offices across the street from the movie studio's back lot in Burbank, the erudite artist enraptured the executive like no other musician, save Frank Sinatra, had ever done. Parks wrote great songs, had a unique voice, and could master any instrument. He could write arrangements for rock bands and orchestras, and he thought like a futurist. Eager to get Parks on board in every conceivable capacity, Ostin engaged him not just as a recording artist but also as a studio musician, arranger, and producer. Who knew where Parks's brains, talents, and ambitions would take the company next? When the musician signed the deal on January 5, 1967, Ostin didn't bother hiding his glee. "We thought he was a phenomenon."

The *Song Cycle* recording sessions began in the spring and continued for more than six months, nearly as much time as it would take the Beatles to record *Sgt. Pepper's Lonely Hearts Club Band* and twice as long as it took Brian Wilson to create *Pet Sounds* for the Beach Boys in 1966. The only reason the Beatles could get away with spending that much time in the studio was because they were the most successful rock band in the world. That an artist with no commercial success would be allowed such a Beatle-size privilege was unheard of—except at the new Warner/Reprise, where artists really did come first.

Sometimes Parks would book a dozen or more session musicians and hand out fully composed scores for them all to follow. Other times, he'd call players in one or two at a time and arrange parts as they went along. Still other times, Parks and Waronker would come in alone so the artist could record keyboard tracks, or the two of them could work with sound engineer Lee Herschberg to find new ways to enhance or distort the sound of what they'd already recorded.

Herschberg, already a seasoned engineer with credits on records by Frank Sinatra, Lawrence Welk, Sammy Davis Jr., and many others, remembers the *Song Cycle* sessions as entirely professional: no scarves over the lampshades, no incense burning, and no colored bulbs screwed into the fixtures—only cigarette smoke in the air and the thrum of group creativity, its pitch elevated just a few cycles by the electrified blood running through Parks's and Waronker's veins.

Parks had opted to record for the Warner Bros. Records side of the company, and when its managing director, Joe Smith, came to hear the just-finished album in the fall of 1967, he took in the thirty-three minutes of musical dream logic and gave Waronker a quizzical look.

"*Song Cycle*, huh?"

"Yep."

"So, where are the *songs*?"

The former Top 40 disc jockey turned promotion man turned company leader couldn't hear the record—or he heard it, but he couldn't comprehend its place in the pop music galaxy. But Smith could definitely see how much money Waronker and Parks had spent in the studio: somewhere between $75,000 and $85,000, which at that time made *Song Cycle* the most expensive album in Warner Bros. history. And for all that money, they'd brought him a record that didn't have a single tune Smith could imagine hearing on even the underground radio stations popping up on the scarecly populated FM dial.

Smith left the room muttering and shaking his head. Waronker looked over at a red-faced Parks and waved it off with a casual hand. *Don't worry, man.* There was no way *Song Cycle* wasn't going to be released, Waronker insisted. As it turned out, the producer didn't have to say a word to anyone. When Jac Holzman, founder, president, and chief A&R man of the still-independent folksy-artsy label Elektra Records, came to visit his Burbank colleagues and heard the *Song Cycle* acetate coming from Smith's office, he sat to hear the whole thing. Afterward, when he heard Smith's grousing about the thing's weirdness, the fucking *eighty* big ones they'd spent, and the complete absence of commercial outlets willing to promote the thing, he interrupted him with the incredulous response, "You don't want to release *that*? Shit, I'll put it out tomorrow. What do you want for it?"

Smith may not have had the taste for musical adventure that Ostin had just then, but he had the rare capacity to understand that he didn't know everything. He was also aware of Holzman's magical ears. Less than a year earlier, Holzman had picked up on the nearly unknown L.A. band the Doors, who had paid him back instantly by becoming one of the top acts in the United States. And as Smith would admit to anyone, including people who hadn't even asked, he was a Jewish kid from a nowheresville suburb of Boston, who had gotten lucky in radio and even luckier when he got into the record business. Parks was obviously brilliant, Waronker had his nose to the ground, and between those two and now Holzman trying to get his beak into it . . .

"*Oh no,*" Smith said. "We're definitely putting it out. That's a Warner Bros. record. For sure."

On November 1, 1967, Smith got the *Song Cycle* ball rolling with a memo to the company's network of promotions staffers, the local reps who hand-sold Warner Bros. vinyl to record distributors, disc jockeys, record store owners, and anyone else who could push a record into the hearts and minds of cash-carrying citizens. The promo men knew the value of the Next Big Thing, but like all professionals plying a fickle trade, they needed delicate handling, especially when the going got weird.

And handle them is exactly what Smith did in his memo. He started with a comic apology for not seeing them more often. ("I run around with only the top people now. Any night I can be seen with the Grateful Dead and other nice guys.") He ran through some news about Peter, Paul and Mary's new single and coming releases from the Association and Petula Clark before coming to a hard pivot.

"In November we have some strange LPs that will have you wondering if we've all gone on pot and acid out here. However, there are some changes in the business as you have learned and are learning from Arlo Guthrie and the Grateful Dead and etc., and a lot of things make sense now that wouldn't have a while back."

Bracing himself.

"We've got this new genius kid, Van Dyke Parks, with the wildest, most overpowering record I've heard in years. It's very, very, very different and you won't be able to drop it off without some explanation. More on that from us later."

But hey, isn't it almost Christmas?

"Keep going with that good product. It's been a groovy year and we can wind it up big. Talk to you guys soon."[2]

When Waronker played *Song Cycle* for Mo Ostin, Smith's counterpart down the hall all but ordered a crate of champagne. He was still a Sinatra man at heart, but Ostin, who had signed Parks and then honored his whimsical request to have his music released through the Warner Bros. Records side of Warner/Reprise, could also hear how special this outlandish music was. Parks's imagist lyrics had the fractal quality of Pablo Picasso's cubist portraiture (misshapen eyes peering in two directions at once, mouths smiling and sneering at the same time), a reality distorted to the point of being the truest thing you'd ever seen or heard. "We thought we had the next Beatles," Ostin says. He could already anticipate the great reviews *Song Cycle* would get. It was, he insisted, the perfect album for the recalibrated record company: artistically ambitious, wholly unique, entirely beautiful. He was sure it would be a smash, but even if it wasn't, that was nearly beside the point.

Released in early 1968, *Song Cycle* hit the small but growing community of serious pop/rock critics like a burning bush. To the *New Yorker*, Parks's creation was "a milestone in American pop music," words echoed almost exactly by *New York Magazine*, who heard "A Milestone in Pop."

*Time* described the album as "all shimmering beauty." *Jazz & Pop* went all in, hailing it as "the most important, creative and advanced pop recording since *Sgt. Pepper.*" *Esquire* included a wink and a nod with its "High Album of the Year," but *Stereo Review* played it completely straight, designating it as nothing short of the "Record of the Year."

The problem: hardly anyone wanted to *buy* the thing. Even after a year, *Song Cycle*'s sales stayed frozen somewhere around ten thousand copies, which would have been disappointing for an album that cost twenty thousand or even fifteen thousand dollars to make. And given *Song Cycle*'s eighty-K ticket, the situation was . . . well, problematic. So, what do you do with an eighty-thousand-dollar critical smash that can't find an audience?

At Warner/Reprise, that's where Stan Cornyn came in. A Grammy-winning author of liner notes and a publicity wordsmith going back to Warner Bros. Records' first months in 1958, Cornyn had recently been tapped to serve as Warner/Reprise's new director of advertising. The fact that he had never before written an advertisement, and in fact viewed the form with contempt, was not just okay with Ostin and Smith; it was what qualified Cornyn for the job. Ads for pop records, to the extent that they existed, had always been dull. Surely any change at all would be an improvement. And the lately fledged adman did not disappoint.

In pursuit of a public voice to reflect Warner/Reprise's changing identity, Cornyn created an entirely new style of record advertisement. Aimed directly at the educated young record buyers whom Ostin and Smith envisioned as their core audience, Cornyn's first *Song Cycle* ad was published on a full page in *Rolling Stone* and in dozens of the local underground newspapers in early 1969, more than a year after its release. Cornyn divided the page into halves, the top devoted to an enormous headline, which in this case was:

### HOW WE LOST $35,509 ON
### "THE ALBUM OF THE YEAR"
### (DAMMIT)

Here's what we did. Put out Van Dyke Parks' "Song Cycle." Enough said? Hardly.

The next dozen paragraphs not only focused on the artist and his music, but also traced the profile of the new Warner/Reprise, a funky establishment with nothing to hide and even less corporate jive to hide it in. So, first of all, Cornyn wrote, don't bother feeling bad about the company's financial losses. But there was a dynamic at work. "Our Mr. Waronker" was the resident genius in charge of the label's "tough sell stuff," and he'd spared no expense to produce *Song Cycle*. The chorus of ecstatic reviews made it clear that the risk had been worth it.

But, as Cornyn admitted, not everyone was equally excited, particularly not WBR topper Joe Smith.

"Our Mr. Smith takes a jaundiced view of Art. After about a month of tub thumping, Our Mr. Smith shook his head and said, 'Van Dyke's album is such a milestone, it's sailing straight into The Smithsonian Institute, completely bypassing the consumer.'"

But the record really was everything the critics said it was, the ad insisted. "You shouldn't—honestly shouldn't—miss 'The Album of the Year.'"

And one last time, beneath the thumbnail picture of *Song Cycle*'s cover, came the final appeal: IT COST US $48,302.

Other than the fudged price tag for the album, had any record company, or any kind of company, ever been that transparent about how it did business? And when the gambit didn't work, Cornyn published a follow-up:

**Two weeks later,**
**And it still looks black for**
**"The Album of the Year"**

"Two weeks ago, in this very space, we shoved it to you pretty good about Van Dyke Parks' album of the year that lost us $35 thou . . ."

Another litany of blurbs followed, and then a delicious new offer. Fans who already had a copy of *Song Cycle*, and who had undoubtedly worn it out from constant playing, could send it back to Warner/Reprise central in Burbank, and if they included a penny in the envelope, they would receive *two* new copies, one for them and the other for a deserving friend.

"We don't expect a flood of mail on this one," Cornyn noted. "Look, we're already down for $35 thou. But if you feel about Parks as we do, send in your old copy and a penny to Our Mr. Cornyn. He'll get right back to you."

And yet the album refused to budge from the record shop shelves. Parks, meanwhile, was growing increasingly furious: Cornyn, with his ads, was trying to destroy his career! And Smith, for his part, continued to grumble about the *Titanic*-size hole *Song Cycle* had left in his annual budget.

Meanwhile, Mo Ostin applauded and called for everyone to take a bow. A cheer to Lenny Waronker for his bravura talent scouting and producing! To Parks for his beautiful weave of classical music theory and avant-garde experimentalism! And to good old Stan Cornyn for the sweetly satirical ads that not only celebrated the music and the artist but also made clear that Warner/Reprise would be like no other record company, or for-profit American company, that ever existed.

Who would have guessed where it would all lead, or that any one record company, let alone one that set out to ignore so many of the industry's established practices, could sell so many hundreds of millions of records and rake in so many billions of dollars? And it wouldn't be just a flash in the pan, its success limited to the cultural moment of the late 1960s. Warner/Reprise, known eventually as Warner Bros. Records, plain and simple, would remain at or very near the top of its industry for close to thirty years. The company would release culture-altering works by Jimi Hendrix, Joni Mitchell, James Taylor, the Grateful Dead, Neil Young, Fleetwood Mac, Prince, Madonna, Paul Simon, R.E.M., Tom Petty, Van Morrison, U2, the Sex Pistols, Frank Sinatra, Black Sabbath, Arlo Guthrie, and many, many more. All the while, Warner Bros. would boast the most productive and loyal staff in the industry, while also being beloved by artists, record buyers, and even its competitors.

How the devil did they do that?

During its peak era of 1967 through 1994, Warner Bros. Records was in both commercial and creative terms the most successful record company in the history of the music industry. And it all began one afternoon in 1967 when Mo Ostin gave the company's producers the most unexpected instruction ever uttered by a top executive in a corporate record label.

*Let's stop trying to make hit records.*

## WELCOME TO THE CHALET

The first time I crossed the threshold of Warner Bros. Records' Burbank headquarters, I felt like I was coming home. There was music in the air, a warm greeting at the reception desk, and luxuriously broken-in leather sofas deep enough to draw you into a warm embrace. Then I noticed the framed photos, album covers, and other WBR memorabilia lining the walls—a visual history of the company, of American popular culture, and, in an abstract way, of my own life.

It starts with Frank Sinatra and the Everly Brothers; folk music superstars Peter, Paul and Mary; the revolutionary comedy of Bob Newhart, Richard Pryor, Steve Martin; and more. Vaulting into sixties rock 'n' roll with the Kinks, Jimi Hendrix, and the Grateful Dead; and then the singer-songwriter seventies with Neil Young, James Taylor, Joni Mitchell, and Randy Newman, plus Van Morrison and the Doobie Brothers, most of them unknown at the time but all made into stars, and then superstars, and then Rock and Roll Hall of Famers. Step down a few frames, and here come the eighties in a nutshell: Devo, Van Halen, Talking Heads, Dire Straits, the Replacements, Madonna, R.E.M., ZZ Top, Paul Simon's globe-trotting epics *Graceland* and *The Rhythm of the Saints*, and right into the next decade with the Red Hot Chili Peppers and Green Day. And all of it came out of this one company, located since 1975 in this airy palace of redwood, concrete, sparkling glass, and California ease nicknamed the Chalet for its resemblance to a luxe European mountain villa. Here they made albums that sold hundreds of millions, close to a billion, copies, unleashing a vast river of green; and made it look like fun, often like frolic. Because, to paraphrase the company's storied chief writer, adman, and executive Stan Cornyn, the money took them only so far. They were, seriously and truly, in it for the music.

Easier said than done, but that ethos was real at Warner Bros. Records, and not just during the shaggy years, when the company's plurality of offbeat, noncommercial artists made it the commercial nexus of the hippie counterculture. The ethos guided the company from the start of the reign of its beloved chairman Mo Ostin. A successful jazz label executive whose love for the music governed every decision he made, Ostin made the quality of the music, rather than the needs of its finance department, Warner/Reprise's central priority. His philosophy signaled a shift that altered nearly everything about how the company functioned, from how it treated its artists to how it spoke to its customers. Ostin expected his executives and staffers to be as creative and daring as he wanted the artists to be. Established practices were fine for the other record companies, but as Ostin liked to tell his employees, no one at Warner/Reprise needed to follow anyone else's lead: "Why do it their way?"[1]

Back in the present tense, a young woman came out to get me. She was the assistant to Lenny Waronker, now back to working as an Artists and Repertoire staffer, but previously the president of WBR and one of the most admired and successful record company chiefs in the industry. The assistant led me down a flight of stairs to the basement, where the A&R team went about their business of listening to demos from unsigned acts and tracking the work of the company's current artists.

Waronker's office was a small, cluttered space whose company-issued chairs and mini-sofa were overwhelmed by the demo packages, studio mixes of albums in progress, executive memos, press releases, finished CDs and DVDs, thumb drives, and all the other detritus of the music-industrial complex.

See if you can find a place to sit, he said, gesturing toward the sofa. At seventy-two, Waronker was old enough to be the father or even the grandfather of many of his colleagues, but that was one of the reasons he loved being there. He wore jeans and a dark T-shirt beneath a button-up shirt he kept open and untucked. His brown hair has gone mousy gray over the years, but even in his eighth decade, he retained the tentative poise of the uncertain young man he'd been when he started at the company nearly fifty years earlier.

I had come to talk to him about an artist, but the conversation kept wandering back to WBR, the company he'd joined in April 1965. Waronker signed on just in time to witness the end of the era controlled by the original crop of executives, jazz-pop men who had no patience for the pounding racket that had exiled their music, *good* music, to the margins of the sales charts. But while you could knock the rock all you wanted, Daddy-o, there was no holding it back—not if you wanted to be in the record business, anyway.

Hired to be a junior A&R man and record producer, Waronker started his job convinced he would soon be fired. He had produced a handful of records for his dad's indie label, Liberty Records, but he'd never made a hit in his life and had no confidence that he would ever figure out how it was supposed to be done. And as he knew, making hit records was by far the most important thing record producers were supposed to do.

Still, Waronker underestimated his own potential and quickly sent Harpers Bizarre's chamber-pop cover of Simon and Garfunkel's "59th Street Bridge Song (Feelin' Groovy)" to the No. 13 post in *Billboard*'s Hot 100. A chain of Top 40 singles followed over the next few months, but Waronker's real strength turned out to be producing full-length albums, a once-overlooked format that was fast becoming the industry's dominant form.

Back in his office in 2013, Waronker spoke at length and with tangible pride about the company's history. "It's quite a story,"[2] he said. One of his favorite parts took place in 1983, when he agreed, after many years of resisting, to become the president of the record company, a position that made him second only to Ostin, by then the chairman of all of Warner's Los Angeles–based labels and their many subsidiaries. Before he started, Waronker, who knew next to nothing about the nonmusical aspects of running a record company, had asked Ostin to give him a detailed description of everything he was supposed to do and how each task should be done.

Ostin agreed. The two were exceptionally close already, driving to work together and consulting with each other repeatedly and while carpooling home at the end of the day. Still, Waronker set a formal meeting, raiding the supply room for an armload of yellow legal pads and multicolor pens.

Waronker hauled his supplies to Ostin's office, sat across the desk from his boss, and waited for him to start what he figured would be a detailed litany that would continue for hours. To start, Ostin gazed through a window to gather his thoughts. He furrowed his brow. Minutes passed without a word. Finally, Ostin looked straight at Waronker and started to speak. Even now, Waronker could remember every word he said. There weren't very many of them.

"Just go do."[3]

And that was it.

So informed, Waronker started his job as the president of the most successful record company of the rock 'n' roll era. Recalling it for me in the cramped basement office where he currently resided, he laughed and shook his head. "*Just go do.* And that's it, right? I couldn't fucking believe it. He knew I didn't know anything about business. I was terrified. I knew I was going to fall on my face."[4]

But he didn't. Instead, Waronker did exactly as Ostin had hoped, leaving most of the business details to his boss while he kept himself, and the company, focused on music. In many ways, it was the same job he'd been doing as vice president of Artists and Repertoire. But as the president of the label, with more clout at the company than anyone except Mo Ostin himself, Waronker was in a position to put into practice all he had learned from Ostin over the years. He wasn't above wielding the corporate blade when he had to, but he was more likely to be the voice of reassurance when the going got tough. Of course they wanted to have hit records, but that wasn't all they were after, not even in the go-go-go 1980s. Did you produce a flop? Waronker would shrug and ask one question: *Is it good?* And if the answer was "yes," especially if the critics had noticed, Waronker would shrug again: *Then don't worry about it. We can't ever get hurt by making good music.*

Talking to Waronker reminded me of something I hadn't thought about in more than forty years. I grew up in Seattle during the 1960s and '70s, and my parents were hippies of the bourgeois subspecies; my dad ic, polkas, big bands, pop standards recorded with a Caribbean lilt, -key guitar, modernist pop, accordion-laced French pop. Soon they close to a hundred songs ready to go, enough to fill a dozen albums ast. Conkling handed the tracks to his small staff. He'd done the best what he had, and now it was their turn.

As the September release date drew closer, the handful of Warner s gathered in a conference room and tried to make sense of things. could they collect this stuff into albums? And even if they did, how they supposed to package them so customers would want to buy m? They certainly couldn't play the game by ordinary means. But what uld their approach entail? They loosened their ties and folded shirt-ves up over their forearms. The conference room hazed over in smoke. y ordered in dinner. They sent someone out to buy a few bottles of skey. The days stretched into evenings, then nights, then into the wee rs. They struggled and grumbled. They laughed a little, then a lot. eone blazing away on his own all-nighter nearby pounded out a note Conkling: Did he know that his employees were drunk and laughing maniacs in the middle of the night? Well, he knew now. Maybe they ld close the windows.

A kid they'd just hired, this tall, blond fellow who wrote liner notes, ss releases, and the like, turned out to be a real crack-up. His name was n Cornyn, a recent Pomona College graduate who had quit an editorial at Capitol Records because his boss was too strict about the rules of nctuation. Smart, a trifle conceited but charming enough to take the ng out of it, Cornyn picked up on the badinage around him and felt mpletely at home. Given a collection of big band instrumentals fea-ring guitar, the secret product of the guitarist Alvino Rey, Cornyn was arged with inventing a memorable album title, a nearly as memorable tist name, and liner notes that would make the whole package come ve. What he came up with was, indeed, truly distinctive. Titled *Music for ople with $3.98 Plus Tax (If Any)*, the album proclaimed itself the debut Ira Ironstrings, introduced in Cornyn's liner notes as an outsize char-ter glowing like neon across the moribund big band scene. His record, ornyn wrote, "is a bromide (alka seltzer, dad) in a mirthless musical aelstrom. It's music to dance to in your living room, music to warm to n a rainy night, or music, as Ira puts it, 'to listen, for cryin' out loud!'"

was a research psychologist at the University of Washington who stud-ied the effects of marijuana on its users' consciousness, while my mom worked at a freaky art school near campus. When they participated in peace marches, my brother and I went on parade, too, sweet-faced tykes thrusting War Is Not Healthy for Children and Other Living Things plac-ards above our heads. They ordered the whole-wheat crust at the Yellow Submarine pizza parlor and took us to puppet shows in Volunteer Park that made Punch and Judy symbolic figures for the oppressed and their oppressors. Counterculture idealism was the water I swam in as a child, and I was certain that it was only a matter of time before it took over all of mainstream society.

One place where I could see it clearly was in *The 1969 Warner/Reprise Record Show*, a double-record sampler of new music my dad had mail-ordered from Burbank. The shiny psychedelic cover only hinted at the music etched into the vinyl, including new cuts by the Grateful Dead, the Fugs, Frank Zappa, and Van Dyke Parks, along with jazz singer Ella Fitzgerald, New Orleans rhythm-and-blues man Fats Domino, folk singer Theo Bikel, and many others. But what stuck with me most were the liner notes, particularly the dust cover essay that promoted the double-disc samplers as the work of a "benevolent" record company that, along with its artists, had decided it was better to spread the music than to make a profit on the two-dollar samplers. But the essay also encouraged customers to be suspicious of big record companies, including Warner/Reprise, which was actually scheming to get listeners to pay full price for the records by the artists included on the sampler because . . . well, "We are not 100 per-cent benevolent." But beneath the wisecracking and self-revelation lay the countercultural idealism that even the six-year-old me knew would soon be taking over the world. Except, of course, it didn't.

But then I met Waronker, heard his stories, and began to wonder if my child's-eye vision of utopia might have come true after all. Because every-thing I was hearing about Warner/Reprise, and not just during its mossy hippie years, told me that those ideals had actually been put into practice right here in Burbank; that Warner/Reprise had lived by those egalitarian values, had made doing good as important as doing well, believed fiercely in their art and one another, and had made this arrangement work for three extraordinarily profitable decades. And here was Waronker, one of the most important players throughout, a man who could currently be earning millions running another music empire, or consulting, or sitting on for-profit boards of vast multinational media groups—except all he wanted to do was hang out in a cluttered basement office talking about bands and records with similarly obsessed kids a third his age.

When it was time to go, I crossed Warner Boulevard and turned around to contemplate the wood-and-glass structure on the other side. I'd spent so many years assuming that all those long-ago visions of a new way of doing things had fallen to nothing. But they had been real for nearly thirty years, less than a hundred feet from where I was standing.

## WARNER BROS. RECOR[
## TERRIBLY SOPHISTICATED

When the original Warner Bros. Records sta[ paring the company's first dozen albums for rel[ 1958, they faced a curious challenge: many of the arti[ making the records didn't actually exist.

Obviously, someone had composed, arranged, and [ that filled the albums' grooves. Some of those people ev[ tations, as bandleaders and soloists whom other record[ built into steady sellers and even low-level stars. The p[ they were all still under contract to those other compa[ for Warner Bros. would be a cardinal sin against their c[ invitation to be sued by the large companies that employe[ label's founding president, Jim Conkling, needed help ge[ label off the ground. A seasoned music executive whose [ fessional singer, he had plenty of friends and family he co[ anyone want to earn a little extra cash by recording som[ tunes? It would all be on the q.t., he promised. No name[ They'd credit the discs to one of the alter egos they planne[ musicians gathered, and tape rolled. The styles varied. They[

mus[
slack[
had [
at le[
with[

exe[
Ho[
wer[
the[
sho[
slee[
The[
whi[
hou[
Sor[
to [
like[
cou[

pre[
Sta[
job[
pu[
sti[
co[
tu[
ch[
ar[
ali[
Pe[
of[
ad[
C[
m[
o[

Cornyn ended with an intriguing question: "By the way, just who the devil is Ira Ironstrings?"

The question hung unanswered. But now they were all into it: the crazy titles, the strange artist names and absurdist liners. What do you call a grab bag of Caribbeanized standards? . . . *But You've Never Heard Gershwin with Bongos*. A collection of cocktail bar keyboard stylings? *Don't Leave Your Empties on the Piano*. Then came an album of sing-alongs called *Songs that Followed the Kids Home from Camp*; then more instrumentals pitched as *The Smart Set*; and in a different approach, its cover adorned with a stock photo of beatniks in shades hunching together at a divey bar smoking what at least appeared to be cigarettes, *The Cool Scene: Twelve New Ways to Fly*.

The appetite for strangeness didn't begin with Cornyn and his colleagues. Months earlier, Conkling had made a deal with a young movie orchestrator named Henry Mancini to work with songwriter Irving Taylor* on an album of gag songs playing off all the familiar pop ballad tropes to what they hoped would be hilarious effect. What they came up with is one of the oddest records in WBR's catalogue, which is saying something, given all that would come in the next few decades. Thinking silly, Taylor composed an album's worth of songs, including the blended love (and gardening advice) song "When the Crab Grass Blooms Again," "I'm Filled with that Empty Feeling," and the indelibly named "I'll Never Forget Those Unforgettable Never to Be Forgotten Memories." Performed by a variety of singers—some of them play it straight, while others all but reach through the speaker to elbow you in the ribs—the album came off as even more absurd against Mancini's elegantly composed orchestration. Titled *Terribly Sophisticated Songs: A Collection of Unpopular Songs for Popular People*, it led to a series of comic and/or unlikely collections of Taylor songs, including *Drink Along with Irving* and *The Garbage Collector in Beverly Hills*, which features songs about folks with strange jobs ("Hawaiian Worm Raiser," "Marriage Counselor in a Turkish Harem," and so on). None of them sold many copies, but they were exceptionally cheap to make, and in WBR's herky-jerky early years that's what mattered most.

---

* Taylor's credits include a cowrite on "Everybody Loves Somebody" and "Kookie, Kookie (Lend Me Your Comb)," both of which would figure in WBR's not-distant future.

○

It took a while for Conkling to get used to the stark conditions at his new company. Capitol Records, the company he had once served as vice president, had its own home in Hollywood, a thirteen-story modernist structure designed to resemble a big, shiny stack of 45 rpm records. But when Conkling came to the Warner Bros. headquarters on its movie lot just over the Hollywood Hills from Los Angeles, in Burbank, he was led to a dingy building whose main floor was taken up by the fast-clacking women of the studio's secretarial pool. One creaky flight of stairs above them, he found a deserted warren of offices once occupied by a team of studio writers. The carpets, in Warner's standard-issue green, had been shredded by decades of shuffling feet. The office walls were blurry with scuff marks and riddled with the holes left by thumbtacks, nails, and what appeared to be hurled staplers, coffee mugs, and other blunt objects. Then came the president's office, the seat of power in the new record company. Here's what Conkling found there: a desk, a chair, one yellow legal pad, and a sharpened pencil. Here's what he didn't find: a pencil sharpener, a telephone, a typewriter, a file cabinet, or a secretary. "I'd never seen anything like it," Conkling said later. "And here I was, supposed to be starting a first-class record company."[1]

There was no money to outfit the place, so Conkling turned to Matt Gilligan, Jack Warner's personal assistant, to mount scavenger hunts around the movie lot. A veteran employee highly enough placed to bear Jack Warner's personal imprimatur, Gilligan led the newcomers on incursions of hidden rooms full of cast-off desks, chairs, and shelves, and then, a bit more surreptitiously, to the prop warehouses where movie producers could get the furnishings to lend verisimilitude to a picture's workplace scenes. Telephones, typewriters, desktop intercoms—Gilligan signed for them like any producer would, and the studio hands delivered the goods by the end of the afternoon.

It wasn't the first time Warner Bros. Pictures had tried to get into the music business. In fact, the Warner brothers, Harry, Albert, Sam, and Jack, had pushed their thriving young movie studio toward sound before most movie company owners had even given it a thought. Then, in 1927, after funneling money to the scientists and inventors trying to figure out how to bring sound to moving pictures, they were delivered a miracle: soundsynching technology precise enough for both spoken dialogue and musical performances. To create maximum impact for the new technology, the studio launched it with *The Jazz Singer*, starring the popular singer/actor Al Jolson, who belted out "Sonny Boy" and the film's other tunes with enough eye-rolling brio to bring wowed viewers back to the theater again and again. And wouldn't they want to listen to the *Jazz Singer* songs in their own homes? The timing seemed exquisite. At the end of the Roaring Twenties, the recorded music industry was just taking off; now the Warners could enter the race with a big head start.

Released to the theaters at the start of October 1927, *The Jazz Singer* was still near the height of its popularity two years later when the American stock market collapsed, marking the start of the Great Depression. Happily, the movie biz rolled forward with nary a hitch. With tickets priced at a nickel, a weekly visit to the neighborhood movie palace was a luxury nearly everyone could still afford. Assuming *The Jazz Singer*'s undying popularity would cross into the record business, the brothers bought the Brunswick record company in 1930 and quickly discovered the error in their strategy. Records cost somewhere between $1.00 and $1.50 in 1930, while record players cost many times more and were well beyond the budget of a struggling Depression-era family. With record sales down to a trickle, the Warners gutted it out for a year and a half before leasing the company to ARC at the end of 1931. They held on to Brunswick for another ten years but kept themselves as far away as possible, vowing to stick with the business they knew best.

Funny how twenty-six years, a world war, and a global economic recovery can change things. By 1958, Jack Warner had sole control of his family's movie empire and a dim view of anyone else making money off the movies and stars his money had created. It was bad enough Warner Bros. had to miss out on such a big percentage of the dough when some other record company released one of its soundtracks. But it was even more of an outrage for Jack Warner to see his own contracted actors, like Tab Hunter and Connie Stevens, scoring hits for someone else's record company. Build me a record company, Warner commanded. And on March 10, 1958, unto Jack Warner was delivered the just-incorporated Warner Bros. Records.

Warner used all his charm to land Conkling, a veteran music executive who had cut a wide swath through the industry since he landed his first job at Capitol Records after World War II. Starting in the company's artists and repertoire department, Conkling needed only three years to become its vice president. Recruited by Columbia Records, the young executive took over the company's presidency in 1951 and succeeded so magnificently that he chose to retire in 1956, when he was all of forty-one years old. Next, Conkling helped found the National Academy of Recording Arts and Sciences (NARAS), including its annual Grammy Awards ceremony, and was pondering what he might do next when Warner called. The prospect of building a new major record label from the ground up got Conkling's imagination spinning, and with Warner pledging $2 million in start-up money, almost exactly what it cost him to produce one full-length, top-grade movie, Conkling grabbed it.

The first artist to join the new label was Warner's contracted heart-throb Tab Hunter, whose hit cover of "Young Love," released on the Dot label, had inspired Jack Warner's urgent desire to start his own record company. No one, including Hunter, mistook the actor for a serious musician. But Connie Stevens, another one of the studio's sexy youngsters, really could carry a tune, and given that she was already the subject of one of Warner's everything-but-the-first-born contracts, they could sign her for free, a price that fit the new company's budget. Conkling also signed up his close friend and Warner Bros. TV actor Jack Webb, who was famous as the gruff Sgt. Joe Friday from *Dragnet*. Conkling figured, or hoped, that no one would notice that Webb's tobacco-stained baritone made Tab Hunter sound like Enrico Caruso. And that was fine with Jack Warner. Everything was fine with him, as long as the company made money—and that nothing they released sounded anything like rock 'n' roll.

Stan Cornyn wasn't the only staffer looking for creative ways to sell the company's first line of albums. Promotions executive Joel Friedman, who had come to Warner Bros. after covering the music industry for *Billboard* magazine, had relatively up-to-date rosters of all the regional and local promotions employees working on the respective staffs of Columbia and Capitol Records. Figuring the Ira Ironstrings record as the clearest shot they had at a hit, Friedman sent telegrams to every name on the other companies' lists, urging all of them to dig deep to get the album moving.

"GET OUT AND TELL EVERYONE ABOUT THE IRA IRONSTRINGS ALBUM," he wrote, signing the missive with the impressive yet meaningless "THE NATIONAL PROMOTION DEPARTMENT."

It went without a hitch for two weeks. Dozens of the other companies' promotions staffers, assuming they were promoting one of their own artists, jumped in with both feet, papering their regions with Ira Ironstrings stickers, urging distributors and retailers to stock the record, putting together events and contests to sell the Ira Ironstrings album. It was going great until Lloyd Dunn, Capitol Records' chief of publicity and promotions, figured out what was going on. One morning, the telephone in Jim Conkling's office rang. "You son of a *bitch!*" Dunn bellowed, by way of a hello. But that only launched the next stage of the Ironstrings caper. The September 8 edition of *Billboard* devoted a feature article to celebrating the scandalous story, noting that the Ironstrings name had already become ubiquitous, and that an anonymous Warner Bros. executive (Friedman, of course) said that the company already had advance orders topping twenty-five thousand, a figure that made him think highly of his competitors' promotions staffs, "when they make up their minds to get out and work."[2]

Still, Friedman's scheming, and the hard work of his unwitting agents at the other companies, couldn't make Ira Ironstrings a best seller. Despite the advance orders, *Music for People with $3.98 Plus Tax (If Any)* did a belly flop in the record stores, as did Jack Webb's intoned love lyrics and both movie soundtracks. Most of the advance orders came back as returns for nearly the whole crop of Warner Bros.' first releases. The only record that wasn't an abject flop turned out to be a generic collection of New Orleans dance numbers called *The Dixieland Sound*, though that wasn't a hit, either. And when Tab Hunter, whose "Young Love" spent six weeks at the top of the *Billboard* charts for Dot Records in January 1957, made his WBR debut with "Jealous Heart," the tune reached only No. 62 in 1958. Hunter would never visit the Top 30 again.

A dismal performance, but what could they do? *No rock 'n' roll on my label*, Warner had proclaimed, just as Elvis, Jerry Lee, Chuck, Buddy, Fats, and all their fellows were locking down the *Top of the Pops* in the name of hound dogs, jailbirds, and Coupe de Villes everywhere. To pretend that the revolution wasn't happening was close to delusional. Still, when the New York–based A&R boss (and celebrated jazz producer) George

Avakian pitched some sure things to the Burbank HQ, he kept his eyes locked stubbornly on the past. How about this new Negro vocal group he figured for the next Ink Spots? Or a Patti Page–like chanteuse whose new song reminded him of "Tennessee Waltz"? And when it came to sure things, here's a fellow who is a combination of Jimmie "the Singing Brakeman" Rodgers and that clean-cut youngster Pat Boone. Wasn't it time for someone to do a modern remake of "Cigarettes, Whiskey and Wild, Wild Women"? Avakian had just the artist for that. He also had David Allen, a middle-aged singer who would be perfect for a song Avakian wanted to commission for the teenage market, "in which David is the understanding old man who recognizes that a teenager's infatuation for him is deeper than mom and dad think, but . . . consoles her that her true love will come along in a more appropriate age bracket."[3]

When they got to the end of the company's first year in business, Warner Bros. Records had lost $1.53 million. And that official number didn't include the boxes of unsold records its distributors were sending back for refunds. With those losses, the number was closer to $3.5 million, which, given the company's original $2 million operating budget, was pretty impressive, albeit in a bad way. The losses continued through 1959, and with no stars or hits to market, Cornyn and friends continued their fiction-writing efforts, looking for new ways to juice up sales of their non-existent artists. In one gothic twist, they prefaced the release of an album of café songs credited to a shady French mandolin player dubbed Raoul Meynard by announcing that the musician had been stabbed to death in a knife fight outside a Paris café. And as if that weren't interesting enough, get a load of Warner Bros.' superior recording equipment! They called it Vitaphonic, "the optimum in modern sound recording technique." The industry media did its best to help. The reviewers at *Billboard* pretzeled themselves to find something, anything, praiseworthy they could add to their WBR critiques. Ray Heindorf's collection of *Auntie Mame* instrumentals, for instance, had "a very sharp cover that should be a real attention-getter." And they were right. The first Grammy award WBR ever won was a Best Cover Design trophy for *Auntie Mame*.[4]

Then they got lucky. Warner Bros. Television produced the TV series

*77 Sunset Strip*, a tongue-in-cheek drama whose cast of L.A. characters included Lloyd "Kookie" Kookson, a parking lot attendant who sported a vocabulary of beatnik-style colloquialisms. As the show became a hit, Kookie's catchphrases (*Ginchy*; *Crazy, man, crazy*; *Antsville*) swept through the nation's schools and offices like a pop culture tsunami. Sensing opportunity, a producer at WBR recorded a mostly instrumental version of the show's finger-snapping theme song. The single sold more than 87,000 copies, making it the largest-selling WBR release by far. With distributors keening for a full-length *77 Sunset Strip* album, they ran back into the studio and emerged a week later with a collection of character-inspired tunes that vaulted to No. 6 on *Billboard*'s Hot 100 album list within a month of its release. It climbed to the top three a few weeks later, and soon moved more than 100,000 copies, thanks to the smashing success of "Lend Me Your Comb," a Kookie-centric novelty single that strung together the character's loopy catchphrases with Connie Stevens's uncredited performance of the central "Kookie, Kookie, lend me your comb" hook. The tune leaped to *Billboard*'s No. 4 slot, ultimately selling 587,000 copies—just about 150,000 more sales than for all the previous WBR singles combined.[5]

This time there were no returns—just a gusher of cash bound for WBR's end-of-year profit-and-loss statement. And more *77 Sunset* records followed, including Edd "Kookie" Byrnes's follow-up, "Like I Love You," which moved more than 182,000 copies. But by then, according to the silver heads at Warner Bros. corporate in New York, it was too late. Summoned in early 1960, Conkling, along with WBR's chief financial officer, Ed West, hopped a plane for Gotham to present their budget numbers and plans for the next year to top executives Hal Cook, Herman Starr, and Ben Kalmenson.

Prepared for a full day of meetings, the Californians were caught short by Kalmenson's greeting. "Gentlemen, before we begin," he said "I just want to say that Warner Bros. has grown disenchanted with the record business. We want you to fold up your tent and get the hell out as quickly as possible." To conclude, Kalmenson distilled everything he'd just said into one word:

"Liquidate!"[6]

So, that was it—or it would have been if West, who came out of Jack Warner's top shelf of finance men, hadn't refused to accept it.

"It won't work, Ben,"[7] he shot back. The success of *77 Sunset Strip* meant the record company still had half a million dollars to collect from its accounts. And what were they supposed to do with their stockpiled inventory, including fifteen new albums they'd already paid to produce but had yet to release? It made no sense to leave that much money on the table.

Kalmenson was taken aback. Like virtually all the top execs in Warner's top echelon, he hadn't wanted Warner to get into the record business in the first place. Unlike movies, the reigning form of American entertainment and the stuff of bejeweled stars, the pop music world was beneath them. They saw it as a place for greasy kids, Negroes, and street hustlers. The whole point of having stationed Ed West in the record company in the first place was to have him know where the money was stashed so they could preserve as much of it as possible when they blew the place up. But West appeared to have had a change of heart—not just because he'd come to like and respect Conkling and the rest of his team, but because he'd figured out how much money there was in the record business. And if Kalmenson couldn't see it yet, they were going to have to fend him off until it became too obvious to ignore.

Conkling stepped in with a last-ditch counterproposal. Give them six months to collect the remaining dough and take the new products to market, and then they'd see where they stood. Six months was exactly what Kalmenson gave them.

Back in Burbank, Conkling and West set out to do everything they could to make the company indispensable. Step one: sign up more stars. To start, they snagged Bill Haley and the Comets, the "Rock Around the Clock" and "See Ya Later, Alligator" stars, who still had enough country swing in them to avoid setting off rock 'n' roll alarm bells in the ears of the senior Warner men. They were soon eclipsed by the Everly Brothers, the country-based rockers whose seven most recent singles included five million-sellers. Ordinarily stars of that wattage would stick with a powerhouse label, but the brothers had an itch to become movie stars. WBR came on strong with a ten-year, million-dollar record deal that also included a shot at the big screen. How Conkling convinced Warner to pony up the million to seal the deal is anyone's guess, but the payoff came just a few weeks later, when the Everlys' first Warner Bros. single, "Cathy's Clown," soared to No. 1 and became the duo's next million-seller.

But even Don and Phil paled in comparison to Bob Newhart. A stocky, prematurely balding Korean War veteran based in Chicago, Newhart had studied to be an accountant and then abandoned the profession to take a stab at what he really wanted to do: write comedy. Newhart partnered with a friend and spent a year writing and performing a weekly show they syndicated to a total of three radio stations, one in Northampton, Massachusetts, another in Jacksonville, Florida, and the last in Idaho Falls, Idaho. When Newhart's partner took a radio job in New York, Newhart began to fret that he would never make it on his own. Then he noticed an advertisement for driving instructors, and inspiration struck. What would a driving instructor's workday be like? What would his *worst* day be like? Composing a monologue in the voice of a driving teacher trying to be calm even as his student sends cars and pedestrians hurtling for safety, Newhart recited his end of the conversation with a deadpan tone that made the unseen chaos doubly hilarious.[8] Soon, he came up with others: a modern Madison Avenue adman giving notes to Abraham Lincoln on his Gettysburg speech; a publicist urging the Wright Brothers to merchandise their newly discovered powers of flight; a hapless navy ship captain trying to downplay a series of recent accidents, collisions, and mutinies.[9]

A Chicago disc jockey played Newhart's bits on his show and was so tickled by what he heard that he typed up transcripts of his favorites and passed them, along with tapes, to his friends Jack White and Seymour Greenspan, who ran Warner's Chicago branch offices. Hearing Newhart for themselves, the pair started preaching the gospel to the Los Angeles–based executives who had come to town with Conkling. One of them liked Newhart enough to get Conkling on the telephone and beg him to get to the branch warehouse as quickly as possible. The chief executive found his way into the industrial district and waited with the others while Newhart rode the bus in from the suburbs. When the radio comedian finally arrived, he came with a portable tape player and a copy of the Abe Lincoln routine. Once he heard it, Conkling forgot all about the flight he was supposed to catch back to Los Angeles. "We had to do something," he said.[10]

A&R chief George Avakian flew to Chicago two days later and struck a deal with Newhart and his manager. Together, they began planning for Newhart's first comedy album. The tapes were hilarious, Avakian said, but in order to add energy, they'd need to rerecord the bits in front of a live, laughing audience. So, where was he performing next? Newhart gawped. He didn't have a next performance planned. In fact, he'd never performed in public before—which meant that no respectable nightclub in Chicago would book him for a set.

Casting a wider net, Avakian found a club in Houston willing to host Newhart as an opener for headliners Ken and Mitzi Welch, who were kind enough to allow Newhart to take their show-closing slot each night. When Newhart got to Texas, he realized he had enough material for only one side of an album and set frantically to writing more. Fortunately, the pressure brought out the best in him, and he came up with enough new bits to fill out the set. On the first night, Newhart was almost too terrified to go onstage, and then the comedian's nerves were tried severely by the constant heckling of a drunk woman. "She kept yelling, 'That's a bunch of crap!'" Newhart recalls.[11] The audience behaved much better after that first night, and Avakian was able to get Newhart's sketches on tape, laughter and all. But months then passed for Newhart without a word from Burbank. He finally called at the start of April to ask why they hadn't released his album yet. What he didn't know was that they had done just that a few days earlier. And *The Button-Down Mind of Bob Newhart* was exploding out of the box.[12]

It began in Minneapolis. A disc jockey named Howard Diken picked up on the record and put it on the air, triggering an immediate rush on record stores. On March 30, the local distribution manager wired in a request for another thousand copies. On March 31, he wired again: they'd sold 4,500 copies in two days and needed another 2,000 copies immediately. NOTHING HAS EVER SOLD AT THIS PACE IN THIS MARKET, he wrote. STATIONS CAN'T CONTROL SWITCHBOARDS. SMALL DEALERS REORDERING BOX LOTS BEFORE INITIAL SHIPMENTS ARRIVE. Another wire zipped in on April 1: the distributors had sold 6,500 copies in four days, and that was just in the Twin Cities. Outstate reorders weren't due for another few days. Meanwhile, the urban dealers were screaming for more, more, more. A rave review, along with news of the Minneapolis–Saint Paul hysteria, hit *Billboard* a few days later. *Button-Down Mind* hit the charts not long after, made it to the top of the album list at the end of July, and stayed on the throne for three and a half months. It wouldn't leave the sales charts for more than two years.[13]

Soon Newhart was performing on the *Emmy Awards* alongside the likes of Steve Allen, Don Knotts, and the duo Mike Nichols and Elaine May, the most popular figures on the comedy scene. Not long after that, Conkling invited the comedian to a dinner with all the company's top executives, including Jack Warner. When he stood up to speak, Warner gestured to the top brass from Warner Bros. Records before pointing directly at Newhart. "You know, I was ready to shut this whole goddamn thing down until this kid showed up," he said with a chuckle. Everyone laughed—just a little higher-pitched than usual.[14]

○

Suddenly, no one at Warner Bros. Pictures was disenchanted with the record business. But that didn't mean there wasn't room for hard feelings to blossom between Warner and Conkling. They had been germinating for most of the label president's tenure. Warner, like the record business–hating Ben Kalmenson, had tormented Conkling for much of his time with the company, even after he stopped trying to shut down the label. The most recent cutbacks, imposed despite Conkling's remarkable successes, sapped the last of his team spirit. When his stock options matured, Conkling moved to sell them immediately, a very public gesture of disloyalty to Warner. He had already been thinking of leaving, but now Conkling didn't have to write a resignation letter. Kalmenson gave him the word, granting the record company's founding president just enough time to recruit the current Capitol Records president, Mike Maitland, as his successor. And with nothing left but the good-byes, Warner had his staff plan a farewell party that Conkling would never forget—whether he wanted to or not.[15]

They rented the main ballroom at the Beverly Hills Hotel for an evening in October 1961 and invited two hundred and fifty of the entertainment industry's most powerful grandees. No women allowed—Warner wanted it to be as unrestrained as possible. Jim Conkling was a Mormon, about as far from Old World Jewish as it gets, but when the testimonials began, he might as well have been having a bris right there at the front table.

Bob Newhart softened him up with his WASPy Midwestern japery: "I haven't been in the record business too long, and so I only know four nice people in the record business," he began. "With Jim retiring I still know four." The songwriter Johnny Mercer performed a mostly generous farewell called "Everybody Loves Our Jim." Jack Warner said he'd been impressed by his record company's president at first. "But as time goosed on, I found we were getting well fucked." But it was all in good spirits, wasn't it? The new president, Mike Maitland, came to introduce himself and pitch in on the convivial trashing of his predecessor with a bit about all the physical and psychological tests he'd had to endure before he'd been officially hired. "All this to prove that I was qualified to replace Jim Conkling. You can imagine my horror tonight to realize that he's a faggot and a first class shit-heel."[16]

Maitland's joke might seem crass, but it was child's play compared to the song performed by Allan Sherman, a little-known TV writer drafted by agent George "Bullets" Durgom. While unemployed, Sherman had started writing gag lyrics to hit songs purely to entertain himself, but he'd shared a few of them with friends, and when Durgom offered him cash to write a joke song about Warner Bros.' outgoing president, Sherman took the assignment. It took him only a few hours to write "Big Bad Jim," a play on country singer Jimmy Dean's recent hit song "Big Bad John."

Too filled with stage fright to perform for the crowd, Sherman made a recording of the song and hung just out of sight as his outrageous tribute played through the speakers. Taking up where Maitland's foulmouthed gag left off, "Big Bad Jim" was wild. It was also filthy—so filthy, in fact, that the guests all swore a vow never to recite the lyrics to anyone else. Someone called out for an encore, and the song played again, then another time, and then again as the laughter and applause redoubled and doubled again. Sherman took the stage to receive his acclaim and to apologize to Conkling, who accepted it all with excellent cheer. All traces of "Big Bad Jim" vanished with the evening. And for a time, so did Sherman. But that would change.[17]

Allan Sherman hadn't expected his big night at the Beverly Hills Hotel to change anything in his life. Indeed, he went back to the same rut he'd been in before, trying to land another TV writing job while his savings account shrank. A few months after the farewell roast, he scored a little more dough performing at a New Year's Eve party for his friend the actor Jim Backus. The pianist who backed him on that recording (Lou Busch, who moonlighted secretly as Warner Bros. Records artist Joe "Fingers" Carr) invited Sherman to make a demo recording of his best song parodies, and the unemployed writer threw himself into the project. Sherman dug most of the laughs out of Jewish cultural references, and his songs were rejected at Capitol Records for being too ethnic to draw a mainstream audience. But when Bullets Durgom set up an appointment at Warner Bros. Records with Mike Maitland in June 1962, the supremely WASPy president laughed just as hard as he had at his predecessor's farewell banquet. His only reservation was that Sherman had set his lyrics to songs from the popular Broadway show *My Fair Lady*, which would make clearing the rights a difficult and expensive task. So, could Sherman try to write some new lyrics to songs from out of the public domain, like folk songs? Sherman certainly could do that, and he came back a week later with an album's worth, including "Sarah Jackman," an adaptation of "Frère Jacques" that went *comme ça*:

> *How's your brother Bernie? (He's a big attorney)*
> *How's your sister Doris? (Still with William Morris)*

"The Battle Hymn of the Republic" was renamed "Glory, Glory, Harry Lewis" and celebrated the passing of a tailor fatally stricken while working a bolt of velvet in the company warehouse. ("His cloth goes shining on!")

Back in Maitland's office a week later, the executive heard the new songs, offered a $1,500 advance, and set up a live recording session in a Hollywood studio large enough to seat a small audience. Busch and Sherman performed flawlessly, the crowd loved what they heard, and with no need for fixes or retakes they finished the recording of the twelve songs in precisely the forty-five minutes it would take to listen to them.[18]

*My Son, the Folk Singer* was released in October 1962, exactly a year after Sherman's "Big Bad Jim" brought down the house at Conkling's farewell roast. As with Newhart's debut, Sherman's songs started blowing up request lines at Top 40 stations. The album sold 300,000 copies in three weeks, spurring a production crisis as the Warner printing presses, album cover plants, and distributors hustled to keep stores supplied with the record.[19]

*My Son, the Folk Singer* sold 250,000 copies in New York City alone, its impact so overwhelming that French schoolgirls were singing Allan Sherman songs in Paris. Meanwhile, President John F. Kennedy, an Irish Catholic, arrived at New York's Carlyle Hotel for a meeting audibly singing "Sarah Jackman" as he strode through the lobby.[20] The album hit the top of the charts in early December, on its way to selling more than a million copies during its run. Sherman's follow-up album, *My Son, the Celebrity*, was written and recorded between dates on his jam-packed touring schedule and came out sounding a bit threadbare as a result. Rush-released in January 1963, just three months after Sherman's debut, the new album didn't sell nearly as well, but it still moved more than 350,000 copies, topping the album sales charts for a week in early March.[21]

Sherman's third album, *My Son, the Nut*, was a return to form, earning Sherman a lasting place in pop culture history. Released in the summer of 1963, it included the smash summer single "Hello Muddah, Hello Fadduh (A Letter from Camp Grenada)," a child's letter home from a highly standard summer camp set to Amilcare Ponchielli's "Dance of the Hours." The song hit No. 2 on the *Billboard* charts in August and sold 600,000 copies, catapulting the album to the top of the heap with 1.2 million copies sold.[22]

○

Sherman's stab at folk songs was an extension of the folk music revival that had been building in the United States and in England for more than a decade. In New York in 1961, the fastest-rising star in the folk scene growing in the downtown neighborhood of Greenwich Village was the arriviste Minnesota folkie Bob Dylan, who soon studded his repertoire of folk traditionals and Dust Bowl ballads with his own portrayals of injustice, incipient nuclear catastrophe, and the aggravating people, places, and situations that caught his witheringly satirical eye.

The folk impresario and artist manager Albert Grossman nabbed Dylan before anyone else got there, and was just as quick to figure out that the budding oracle's hard-eyed wit, scruffy appearance, and splintery singing voice left plenty of room for a new pop-folk hybrid to take root. In search of an edgier, sexier kind of 1960s Kingston Trio, Grossman combed the folk clubs to find three singers with the right look, sound, and presence to bring modern folk to the masses. Soon, he narrowed his field to a trio. Peter Yarrow, a psychology student from Cornell University, had already performed as a solo act at the 1960 Newport Folk Festival. Noel Paul Stookey had worked his way through Michigan State University by playing in rock bands, before moving to New York to work as a musician and comic in Greenwich Village folk clubs. Grossman rounded out the trio with Mary Travers, a strikingly beautiful young woman whose sky-blue eyes and straw-blond hair couldn't mask the depth of her intelligence and political commitment. Her strong, clear voice made her as welcome on the Broadway stage as it did in the folk clubs of Greenwich Village. The hulking Grossman, whose Olmec-scaled head telegraphed his domineering personality, proved a canny matchmaker. He called the group Peter, Paul and Mary.

Yarrow's, Stookey's, and Travers's voices blended just as sweetly as their personalities, and when Warner Bros.' New York A&R man Artie Mogull followed a tip to the Village's Blue Angel nightclub to see one of their early shows in December 1961, he staked his new job on the trio. Mogull tracked down Maitland, who happened to be in the city, and all but ordered his boss to hear the singers' midnight set. Six songs later, Maitland struck a handshake deal with Grossman out on the sidewalk, agreeing to the manager's extraordinary demand for a fifteen-thousand-dollar advance, a guaranteed fifteen-grand promotional budget, and control over the contents and cover designs of their albums. How could he know that Grossman's new folk group would connect as strongly with record buyers a third his age as they had with him? Some people just know, despite everything.[23]

Warner Bros. Records' new president, John K. "Mike" Maitland, a Detroit boy who grew up to be broad-shouldered and movie star handsome, flew fighter planes during World War II. He joined Capitol's sales division in 1946 and rose quickly on the strength of his managerial and organizational skills, which were set off by his easygoing warmth and charm. Maitland never presented himself as an expert in popular music, but by the early 1960s he had a solid grasp of the artists on the top music charts and of the sounds bubbling up next in the ears of tuned-in radio programmers and record buyers.

For Maitland, the core of Peter, Paul and Mary's magnetism lay in how they combined the moral fervor of modern folk music with such captivating euphony. The grad school trio could speak the rhetoric of revolution in the cultivated tongues of a Manhattan cocktail party. And while Dylan hid the stately melody of "Blowin' in the Wind" behind his prairie honk, Grossman's pop-folk outfit draped it in harmony and made it shimmer with hope. As the Kingston Trio had done with old-fashioned folk in the 1950s, Peter, Paul and Mary had the capacity to make modern folk music like Dylan's palatable to a mainstream audience.

By positioning the unheard-of Peter, Paul and Mary as one of his label's marquee acts, Maitland pushed the company's focus into a future that had yet to be fully imagined. Now all he needed was a promotions man with enough drive and imagination to launch the group into the ears, minds, and hearts of the listeners who would turn them into stars. Fortunately, he had hired that very guy just a few months earlier. His name was Joe Smith, a highly educated former disc jockey whose intellect, pop savvy, and razor-sharp wit were already sending up sparks in the WBR offices.

The only child of a middle-aged Jewish couple in Chelsea, Massachusetts, near Boston, Smith jumped from his public high school to the upper-class sanctuary of Yale University. He spent his freshman year sharing a suite of rooms with future conservative pundit William F. Buckley, whose patrician airs Smith twitted by singing "God Save the King" whenever his roommate came through the door. Smith continued his teasing on his campus radio show by reading Buckley's *Yale Daily News* column to his listeners in a ridiculously plummy British accent. Rather than use his Yale diploma to get into the upper echelons of business or law, Smith went to rural Pennsylvania to start a career as a radio disc jockey. Funny, sharp, and innovative, he ran against the flood of shrieking AM jocks who clanged bells and cranked sirens to get their listeners' attention. Instead, he emphasized his own wit, taking listener calls on the air and trading wisecracks with a regular coterie of high-profile guests. By the mid-1950s, Smith had worked his way up to WMEX, the most popular Top 40 station in Boston, where the city's most powerful figures, including Cardinal Cushing, Boston's reigning spiritual leader, came onto Smith's airwaves once a week. But Smith's run on the radio came to an abrupt halt as the decade ended. Following the conventional practice of accepting money to play certain records on his show, he got caught up in the federal payola investigation. He had committed no crimes—payola wasn't illegal then, and he had kept track of what he'd earned and paid income tax on every dime. But he'd already lost his taste for both radio and the east coast and Smith headed west to make a new start.

He moved to Los Angeles in 1960, hoping to jump to the other side of the record promotion business. In October 1961, Mike Maitland, himself freshly installed at Warner Bros. Records, hired the former disc jockey to take over the company's promotions office, and three months later, he handed him Peter, Paul and Mary with instructions to do everything morally, ethically, and humanly possible to get them seen, heard, and then—in the form of their debut album, *Peter, Paul and Mary*—bought.

The best way to do it, Smith figured, was to bring the music directly to the people. He rented a station wagon and loaded in everything they had—Yarrow, Stookey, Travers; a couple of acoustic guitars; a compact PA system; and as many boxes of their debut album as would fit. Then he drove to the center of the country and hit every college campus he could find.

After calling ahead to figure out the best time and place to play, Smith and company would set up their sound system and microphones and then prop up an easel with a poster board reading NOW PLAYING! PETER, PAUL AND MARY—WARNER BROS. ARTISTS. Smith would make an announcement, the group would start singing, and, as Smith recalls, students would run over from every direction to listen. By the end of the group's forty-five-minute set, thousands of kids would have filled the quad and be hanging out of dorm and classroom windows, cheering for more—and lining up to buy albums from the back of the station wagon. Smith's audience-building strategy worked. *Peter, Paul and Mary* snatched a low rung on the *Billboard* charts in late April, climbing slowly but steadily until it claimed the No. 1 spot in the magazine's October 28, 1962, issue. The album straddled the top of the charts throughout the Christmas shopping season, selling more than two million copies before its *Billboard* run was over more than three years later. The success established Yarrow, Stookey, and Travers as stars, and also proved the mettle of Smith, whose career at WBR was now on the same steep trajectory.

No longer the saddest sacks not on the hit parade, Warner Bros. Records had become a thriving entertainment company. And that's when Jack Warner broke the news to his staff that they were about to go into business with Frank Sinatra's Reprise Records.

It might have sounded flashy on the surface, but Reprise was a mess, perhaps the one record label whose history of futility rivaled WBR's. Reprise had never made a profit, and as Warner assured his staff, the company's $1.5 million debt was headed directly to WBR's books. In that one stroke, every WBR executive who had been imagining the year-end bonus he was due for an immensely profitable year felt his dream collapse. WBR was back in the hole to the tune of $1.5 million, with nearly twice as many staffers as necessary and nothing but struggle ahead.[24]

# REPRISE RECORDS:
## NEWER, HAPPIER, EMANCIPATED

Once he realized that Mickey Rudin wasn't pulling his leg, Mo Ostin's heart thudded like Buddy Rich's tom-toms. Did he want to be the general manager of Frank Sinatra's new record label? Ostin was thirty-two years old. It was 1959. Sinatra was the biggest pop star in the world—and not just with his singing but also his acting and all that ineffable coolness: the tuxedo, the icy blue eyes, the Camels and Jack Daniel's whose essence he wore as cologne. Ostin didn't smoke, and he barely drank. He wore heavy horn-rim glasses that, combined with his ebbing hairline and humble features, put people in mind of Phil Silvers, TV's Sergeant Bilko. But that didn't bother Ostin at all, which was one reason Rudin had decided to hand him this life-altering opportunity.

Sinatra would be the company's titular president and decide which artists deserved to record for his label. But the company would need a full-time executive to tend to the front office, negotiate contracts, work with the artists, and more. Ostin made it through a meeting with Sinatra's manager, Hank Sanicola, in one piece, but when Rudin took him to his climactic audience with Sinatra everything started going wrong.

They went to Columbia Studios, where Sinatra was filming *The Devil at Four O'Clock* with Spencer Tracy. The day's filming obviously wasn't going well, because when Rudin and Ostin walked onto the soundstage, they found Sinatra in the midst of a vein-popping argument with the movie's director, Mervyn LeRoy. "He was out of his mind," Ostin recalls of Sinatra: screaming, swearing, reducing LeRoy to a spot on the heel of his shoe, and not one of the nicer pairs, either. Watching from just beyond the lights and cameras, Ostin was overcome with the terrors. "I've got this life-changing opportunity and *this* is what I'm faced with?" he told me.

Rudin shrugged. "Frank's busy," he said breezily. "Why don't we go wait in his dressing room?" Ostin nodded and skittered after him.

The next hour passed uneasily. Inside the star's trailer, Ostin flinched a bit when he heard the doorknob twist, but the Sinatra who stepped in bore no resemblance to the maniac Ostin had just seen on set. This fellow was all sparkling eyes, smiles, and handshakes, his baritone velvety as he fixed his guest a drink and told him how owning a record company had always been his dream, how he'd already made a list of the artists he wanted to sign, all of them the best at what they did. His life had always been about music, and so would his record company, where the artists and music would always come first. As a Verve man, Ostin already knew how that worked, and also how to deal with a willful boss. He listened and nodded, made some mental notes on his new boss's passions, how intent he was on supporting the music he loved and the artists he admired—and also how determined he was to stay away from the one form of music he hated most: rock 'n' roll.

"It was the one thing he wouldn't tolerate," Ostin says. "And I wasn't hip enough to figure out what a terrible idea that was."

For now, Sinatra knew it was going to work out beautifully. He climbed to his feet and offered another handshake. "Welcome aboard, Mo, I'm glad to have you."[1]

●

He hadn't set out to be a record man. When the twenty-two-year-old Mo Ostin, né Ostrofsky, graduated from the University of California at Los Angeles with an economics degree in 1949, he signed up for the university's law school.

Like so many American immigrant stories, the Ostrofsky family's journey through the twentieth century was built on a combination of vision, work, and luck. The son of Julius and Bertha, Russian immigrants who got to the New World in 1920, Morris Meyer Ostrofsky was born in Brooklyn, New York, in 1927. The family settled into a Jewish section of the Bensonhurst neighborhood, close to family members who had arrived earlier and were already finding their way toward the American middle class. Julius could have taken a job with one of his uncles, but chose instead to strike out on his own, pushing a junk cart through the streets, each step taking him closer to owning a real store with a door, windows, and a fixed location in the United States of America.

Mo spent his first fourteen years in working-class Brooklyn, where he discovered a talent for school. The work came easily to him, and though he was smaller than the other kids, the As his teachers inked on his schoolwork girded his confidence. Then, just before he was set to start high school, Julius decided to pursue opportunity to California. Settling into a Jewish enclave of central Los Angeles in the fall of 1941, he sold produce and other groceries at the city's Farmers Market until he'd saved enough to open his own small grocery store. Soon, he was able to set up shop not far from the family home in Fairfax.[2]

Mo entered Fairfax High School's freshman class two months after the start of the school year, but he found it easy to make friends. Conveniently, the Granz family next door to the Ostrofskys' new home had a son, Irving, who was Mo's age, and the boys became fast friends. Together, they joined a neighborhood teen club called the Rams, where Mo met Benny Abrams, another Fairfax High kid known throughout the neighborhood for his passion for music. Pop, jazz, and particularly classical—Abrams dug it all. And he loved nothing more than passing his knowledge on to others. He found a particularly eager student in Mo Ostrofsky. As Mo's interest grew, Abrams encouraged him to join the school's music appreciation society, the Sharps and Flats. The school's administrators welcomed the young sophisticates in the building when classes ended and allowed them full use of the institution's sound equipment and collection of classical music records.

Made from solid eastern European material, Mo was about as far from the brawny, sun-kissed Southern California ideal as a teenager could get. No matter—he rose quickly in his schoolmates' estimation, borne up on his brains and warm-spirited charm. He was elected president of the Sharps and Flats at the start of his senior year and turned to fellow member and resident jazz fan Irving Granz to lead the discussions of America's latest homegrown music.

Irving had gotten his love for the music through his brother Norman. Ten years older, Norman Granz was fast making a career out of his love for music, launching the Jazz at the Philharmonic concerts in 1944 with an all-star lineup featuring Nat King Cole, J. J. Johnson, Buddy Rich, Barney Kessel, and Les Paul. The demand for tickets outstripped the size of the hall and opened an array of new opportunities for the young impresario. Norman Granz went to his baby brother to find some kids to sell concert programs and serve as ushers. Both Irving and Mo signed on immediately.

Norman Granz liked what he saw of Mo's brains and work ethic and gave him more to do, including the end-of-night counting of receipts and cash. The high schooler liked stretching his skills, even if it meant missing some of the music during the shows. But when he graduated high school in 1945, Mo headed to UCLA with no thought of working his way up in the music business. He pledged the all-Jewish fraternity Zeta Beta Tau for the social and professional benefits, and when one of his frat brothers took note of his last name, he suggested Mo make a change. "Ostrofsky" was too long, the frat brother said, and maybe too ethnic for the WASP-controlled world of business and finance. *Why not change it to something shorter and easier to spell?* Mo, therefore, revised "Ostrofsky" to "Ostin" and assimilated himself that much deeper into the mainstream of American commerce.

Norman Granz launched Clef, his jazz-focused record label, in 1946, but Ostin paid little mind. He was studying economics at UCLA at the time, while also falling in love with Evelyn Bardavid, a slightly younger woman who was pretty, smart as a whip, and radiant with a sweetness that most everyone she met found irresistible. They married in 1950, Evelyn setting up their home while Ostin pursued his classes at UCLA's law school. Then Evelyn got pregnant, and both their lives took a sharp turn. Now Ostin had to earn enough money to support his wife and a baby. He'd need a full-time job, but doing what? When he mentioned his plight to Irving Granz, his high school buddy told him that his big brother's new record label was doing so well that he was looking to hire a new staffer. Ostin set up a meeting with Norman Granz, and by the time it was over he had a job. He'd start at Clef Records the next Monday, earning a hundred dollars a week to do whatever Norman needed him to do. Mo was thrilled, almost entirely with having scored a regular income, any income. "I was looking for a job," he says. "I could have been an insurance agent."[3]

Mo began his career at Clef as the company controller. The title was a ruse. Controllers are almost always credentialed bookkeepers, which Ostin wasn't. But because he'd be dealing directly with the company's distributors and the bosses of pressing plants, song publishers, and so on, often about the cash or services they owed Clef, Ostin, Granz figured, would get more of his calls returned if the messages came from a top executive, or someone who sounded like one. And as it turned out, Mo's economics studies at UCLA had taught him more than enough for him to tend to the company's financial dealings. Given Clef's skeletal fifteen-member staff, Ostin took on new duties on a nearly weekly basis, negotiating with the artists' managers and lawyers and making decisions about marketing, sales, and advertising. He also got involved on the music side, listening to demo reels with the A&R staff and tossing in his two cents on which artists should or shouldn't be offered contracts.

Granz, who changed the name of the label to Verve in 1956, made for an exciting boss. Brilliant, sophisticated, and temperamental, he could be kind and supportive one minute, then erupt the next, a geyser of shouts and recriminations he sometimes punctuated with hurled papers, hole punches, and staplers. But Granz was fiercely dedicated to his artists, always dealing with them on the square and working to build their careers and spread the gospel of jazz. A fierce campaigner for African American equality at a time when institutional racism still thrived in daylight, Granz required all the venues hosting his Jazz at the Philharmonic road shows to allow integrated audiences. And if some hall manager tried to evade that commitment, Granz pulled his artists on the spot, even if the curtain was just hours or minutes away.

Granz was also a gifted businessman. By keeping costs low and the marketing tightly focused, his company could make money on an album that sold as few as twenty thousand copies and from a single release that moved just fifty thousand discs. Granz never bothered to explain his methods to Ostin; he trusted his recruit to learn by being present and attentive. The younger man was a quick study, and it wasn't long before Granz promoted him to director of the company's finance and administration departments. As Verve's reputation grew, so, too, did Ostin's. Now when he introduced himself at industry affairs, the other record men already knew who he was.[4]

Sometimes fortune comes from the least expected direction. For Verve Records in the spring of 1957, it walked through the door with Barney Kessel, an elite jazz guitarist and top session musician at L.A.'s recording studios. When he came in to pitch Granz on a project, the Verve boss was all ears. Ricky Nelson, the real-life son of Ozzie and Harriet Nelson, who played the titular roles on their highly rated television sitcom, *Ozzie and Harriet*, wanted to make a pop record. The Nelson boy was strictly a pop musician, but why not give him a shot? If his record hit, the cash would help float the jazz operation. Granz shrugged. Sure, why not? Kessel booked the session, and when Nelson's double-A-sided single "I'm Walkin'" and "A Teenager's Romance" came out in early April, the Fats Domino–written "I'm Walkin'" rocketed to No. 2 on *Billboard*'s Hot 100, with "A Teenager's Romance" rising to the No. 4 slot two months later. The record sold more than a million copies, and for the first time in his company's history, Granz had more money than he knew what to do with. And what might happen next? The Nelson boy had signed a contract that guaranteed Verve the rights to his work for the next few years! Or that's what they had been led to believe.

A few weeks later, Ozzie Nelson came in with an executive from MCA Records. The thing was, Ricky was only seventeen years old. Neither of his parents had cosigned his contract, so, as the law made clear, the document was meaningless. Granz could either give Ricky a lot more money or lose him to MCA. Furious, but unconvinced that the boy would have a second hit, Granz shook his head. Ozzie nodded and stalked out with the other record man. Once Granz's face stopped turning colors, he looked across his desk at Ostin and pointed to the office of Verve's attorney, who had negotiated the original Nelson contract. "Fire Jerry Rosenthal!" he snapped.[5]

Asked to find a new attorney for the company, Ostin came back with Mickey Rudin, a thirty-seven-year-old lawyer whose street-tough exterior disguised a powerful, Harvard-honed intellect. Moving to Los Angeles, Rudin signed up with the powerful entertainment law firm that would soon be known as Gang, Tyre, Rudin, and Brown. Already serving as Frank Sinatra's personal lawyer, Rudin took on the Verve account at a fortuitous time for both clients, and particularly for the thirty-year-old Ostin.

Granz had a lot going on. That's what it's like when you're a polymath, helping produce an Academy Award–nominated jazz performance short, *Jammin' the Blues*; promoting jazz concerts all across the world; and at the same time becoming close enough to Pablo Picasso to volunteer your (and Ostin's) services to help the artist create a feature-length animated movie of *Don Quixote*. *Life* magazine had already committed to publishing a ten-page spread about the movie's production, but Hollywood yawned. "Picasso?" one executive asked. "How do you *spell* that?"[6] Picasso's *Don Quixote* languished, but Granz had even more projects in mind, and as the 1950s waned so did his interest in running a record label. This news made Rudin think of his other client, the singer who was desperate to free himself from Capitol Records. The lawyer came back to Granz with news: Frank Sinatra would be very interested in buying Verve Records.

By the late 1950s, Sinatra was, as Gay Talese would write a few years later, the model of the "fully emancipated American male." He had it all: success, money, celebrity, the admiration of men, and the adoration of women. "The man who can do anything he wants," in Talese's words.[7] And it was true, except for the one thing Sinatra wanted more than anything else: a fair shake from Capitol Records. When he'd signed with the label in 1953, he was still recovering from the late 1940s slump in his career. But he'd come roaring back soon after, scoring hit after hit after hit for the company. You'd think they'd show him a little appreciation. But no.

And it was always no. No, he couldn't get a bump in his royalty rates. No, they didn't want to distribute albums by the artists Sinatra had signed to his independent production company. And no, they wouldn't let him out of his contract. He was locked in until 1961, whether he liked it or not. Brought low by the corporate blues, Sinatra took ill, overcome by a sore throat that made it impossible for him to sing. All his Capitol recording sessions were canceled until further notice, though Sinatra managed not only to play a lead role in *Can-Can*, but also to sing all his songs for the film's soundtrack, the rights to which belonged to his own production company. Increasingly desperate for a new Sinatra album, Capitol worked a deal with its cranky star, bartering the rights to the *Can-Can* soundtrack in exchange for a new clause in his contract that allowed him to alternate his Capitol releases with albums recorded for another label.[8]

Sinatra already knew which label he wanted it to be: one he owned. And when he did start his own label, he'd give his artists the respect the apes at Capitol never gave him. They'd all be in it for the music, for the sake of the art that had given their lives meaning and purpose—just like Norman Granz was doing for his artists at Verve.

So, when Mickey Rudin learned that Granz wanted to sell his business, Rudin arranged a sit-down between his two clients. As usual, the negotiations dragged on. Granz left town for a planned trip to Europe. Waiting for his flight at Los Angeles International, he bumped into Arnold Maxim, the president of MGM Records. Maxim was a jazz fanatic, too, so when he heard that Verve was on the block, he dove right in. Did Granz want two million? No problem. MGM had plenty of dough. Granz loved the sound of that, but he then had to tell Sinatra that another bidder had stepped up. Granz called Rudin the next day, but the streetwise lawyer, suspecting a bluff, told him to go to hell. *Go ahead and make that deal!* Rudin snapped. So, Granz did, sealing the bargain with Maxim less than a week later.

"Sinatra was furious beyond anything you can imagine," Ostin recalls. Granz had double-crossed him, and Rudin had let him do it! But wait, but wait, Rudin spoke soothingly. *Forget it, Frank,* he said. *You don't need to drop two million bucks on someone else's record company when you can start your own for so much less.* Once Sinatra had simmered down, he realized his lawyer was right again. Rudin got the project started and came back to Sinatra with a candidate to run the place. He was young, but he'd been working for Granz for nearly a decade and knew what he was doing. Better still, he knew how to follow directions and not be a pain in the ass. *That's the guy you need to run* your *label*, Rudin said. And, indeed, Sinatra liked Ostin fine. Offered five hundred dollars a week, significantly more than he'd been making at Verve, Ostin shook hands on the deal and floated home with his big news. Evelyn, now the mother of three energetic young boys, gave her husband a big kiss and a fervent request: "Let's go buy a house!"[9]

Given the title of administrative vice president, Ostin started his new job on January 1, 1961, and proved his mettle from the start, judiciously using his $300,000 start-up budget to recruit the best of his Verve colleagues and find other executives who would be hungry and ambitious enough to help make the new label into a serious competitor. As Sinatra assured him, Ostin had authority to do anything except sign the new label's artists, a job the label's president kept for himself.

They called the new label Reprise Records. In musical terms, a reprise is a repeat of an earlier passage, which fit with Sinatra's vision of making records that people would want to hear over and over again. It also served as shorthand for *reprisal*, which appealed to Sinatra's desire to extract revenge on Capitol Records. "Hey, Mo, see that tower?" Sinatra observed one day as Capitol's gleaming headquarters came into view. "One day we'll have one just like it!"[10] The singer still owed the bigger company more albums, but the next time he dragged himself into a recording session at Capitol's Studio A, he came sporting a necktie with a sleek sans serif FUCK YOU stitched across it.

Renting half a floor of office space above a carpet store on an unstylish block of Melrose Boulevard, Sinatra set his new record company into digs somewhere between cozy and cramped. With fewer than ten staffers on board, the two-man A&R crew gathered into one little office, the financial guys in another, and Ostin in a third. Sinatra loaded the roster with his friends and other artists whose work he'd admired for decades. Sammy Davis Jr. and Dean Martin signed up, along with Dennis Day, Ethel Merman, and Danny Kaye, plus jazz eminences Duke Ellington and Count Basie, Jimmy Witherspoon, the Modern Jazz Quartet, and a few others.

When Reprise released its first batch of records in March 1961—just when Chubby Checker and Elvis Presley were battling for *Billboard*'s No. 1 spot, with the Shirelles, the Everly Brothers, and Ben E. King in close pursuit—the new label's list featured Dadsville duds, including Sammy Davis Jr.'s *The Wham of Sam* and Calvin Jackson's *Jazz Variations on Movie Themes*. The only bright spot was Sinatra's own *Ring-a-Ding Ding*. The next release, four months later, was an even less promising group: *The Exciting Sounds of the South Seas*, Lou Monte's *Great Italian-American Hits*, *The X-15 and Other Sounds of Missiles, Rockets and Jets*, and Sande and Greene Fun-Time Band's *The Ol' Calliope Man at the Fair*. October's releases included *America's Favorite Organ Hits* and *Themes from Great Foreign*

*Films*. Again, the sole hit in the bunch came from Reprise's chief executive. *I Remember Tommy*, a tribute to the late orchestra leader Tommy Dorsey, moved 220,000 copies, more than the combined sales of all the other records.

"A Newer, Happier, Emancipated Sinatra," sang the ads for the company president's first Reprise album. "Untrammeled, Unfettered, Unconfined—on Reprise."[11] But the boss's reputed cheeriness was tested when he took on the task of creating an elaborate album package to commemorate President John F. Kennedy's inauguration in January 1961. The president and his family loved the sound of Sinatra's vision: an all-star cast of celebrities (Sinatra, Ethel Merman, Sammy Davis Jr., Sir Laurence Olivier, Harry Belafonte) to present recitations and sing hymns and patriotic songs. The album, as Sinatra imagined it, would serve both to celebrate the man whose cause he'd made his own and to raise money for the cash-strapped Democratic Party. Ambassador Joseph Kennedy, the president's empire-building father, was especially enthusiastic, and not just because he liked celebrating his son's triumph. He'd put so much of his own money into the president's campaign, much of it through the Democratic fundraising apparatus, that he was eager to get some of it back. The ambassador took the lead on the family's end of the project.

But while Joseph Kennedy connected Ostin with presidential spokesman Pierre Salinger and presidential younger brother and U.S. attorney general Robert F. Kennedy, and helped convince the inaugural performers to give Reprise the right to market their performances, he also demanded approval on everything, from the photographs to the text and feel of the songs. Joe eventually calmed down, and at long last the album was ready. Salinger made plans for the all-star party that would herald its release in Washington, DC.

Then, at the last minute, catastrophe. When President Kennedy came to Palm Springs, he withdrew his longtime promise to stay with Sinatra. Kennedy had his reasons. Sinatra, who owned a casino straddling the California–Nevada border, had been charged with cozying up to Chicago mafioso Sam Giancana. Obviously, the new president couldn't be seen with him in those circumstances and wound up bunking with the cardigan-clad crooner Bing Crosby. Enraged by the public slight, Sinatra canceled the inauguration album. He never spoke to Kennedy again.[12]

The implosion of the inauguration album only added to the young record company's financial troubles. And while Sinatra had better things to do than sweat the company's day-to-day machinations, Mickey Rudin kept a hawk's eye on the label and especially its administrative vice president. The lawyer didn't visit the Melrose Boulevard offices very often, but he called in constantly, mostly to yell at Ostin for whatever real or perceived mistake he was making with their struggling record label. And he wasn't nice about it, either, screaming about the latest bum sales report, enraged that Ostin still hadn't figured out how to sell the albums they were producing. Rudin was a lawyer. He had no idea how the record industry worked, or why dusty performers from out of the past couldn't possibly get across to the increasingly young majority of record buyers. One thing he did understand, though, was that he was the one who had brought Ostin to Sinatra, which meant that his own fortunes were tied to how well Ostin did, or didn't do, at Reprise. Eventually, Rudin's barrage got under Ostin's skin, to the point where his mood grew dark, his glasses seemed permanently smeared, and his self-confidence lay heaped around his ankles. And yet he never even contemplated quitting. No matter how mean Rudin could be, his snarls and insults couldn't be as bad as being unemployed or, worse, a self-admitted failure. And there was still so much to do.[13]

The Reprise hits kept on not coming. The winter 1962 releases included Jack de Mello's *Music from the Land of the Rising Sun*, *Eddie Cano at P.J.'s*, and *The Ol' Calliope Man Visits a German Hofbrau*. Meanwhile, the Top 40 was jumping with Chubby Checker's "The Twist," the Shirelles' "Baby It's You," Dion's "The Wanderer," and more. *Welcome to the record store, kids! Would you rather spin Elvis Presley's "Jailhouse Rock" or the Sande and Greene Fun-Time Band's* Ol' Calliope Man Visits a German Hofbrau?

The conundrum was obvious. Reprise was Sinatra's label, and if he didn't want any part of the day's most popular music, that was his decision to make. But Sinatra could also read sales statistics and profit-and-loss statements, and after a year and a half of futility he began to reconsider. When his musical adviser Murray Wolfe, who found and secured the rights to the songs Sinatra wanted to record, suggested hiring a young producer who knew how to weave rock 'n' roll elements into sophisticated pop songs, the singer gave him the nod.

Reporting for work in Burbank in the late summer of 1963, Jimmy Bowen came through the door with two vital assets. First, he was a sensitive and inventive producer, able not only to tune in to each artist's unique character, but also to guide them into horizons they might otherwise have avoided. Also, he was a tough son of a bitch, coming out of the Texas Panhandle in the mid-fifties with the Rhythm Orchids, a teenage pop combo that topped the *Billboard* charts with their first single on Morris Levy's Roulette Records in 1957. When Reprise's founding A&R chief resigned, Bowen took his job, and spent the next few days digging into the works of the McGuire Sisters, Art Linkletter, the Ivy League Trio, and the like. He noticed the most obvious problem: there was no way they could turn a profit while paying for all these old-school acts. Ostin knew this already, but all those artists were Frank's friends. How was he supposed to tell his boss that he wanted to dump them from his label? Bowen, full of the confidence of the freshly hired, said he'd deliver the news. Ostin set up the appointment, and Bowen pointed his car east to visit Sinatra's mansion on the tenth hole of the Tamarisk Golf Club, in Rancho Mirage.[14]

While on the road, Bowen got nervous. He'd just gotten his dream job. Was he really about to march into the living room of one of the most powerful people in show business and tell him his friends were going to kill his business? And it wasn't as if *all* Reprise's old-style records had swan-dived onto the rocks. Lou Monte, arguably the hoariest act on the label with his Italian-ish song parodies, had scored a hit with "Pepino the Italian Mouse," a sort of Chipmunks-by-the-Mediterranean novelty song in which an invading mouse squeaks in *Italiano* (more off-label use of helium) while Monte grouses about the rodent's appetite for his Parmesan cheese. Not exactly a candidate for the American Songbook, but it sold just shy of 700,000 copies, more than three times what any other Reprise single had moved, Sinatra's included. The influx of cash took the financial pressure off the company long enough for its founder and CEO to consider the impact a hit record could have on a cash-starved record label.

After crunching up the gravel driveway, Bowen was greeted by Sinatra's chief assistant, George Jacobs, who showed him into a richly furnished sitting room that had a full bar at one end. Sinatra breezed in after a couple of minutes, made straight for the bottles, and asked his guest what he'd like to drink. Bowen, knowing what Sinatra's choice would be, asked for the same thing: Jack Daniel's, straight up. Delighted by Bowen's excellent taste, Sinatra led him to a couple of armchairs. *Great to see ya, kid*, he said. *What can I do for you?* Bowen gave it to him straight. He knew Sinatra had signed all the label's artists and that many of them were his friends, but the numbers were the numbers, and they would never add up to a profit until the label got rid of the artists whose records didn't sell. Sinatra, as much a businessman as an artist, took another sip of bourbon and nodded. "Well, you take care of it. Thanks."[15]

He then vanished as quickly as he'd arrived, leaving Bowen to reflect on where he was and what might have happened if his host had taken the news in a different way. "I'd never had Jack Daniel's before, but I slugged it down like milk and thought I'd die for about thirty seconds," Bowen says. "George was laughing at me. Then I got up and went home."[16]

Bowen took a machete to the deadwood on the label's roster, then set to freshening up the sound of the artists who still had enough snap to launch a new record up the charts. Starting with Dean Martin, Bowen took a newly written tune called "Everybody Loves Somebody," put a strong backbeat into the orchestral arrangement, and turned it into a smash big enough to claim the top of *Billboard*'s Hot 100 at the height of the British Invasion. It was Martin's first No. 1 in nine years. Bowen did it again with Sinatra, launching the company's chairman to the No. 1 spot with "Strangers in the Night," and then again with "Somethin' Stupid," a duet with his daughter Nancy. The raucous "That's Life" took Sinatra to No. 4 a couple years later, and suddenly things were looking much brighter around Reprise.

Still, the run of crossover hits Bowen produced didn't come soon enough to solve Sinatra's most pressing problem in 1963. Along with paying Reprise's bills for nearly three years, the singer continued to struggle with the Nevada Gaming Commission, which ruled that he had broken the law by allowing Giancana into his Cal Neva Casino. Stripped of its gambling license, the casino foundered, and the loss of that income, along with the mounting bills from his record company, was about to bankrupt him.[17]

And this was where Jack Warner stepped in with the perfect solution. Craving a star guaranteed to draw audiences to the box office, Warner had spent years trying to sign Sinatra to a long-term movie contract.

And while Sinatra still treasured Reprise and was determined to protect its future, he also needed to plug the hole it had become for his money. So, why not solve both problems at once? If Sinatra agreed to sign with Warner Bros. Pictures, Jack Warner would take Reprise off his hands and merge it with his Warner Bros. Records.

Soon the two worked out a deal that was so favorable to Sinatra that it's hard to imagine what Jack Warner was thinking. Instead of a purely cash deal, Sinatra would trade his two-thirds ownership of the money-bleeding Reprise to Warner for one third of Warner's much larger and profitable company, which would include Reprise. What's more, Sinatra's 33.3 percent share of Warner would give him a voice in all Warner Bros. dealings, plus a share of the company's annual proceeds, and ongoing authority over his beloved Reprise.[18]

Riding high in April, shot down in May, then back on top in June—it was Sinatra's story even before he belted it out in "That's Life," one of the smash singles he'd record for the company that would be known as Warner/Reprise Records.

# 5

## WARNER/REPRISE:
## A QUITE UNLOSABLE GAME

Even fifty years later, there was that edge of competition between them. Joe Smith, sipping a glass of wine in the living room of his luxury apartment a dozen floors above Wilshire Boulevard, was dressed impeccably, twinkling and cracking wise like the streetwise kid turned Yale man he'd always been. Even with his memory fading, Smith could tick off the big acts he'd signed and Mo Ostin hadn't. They both had their strengths, you see. "Mo was a great talent finder, and so was I," Smith told me, recalling how he'd signed the Grateful Dead, James Taylor, Black Sabbath, and too many others to count.

When Ostin settled down in the living room of his hilltop home a year later, he had his own story to tell. True enough, you could build an entire hall of fame from the artists he'd signed. He was the one who'd found Jimi Hendrix, Joni Mitchell, and the Kinks, the first real rockers at the company, who he'd picked up in 1964 soon after convincing Sinatra to let him release rock 'n' roll records.

Mo and Joe, as everyone in Burbank called them during those dreamy years, were great pals and knew how their unified tastes and strengths made them such a powerful team. "One of us had to be president, and it turned out to be Mo," Smith said. He had offers to run other record labels, but for that moment, just when they were sailing into an orbit far beyond where any other record company had ever spun, he was happy to be number two.

"We were basically equals then, and it worked beautifully," Smith said.[1]

Ostin agrees: "Theoretically, I was his boss, but I never treated him like that. We worked as if we were partners."

Ostin: "There was never any question that his leaving would be a great loss. But when Joe did leave, I was chairman and president for four years and did it all myself."[2]

Smith: "No matter what happened after I left, the years we were together were really the golden years."[3]

○

When Rudin told Ostin in 1963 that Sinatra was going to sell Reprise to Jack Warner, the executive was dismayed. What would happen to him and his staff? They had worked so hard to get Reprise on its feet, and their efforts were starting to pay off. Trini Lopez, a young nightclub performer who combined rock 'n' roll and Latin music into a dynamic sound, was amassing fans and racking up sales at an exciting pace. Ostin had also been staffing up, adding enough new bodies to require a move from the label's cramped HQ on Melrose Avenue to larger, if not fancier, digs on the second floor of the Pacific Radio Store, on Cahuenga Boulevard in Hollywood. They'd been in the new offices for just a few months when news of Sinatra's plan to sell Reprise to Warner Bros. came out of the sky. Rudin said that no one on the Reprise staff would be laid off, but that sounded aspirational at best. Merging two fully staffed record companies meant having close to 100 percent more employees than necessary. And if the Warner executives had to choose between their own people and the newcomers from Reprise, their loyalties would be obvious.

Still, there was one colleague Ostin wouldn't be sorry to lose: his perpetually unhappy supervisor, Mickey Rudin. Attending a Dodgers game in Sinatra's box the day after news of the Reprise sale hit the papers, Ostin sat near Art Minella, a tax accountant whose firm had the Sinatra account. So, the other man wanted to know, how did Ostin feel about being sold to Warner?

Ostin shrugged. He hadn't expected it, he admitted, but he didn't think it would be a *complete* tragedy. "At least now I'll have Mickey off my back."[4]

When moving day came, the Reprise staffers formed a motorcade up Cahuenga Boulevard to the Valley side and then east for a couple of miles before rolling into Burbank and the parking lot outside the squat two-story building at 3701 Warner Boulevard. After gathering in the parking lot, the Reprise staff shuffled in together and were led into an open room with a bunch of small cubicles stationed around the edges. Everything was green—the walls, the carpet, the cubicles—and noticeably threadbare. No one came out to greet them, so they sat on the floor, waiting for something to happen. An hour passed. Every so often, someone would appear in the doorway, gaze at them for a moment, then duck out again without saying a word. After ninety minutes, a woman who seemed to be a receptionist came out and said hello, then invited the newcomers into the kitchen to help themselves to coffee. Then she vanished, too.

The movers arrived and started hauling the Reprise furniture through the door. Sinatra had outfitted his company's offices with sleek modern sofas, desks, and chairs, which were a striking contrast to the standard Warner Bros. carpets and cubicles. Some of the Warner employees took to ogling the elegant furnishings and whispering, *Maybe if they hadn't spent all their money on furniture they'd still be in business!* Ostin, standing at the center of the room with his arms folded across his chest, didn't say a word.[5]

He was already a marked man. Herman Starr, the president of Warner's song-publishing company and one of its most senior executives, recognized Ostin's name from his days at Verve and blamed him for Verve's and then Reprise's unwillingness to pay publishing royalties on time. Ostin hadn't been responsible for how either company paid its debts, but that didn't occur (or matter) to Starr. He just didn't want Ostin anywhere near the Warner operation. When he met with WBR president Mike Maitland, Starr made his position clear: "Get rid of the bum!"[6]

Instead, Maitland took the Reprise executive out to lunch to hear his thoughts on his company's strengths and flaws, while sharing his own take on Warner Bros. Records. It was unclear if Maitland was really interested in learning to work with Ostin, or whether Sinatra had, in a typical display of the loyalty he showed to friends and allies, added a clause to the Reprise deal ensuring that Ostin kept his job after Warner took over. Mickey Rudin insisted such a clause was in the contract, though Maitland would always deny it. Ostin can't say for sure either way, but the one thing everyone knew was that once the companies merged, there were only two people Sinatra would speak to when he called the Warner Bros. offices. One was Jack Warner, and the other was Mo Ostin.[7]

Whatever the reason, Maitland worked closely with the Reprise executive to figure out how their conjoined record companies should operate together. And he paid special attention to Ostin's insistence that the labels continue to work independently from one another. That way, Ostin reasoned, the two operations would continue to appeal to record buyers from different angles. Warner Bros. offered pop-oriented acts like the Everly Brothers, Bing Crosby, and Jimmy Durante and popular comedians Bob Newhart and Bill Cosby, while Reprise focused on jazzier artists, including Sinatra, Nelson Riddle, Juan Esquivel, and the Buddy Cole Trio. Maitland agreed that it was a good idea. And when Ostin asked for money to buy out the contracts of Reprise's older artists and pay for younger acts more in tune with the times, Maitland agreed to that, too. Even so, Ostin assumed he'd be tossed out sooner rather than later.

Instead, Maitland—in the process of being elevated to a new role as chairman of a new corporate entity that would contain both record companies—made Ostin the top executive, known as the general manager, of Reprise, while Joe Smith, then WBR's head of national promotions, would be *his* label's general manager. Each label chief would get one executive assistant and two secretaries, but the labels would share everything else, including a commitment to rebuild their rosters with artists who would sound like the 1960s—except for the rock 'n' roll part. That was still off limits.

●

One of the most striking moments in *What's Happening!*, Albert and David Maysles's great documentary about the Beatles' first American performances in February 1964, takes place after the group's *Ed Sullivan Show* debut on February 9. The young British rockers, just through the jostling gauntlet of teenagers and news reporters squeezed outside the Plaza Hotel, are waiting to take one of the operator-manned elevators up to their suite—except the twenty-one-year-old Paul McCartney can't stand still. Eyes alight, laughing and rattling off unintelligible jokes for the reporters and cameras, he makes a tight oval orbit of the elevator bank, back and forth, back and forth.[8]

He is a human electron, sent skittering by the current of a newly born epoch. And he is a harbinger of the energy that would soon be visible everywhere: in the hair, the clothes, the stacked-heel boots, the sparking eyes, the unspoken understandings and secret languages of sounds, styles, and beliefs; in the need to go further, to see more, to shrug off the cloak of the past, to jump and spin and laugh and go skipping off to whatever was next. As Philip Larkin wrote in his poem "Annus Mirablis," the feeling was as widespread as it was intoxicating, a shared sense that life had become, ". . . A brilliant breaking of the bank / A quite unlosable game."[9] And at the start of 1964, it was right there, humming all around you, just waiting to be found, felt, taken up, and passed from hand to hand, ear to ear, and mouth to mouth.

○

Here's a quandary: How does a record company that refuses to release rock 'n' roll records begin to compete in a music marketplace that is almost entirely defined by rock 'n' roll records? Jimmy Bowen had helped drag the Reprise sound closer to the modern world, though his works stopped short of being actual rock 'n' roll. Ostin had also worked an international distribution deal with Pye, a small British pop label whose owners were a lot more interested in making money than in shaping the tastes of its listeners. The Brits there were thrilled to be the UK home for Sinatra, and Ostin was just as happy to have access to Pye's growing collection of British rock groups, to whose records Reprise owned the American rights. Jack Warner might have fancied his role as a guardian of cultural mores, but he was even more eager, Mike Maitland knew, to stop tossing his money away. And if his company owned the American rights to a potential chart-topper, he almost certainly wouldn't want to give those profits to a competing record label, right?

When Ostin first heard the buzz saw chords and lusty-snarly vocals in the Kinks' "You Really Got Me," he knew he was hearing a hit song. And it wasn't just his intuition telling him that. When he heard about the song a week after its British release on August 4, 1964, it was already bouncing into the middle reaches of the British singles charts, selling so fast that Pye's top executives suspended production on their other records so they could press, package, and deliver Kinks 45s around the clock. Ostin snapped up his option to release the song on Reprise, then wrote a letter to Pye president Louis Benjamin to thank him for "You Really Got Me," promising that the entire Warner/Reprise staff was wild for the record, particularly the sales staff, who, he wrote, "are so happy to have their teeth into a piece of hit English material that they have dedicated themselves to knocking off the Beatles." Ostin, feeling increasingly free to stretch the boundaries of acceptability, also urged Benjamin to send along any and every other rock 'n' roll song that struck his ears as hit material. "You don't even need to worry about making a deal or having us listen to it," he continued. "Just realize that if you think a record has it, it will be automatically released here by Reprise."[10]

Ostin's confidence was well placed. "You Really Got Me" leaped into *Billboard*'s Top 10, getting as high as No. 7, with follow-up "All Day and All of the Night" climbing exactly as high and "Tired of Waiting for You" going one better, at the No. 6 slot. And the Pye roster offered more than rock 'n' roll acts. Joe Smith scored even better when he found Petula Clark's "Downtown" during a listening session at the offices of French licensee Vogue Records in Paris. Clark was ten years older than the rock stars of the moment, and her tune was closer to Bowen's hybrid productions than to the metallic crunch of the Kinks, but the latter's British-ness made them Beatles-adjacent, while their song's ascending melody was impossible to deny. Released in the United States in mid-December, "Downtown" made *Billboard*'s No. 1 spot in little more than a month, a supersonic pace in those days.

Closer to home, the Mexican American nightclub singer Trini Lopez (one of the other guests on *The Ed Sullivan Show* the night the Beatles jump-started the youth generation's pulse a few months earlier) skirted the boundaries of rock 'n' roll. He goosed his repertoire of standards, Mexican favorites, and modern folk songs with Ray Charles belters and an electric band. The combination brought a wild energy that could transform his showroom crowds into, as Stan Cornyn wrote in his liner notes, "Hundreds of cravers, united in the sensual act of rhythm."

Still, Maitland knew his bosses were adjusting to the idea of bringing full-bore American rock bands onto their company's two labels. For the time being, they'd have to start with lighter-gauge groups. And what better group to start with than a poppy band whose members happened to include the son of one of Sinatra's closest friends?

The pop-rock trio Dino, Desi, and Billy was a group of well-to-do teens who, in the first year of Beatlemania, got themselves a guitar, bass, and drum kit and set them up in one of their parents' basements to try to make like their British heroes. They were in that basement practicing when a good friend of Dino Martin's dad came over for a drink and a schmooze. So, there they were, Frank Sinatra and Dean Martin, cigarettes and glasses of bourbon in hand, when the music came pounding up through the floor. Sinatra was curious, so down the two pals went to check out the kids' music. There were Dino Martin, Dean's boy, on guitar; Desi Jr., the son of Desi Arnaz and Lucille Ball, on drums; and their friend Billy Hinsche playing second guitar. And they weren't half bad, either.

"You guys have been practicing!" Sinatra called out when they finished the song. "Ever think of making a record?"

Well, of course they had *thought* about it, but—

"Great. Keep practicing." Sinatra turned to Dean and said, *sotto voce,* Let me talk to Mo.[11]

Not long afterward, the boys were summoned to the dumpy building across the street from the Warner Bros. Pictures lot and handed a recording contract. Reprise released the combo's first single a month or two later. That tune didn't connect with anyone, but their second try, a "Louie, Louie"-lite number called "I'm a Fool," made Ostin "hit the roof,"[12] as he wired to the three teens. Record buyers sent it into the Top 20 (No. 17), and were nearly as enthusiastic about its follow-up ("Not the Lovin' Kind," No. 25) before the tide started turning in a different direction. DD&B were kids, still shy of their fifteenth birthdays, when their first two singles visited the upper reaches of the pop charts. But the boys' covers of "Like a Rolling Stone" and "Satisfaction" succeeded only in showing the distance separating the three high schoolers from what actually mattered in the fall of 1965. Dino, Desi and Billy had had their fun, but fun was going out of style.

The rock 'n' roll kids were older now, a lot of them on the way to being their family's first-ever college graduates. Their eyes were open, and it all came flooding in: the slaughtered natives, the enslaved Africans, the degraded environment, and the brutalist sweep of American capitalism. That, plus the horror of seeing your heroes assassinated, your fellow citizens beaten by the police, and your own tender ass perpetually at risk from the Vietnam War or instant nuclear catastrophe. The breezy harmonies Peter, Paul and Mary had draped over "Blowin' in the Wind" and "The Times They Are A-Changin'" had given way to Dylan's own sardonic derision: "Something's happening but you don't know what it is, / Do you, Mr. Jones?"

○

As big and loud as a bear, Tom Donahue came to San Francisco in the early 1960s with an immaculate pompadour and a goatee that would soon stretch into a full beard. An immensely popular disc jockey in Philadelphia who was run out of town by the payola scandals of the late 1950s, Donahue had landed at KYA-AM and soon made himself the Top 40 station's dominant personality, as renowned for his sharp taste in pop music as for his bombastic on-air presence. A fixture in the bars and theaters and anywhere else rock 'n' roll could be found, he kept on top of the San Francisco music scene as it evolved in the 1960s, and he was quick to figure out how much voltage the new generation of bands was bringing to the city. Just as quick to recognize the opportunities opening up backstage, he teamed up with his longtime on-air partner Bob Mitchell and started booking sock hops around the Bay Area, bringing in well-known stars who were willing to sing (or lip-synch to) a few songs to endear themselves to the local fans and, more important, to the guys who wrote the playlists for the region's hottest AM station.

There was a nice stream of cash flowing through the sock hops, but for Donahue, who preferred bespoke suits, it was only a first step toward the great green ocean he knew was just waiting to be discovered. He made his first move in the summer of 1963, investing thousands of dollars to rent the Cow Palace, the 16,500-seat arena on the southern edge of San Francisco, for a September 28 concert he billed as the Surf Party. Donahue booked the hall without any commitments from the acts who might actually draw fans to the box office, but he and Mitchell were the top dogs on the Bay Area's top radio station, so when the big man rang up his pals at the big record companies he had no trouble getting commitments from virtually every act populating that week's Top 10—the Beach Boys, Jan and Dean, the Ronettes, Bobby Freeman, Little Stevie Wonder, Dionne Warwick, the Righteous Brothers, and more than a dozen others—and by the time the big night arrived, there wasn't a ticket to be found anywhere.

Soon there were more arena concerts, then a national radio tip sheet Donahue and Mitchell dubbed *Tempo*. But the real action lay in the music itself. And with so many bands coming out of the city and all the nearby towns, and with so many kids flocking out to groove both to the music and to the generational solidarity, it seemed like it would be easy to make a success out of a halfway decent band. So, Donahue and Mitchell decided to start their own record label.

Declaring themselves the cofounders and chief executives of Autumn Records in early 1964, Donahue and Mitchell only had to look to KYA's staff to find their lead A&R man and producer in Sylvester Stewart, a twenty-one-year-old disc jockey who moonlighted as a record producer and occasional artist, the latter under the stage name Sly Stone. Working together, the three of them found a starting roster of acts, some of whom, like Bobby Freeman, best known for "Do You Want to Dance," had been at it for years, while the Beau Brummels, the Mojo Men, and a harmony-singing surf group called the Tikis were fresh out of the garage. Donahue, already tuned in to early psychedelic music, also signed up the Great Society, a reality-bending group whose icy-hot singer, Grace Slick, would soon join Jefferson Airplane.

The label made a promising start, scoring hits with Freeman ("C'mon and Swim") and the Beau Brummels, whose first two singles ("Laugh Laugh" and "Just a Little") made it onto *Billboard*'s Top 20. But while other record company presidents would invest their proceeds into building up their label's roster and staff, Donahue and Mitchell thought nothing of using company cash for pricey dinners, pricier women, cars, and the occasional washer-dryer set, and it took less than two years for Autumn to hit the edge of bankruptcy. With all the money spent and nothing coming in but more bills to add to their $10,000-plus debt, Donahue dialed the number of an old deejay turned record company executive he'd known for years. He had the right guy. Joe Smith was happy to fly up from Burbank to see if they could strike a deal—which they did, almost immediately. For the cost of Autumn's debt ($12,749.30), the company's logo, name, artists, and all the music made after April 1, 1966, would belong to Warner/Reprise. Donahue and Mitchell would stay on as executive producers with a 2 percent cut of every record that came from their former artists.

Donahue also threw in a hot tip for Smith and Warner Bros.: a few months earlier, he'd sat in on a live audition by a Palo Alto group called the Warlocks, a folk-blues-rock band whose members spanned the worlds of the Hells Angels and the Mills College classroom of the avant-garde composer and academic Luciano Berio. Donahue could sense the group's promise: they made a rollicking sound like no band he had heard before. Lacking the money to sign the group to Autumn, Donahue befriended the musicians and said he'd do everything he could to help them build their career. The group, lately renamed the Grateful Dead, was making a stir in San Francisco's galaxy of rock 'n' roll clubs, ballrooms, and theaters—and no wonder. Their music was truly unique, a runaway train of blues, soul, and folk tunes with careering solos featuring the group's glitter-eyed lead guitarist, Jerry Garcia. But there was something else going on, too, something beyond the mind-scrambling effect of the LSD tabs they gobbled by the fistful. It wasn't just their fans' ecstatic dervishing but the way the musicians made the walls bend and shimmer, loosened gravity's crush, and set you on the moonlit trail to the edge of a new existence.

One day in 1966, chief liner note writer Stan Cornyn got a call from a development executive at Warner Bros. Pictures, just across Warner Boulevard from his desk in the ex-machine shop. The studio had just bought the rights to *Night Moves*, a novel set among the beatniks in San Francisco, and they needed a reasonably hip writer to turn it into a movie script. Was he interested? Cornyn had never written a movie before; he was best known for the promotional tone poems he composed for the covers of Frank Sinatra's *Strangers in the Night* and *Sinatra at the Sands* albums. But he was a youngish music guy with sprigs of oil-free blond hair bristling over his shirt collar, and he knew something about the poets, drunks, and free-livers they had in mind. Cornyn took the gig, demanding only that the company pay for him to spend a weekend exploring the hilly streets and wiggy scenes in the bay city to the north. *Sure, fine*, the production executive said. *Whatever you want.* The guy could have told him to sleep in a Dumpster, and Cornyn would have done it.

Born in 1933 to a conservative lawyer and a strict Christian Scientist mother, Cornyn grew up on an oak-shaded block of Pasadena, where as a teenager he balanced his upper-class equanimity with a passion for writing, theater, and jazz. He studied writing at Pomona College and then spent a year at the Yale School of Drama learning that he wasn't cut out to be a playwright. He passed the next year failing to write a novel in Paris and then returned to Los Angeles in 1956 to try his hand at television writing. Much typing ensued, but his most successful composition that year was the application he filled out for a liner note writer's job at Capitol Records.

The job had its dreamy moments, but Cornyn didn't take well to editing, so when his boss wouldn't stop complaining about his creative punctuation, the stubborn young writer submitted his resignation in early 1958, storming out of the Capitol Records Tower just a year after he'd arrived. Hearing of the just-launched Warner Bros. Records from a friendly Capitol A&R man, he got an interview and was hired to be the new label's editorial director. A steep layoff disrupted his career in 1959, but Cornyn had made such a good fit with the company that then chief Jim Conkling invited him to freelance out of the office he was already in, pledging to throw him as much work as he could until they had the money to put him back on staff. He was rehired in the post–*77 Sunset Strip* boom, and his writing matured into a distinctive blend of New Journalism, beat poetry, and *Mad* magazine spoofs.

For his latest assignment, Cornyn spent his days in San Francisco following his feet through North Beach, where Kerouac, Cassady, and their dharmic buddies had come together to imagine, write, and rant. Most of that scene had evaporated since its 1950s heyday, but Cornyn took it in and kept moving, first to the Mission Flats, then up to the ramshackle Victorians lining the hills south of Golden Gate Park's panhandle. Here, he discovered a different scene. It was the leaflets on the telephone poles that first drew his eyes. "Squiggly-lettered posters," Cornyn recalled in his 2002 memoir, *Exploding*,[13] printed in eruptive shades of yellow, orange, red, and purple. He had to squint to figure out that they were advertisements for the weekend's concerts at the Avalon Ballroom and the Fillmore Auditorium, crumbling venues being revived by young impresarios Bill Graham and Chet Helms, whose production company was called the Family Dog. The acts had uniformly bizarre names: Jefferson Airplane, Quicksilver Messenger Service, Moby Grape. Intrigued, Cornyn marched off to check it all out.

Cornyn might have been younger than the production executives at Warner, but he was still a man of the 1950s, with ingrained appetites for Sinatra, martinis, and women who knew how to put the shimmer into an evening gown. But when he got past the Avalon's box office, he headed for the door with his inner anthropologist on high alert. Inside, he found an unbelievable scene. "I walked into screaming," he reported later. "Electric guitars feeling up speakers and speakers screeching back 'rape.'" The next morning, he ventured to the Haight-Ashbury district and spent the day drifting through the head shops, hippie boutiques, and esoteric bookstores stacked with underground newspapers, mystical tracts by Indian gurus, and jewelry cases stocked with twined love beads, ankh necklaces, and hand-carved marijuana pipes. "My personal mantra," he wrote later, "became 'wow.'"[14]

When he got back to Burbank, Cornyn went straight to Ostin and Smith and spilled everything: the formless music, the sweet aromas, the colors, and the legions of kids gone wild with it all. Intrigued, Ostin set up a weekend trip to San Francisco for Cornyn, himself, and both their wives. "It was like going to *Mars*," Ostin says.[15] But it turned out he liked space travel, and he returned to the city by himself a week or two later, wandering the ballrooms, clubs, and record stores for days on end, taking in as much of this new world as he could. Working among artists had taught him to keep his doors of perception cracked open; you never knew when genius was going to walk into the room. And when it did, you needed to recognize it, understand it, and embrace it like the love of your life.

Thanks to Tom Donahue's tip about the Grateful Dead, Joe Smith was already on the case. Following the disc jockey's suggestion that he head north before another record label snatched the psychedelic band from Warner's clutches, the executive booked a weekend trip with his wife, Donnie, and was dining with her at Ernie's, San Francisco's most elegant steak house, when the maître d' called him to the house telephone. Donahue was on the other end urging Smith to get to the Avalon Ballroom as soon as possible. The Grateful Dead were playing, and the group had agreed to meet with him during their set break, even though they didn't exactly approve of corporate record companies. At first Smith protested. He was with his wife, and they were both dressed to the nines—Joe in a dark business suit, Donnie in a formal gown and white gloves. How could they possibly go to a rock concert dressed like that? *That won't be a problem*, Donahue said. *If anyone notices, they'll just assume you're in costume.* Smith paid the check, retrieved his wife, and hailed a cab for the Avalon Ballroom.

Exiting the cab at the doorway of 1168 Sutter Street, the Smiths climbed the stairs to find what Smith compared to a scene from one of Federico Fellini's surrealist films. A glutinous light show oozed behind the musicians. In the foreground, men dressed as jesters danced wildly alongside young women in skirts, tight blouses, and no bras. Lasers raked the fog while a strobe light made herky-jerky cartoons of the dancers. And all of it was swept aside by the music, that freight-train-that's-lost-its-rails sound that Donahue had tried to describe over the telephone just a few days earlier.

The Smiths located Donahue in the throng. Thoroughly gobsmacked by the sounds and the scene, Smith put his arm over the disc jockey's shoulder. "I don't think Jack Warner will ever understand this," he shouted over the clamor. "I don't think *I* understand it, either. But I just feel like they're really, really *good*."[16] Hauled backstage by Donahue at the end of the set, Smith came on per usual, crinkling his eyes and flashing his incisors, shaking every hand in sight and reciting the incantations that record company executives employ to seduce their quarry: words of love, faith, and everlasting fame and wealth. Smith had seen strong young men shed tears of joy to hear it, but this time he ran up against a wall of blank-faced indifference.

"My grandmother warned me about guys like Joe Smith,"[17] the Ichabod Crane–resembling bassist Phil Lesh snapped. The other band members snickered, but added nothing. Still, the group's managers, Danny Rifkin and Rock Scully, gave Smith a friendlier greeting, softening him up for the many demands their group would need addressed in their contract. A lot of it was basic stuff: the size of the group's advance, recording budgets, recoupable expenses, and royalty percentages. But Smith also had to realize that the Grateful Dead wasn't just a rock 'n' roll band; it was a *community*. Everyone in the band's circle had his or her own needs, and their requirements mattered just as much as those of the band members—if only because the band members had a vote in every decision, including whether they were going to become Warner Bros. recording artists or not.[18]

"Well, that sounds great!" Smith enthused.[19] If this was how San Francisco worked, he figured, he'd get used to it. When the group's self-titled debut album came out a few months later, Smith flew back to San Francisco to lead the celebration at Fugazi Hall.

"I want to tell you all, Warner Bros. Records feels privileged to take the Grateful Dead out to the world!"

At that, band manager Rock Scully took Smith's place at the microphone. "And the Grateful Dead feel privileged to introduce Warner Bros. Records to the world!"[20]

Scully didn't know how right he was.

# CHRISTMAS AND NEW YEAR'S
# AND YOUR BIRTHDAY ALL TOGETHER

To see it now, D. A. Pennebaker's *Monterey Pop!* documentary looks like a dispatch from another society, maybe on another planet. The early gathering crowd is young and hale and frocked in caftans and oozingly patterned blouses, sitting beneath the flying fish flags and rainbow banners, not far from the hand-painted signs listing the day's performers and the times they're due onstage. And what a lineup! Just thinking about it sends one blond teenager, neat as a pin in her blue denim jumper, into paroxysms. "Gaahhhhh!" she says through a Pepsodent smile. "I think it's gonna be like Easter and Christmas and New Year's and your birthday all together, y'know . . . It's like all the vibrations are gonna be flowing *everywhere*, y'know."[1]

She's sitting outside the Monterey County Fairgrounds on the morning of June 16, 1967, the first of the three days set aside for the Monterey International Pop Music Festival, an extended concert that has taken on the heft of a generational event. Planned originally as a profit-making counterpart to Monterey's annual jazz festival, the pop music fair evolved into a nonprofit fund-raiser featuring the most successful and innovative artists at the fore of the rock, pop, and soul music scenes.

It's not just about the music. The long-haired guys constructing the stage are building something so much more important than a concert venue. It's the steel-and-plank foundation of a new civilization: liberated, governed by a shared commitment to free expression, free spiritual exploration, free love. They're a whole generation with a new explanation, according to singer Scott McKenzie, whose "San Francisco," composed by Mamas and Papas leader and festival cofounder John Phillips to promote the festival, has already become an anthem for the summer of '67. "People in motion." And it's so, so much better than ever before. Just watch the Byrds' David Crosby, a study in buckskin, denim, and golden walrus 'stache, bouncing in his suede boots during the vocal sound check. "Oh *groovy*!" he effuses. "A nice sound system at last!"[2]

At first Monterey's chief of police frets about the chaos headed into his peaceful jurisdiction. Chief Frank Marinello, tight as a tick from the shiny black visor of his hat to his epaulets, medals, and snapped-down sidearm, lists the potential horrors: radicals, Black Panthers, bikers, chaos in his sweet village. But when Marinello pays a visit to the fairgrounds, the hordes greet him with hugs and handshakes and freshly plucked daisies. Now he's joking with them, and everyone's laughing it up. The immensely relieved Marinello, who had placed his entire force on twenty-four-hour duty, orders half of them home to their families. "When I go up to that Haight-Ashbury," he tells *Newsweek* reporter Michael Lydon later, "I'm gonna see a lot of friends."[3]

But there's still a wariness in there, the us-and-them, the chill wind of what we can't see but still know is going on. When the Byrds take the stage, Crosby starts talking about something he saw in *Life* magazine, a statement, he adds, "that's gonna affect our times. It's gonna cause a lot of trouble." He recites from memory: "'I believe that if we gave LSD to all the politicians and statesmen around the world, we might have a chance of stopping war!'" Crosby has to shout over the cheers. "That's a quote from Paul McCartney!" The ovation doubles, triples, and Crosby rides the crest like a surfer. "I concur! Heartily!"

We're at peak *Gloria in excelsis iuvenis*, people, and Philip Larkin's quite unlosable game is paying off in every conceivable way, as the Mamas and the Papas' delightfully zaftig Cass Elliott crystallizes when she introduces the band's million-selling 1965 single "California Dreamin'." She describes it as a song that is both about the blessed land around them and also, ha ha, "a source of our great wealth."[4] But Mama C isn't kidding, and neither are the dozens of record company executives, unseen in the documentary but thick as moths backstage, hurling themselves and their checkbooks at every guitar-toting incandescence in sight.

○

Both Mo Ostin and Joe Smith could sense what was coming. In 1965, Ostin had even walked into a Sinatra recording session and handed the grouchiest rock 'n' roll hater in showbiz the sheet music for the Beatles' "Yesterday." Once he saw the writers' credits, Sinatra wouldn't look any further and merely tossed the pages to the floor. Ostin let it go, but he still knew that the hands of the clock would never spin back to jazzier times. The realization had finally spread up the Warner executive chain, too, so Ostin worked hard to develop his expertise in the new rock 'n' roll. He pored over all the music trades and dialed friends around the industry to discuss what he was seeing. Why *were* the Beatles so popular? How had their success changed the other acts in the Top 40? He kept reading, and after a while, Ostin could hear the difference between the same old thing and the new thing that could cut through the noise and maybe even stick around for a while.

In the fall of 1965, Ostin signed the Electric Prunes, a handful of musically ambitious kids from the San Fernando Valley, and saw their quasi-psychedelic first single, "I Had Too Much to Dream Last Night," hit No. 11 on the *Billboard* Hot 100. Joe Smith got to the Grateful Dead at the end of the summer of 1966, just when Ostin was fixing on an up-and-coming rock trio he had discovered in the British music newspapers. He couldn't hear how they sounded by reading the stories, but he could see the cornea-bending portraits of three young men dressed in spangled iridescent coats and heavily ruffled shirts. The leader was Jimi Hendrix, a young Black man from America whose Afro erupted from his skull with a force that had electrified the hair of his two fair-skinned bandmates until the three of them resembled dandelions in full puff. Entranced, Ostin asked his British contacts to send whatever information and music they could find. He received a copy of Hendrix's sole release, a cover of the popular modern blues song "Hey Joe" that only seemed to hint at the psychedelic marvels he'd been reading about. But reports of the Hendrix trio's concerts, which attracted members of the Beatles, the Rolling Stones, and other top British musicians, were even more enticing: if the most popular musicians in England were that entranced by him, Hendrix had to have something extraordinary going on.

A problem emerged for Ostin, though. Hendrix was managed by Chas Chandler, former bassist of of the popular UK group the Animals, in association with Mike Jeffries, who had worked a deal with Polydor Records to release the "Hey Joe" single. Since then, they'd signed another deal with Kit Lambert and Chris Stamp, managers of the Who and recent founders of the independent label Track Records, which was distributed in the UK by Polydor and in America by Atlantic Records. This gave Atlantic dibs on the American rights to Track Records releases, so no deal could be made unless Atlantic passed.

Hendrix's record and a reel of new songs went out to chief Atlantic A&R man Jerry Wexler, whose ears had identified some of the greatest rhythm and blues acts of the twentieth century, including Ray Charles, Aretha Franklin, and Wilson Pickett. But to Ostin's relief, Wexler couldn't hear Hendrix. "Lower-case BB King" was his judgment. So, Ostin pounced immediately. He offered a fifty-thousand-dollar contract for three albums, a pretty rich deal for an untested artist, but Ostin had faith, even when his fellow executives had severe doubts.

Hendrix and his bandmates finished their first album for Ostin in the spring of 1967, and when Ostin played the tape at a budget meeting, the room went berserk. But not in a good way. As Reprise's chief financial officer, Murray Gitlin recalled to Cornyn, he and the other executives could only gape at one another. Hendrix was nothing like any other guitarist they'd ever heard. He didn't bend notes, like an ordinary blues-rock player, as much as melt them, stretch them like taffy and turn them inside out in brain sizzlers like "Foxy Lady," "Manic Depression," and "Purple Haze." (And what *was* that, anyway?) Gitlin and Ostin had been friends since they were kids, friends from Fairfax High, where they connected in the teen club the Rams. But even a finance guy with soul, as Ostin describes his old friend, had his limits. They'd dropped fifty large on *this*? "We'd listen to the tapes and it was *What the hell?*," Gitlin told Cornyn. "It was just a bunch of screeching and screaming."[5] To them, perhaps. But when Ostin brought the music home to his boys and the mob of high school friends who passed their afternoons in and around the Ostin pool, he called them into his living room and dropped the needle on the Hendrix acetate. Did they like it? *Yes!* Did they think their friends would like it? *Yes!* Then a clamor: *Can we hear it again?*

*Are You Experienced* was released in England on May 12, 1967, but Ostin held the U.S. version until September 1, figuring that the group's summerlong American tour would stoke interest in the guitarist and the Jimi Hendrix Experience's first album. To make sure the season of touring would have as high a profile as possible, Hendrix's managers accepted a pro bono booking at that weekend-long benefit festival set for Northern California in the middle of June. Hendrix and company flew out of London's Heathrow airport a few days beforehand and made the rest of the journey to Monterey in time to play on the festival's closing night, along with the hard-rocking likes of Buffalo Springfield, the Janis Joplin–fronted Big Brother and the Holding Company, the Who, and the Grateful Dead.

The Rolling Stones' regal imp Brian Jones heralded Hendrix onstage as "a brilliant performer and the most exciting guitarist I've ever heard." What started a minute later left Ostin, watching from a seat near the stage, flabbergasted. "We were all up there, and the guy absolutely exploded," Ostin says. Hendrix took the stage in his frilly yellow shirt, bolero-style black vest, and red velvet pants, with his multicolor headband all but over-whelmed by his cloud of hair and his Stratocaster guitar strung upside down to accommodate his left-handedness. He played the thing behind his head, between his knees. He plucked the strings with his teeth, cunni-lingus style. Then he sprayed it with lighter fluid, struck a match, and knelt close, his long, waggling fingers calling the flames upward as the dying beast's howls filled the night.

Hendrix's summer tour did indeed build excitement for the coming American release of *Are You Experienced*. Only, none of Hendrix's fan base worked in the pop music industry. So, when Ostin brought the new album to the Warner/Reprise sales force and distributors, all those guys just shook their heads and grumbled. They may have heard a lot of wild stuff over the years, but *c'mon*. When they got a load of "Manic Depres-sion" and "Third Stone from the Sun," their eyes didn't glaze over so much as turn to granite. Most of the distributors took minimal shipments of the album; one ordered the bare minimum of eight. Then the record store reorders started coming in. As the kids in the Ostins' living room had promised in the spring, Hendrix's audience was out there. His debut was a record that kids would buy to play for their friends, who bought their own and played it for *their* friends. By the end of the year, *Are You Experienced* was on its way to selling three million copies. As Gitlin would admit, "Hendrix turned out to be one of the best decisions we ever made."

The distributors' inability to grasp Hendrix's appeal wasn't the first time the traditionalist sector of Warner/Reprise was blind to its own future. After Joe Smith's pursuit of the Grateful Dead put him in the middle of the blossoming music scene in San Francisco in the fall of 1966, he marched straight to Mike Maitland to tell him that the city was so full of promising unsigned bands that he'd need only $250,000 to nail down a dozen of them. There was Big Brother and the Holding Company (featuring Janis Joplin), Jefferson Airplane, Quicksilver Messenger Service, the Steve Miller Blues Band, and a score of others to choose from. Just one of the groups had to break through to pay for all the rest, but Maitland wouldn't go for it. "Let's see how the Grateful Dead do first," he said. It took six months and one music festival for Smith to be proven correct. But by Monterey, all he could do was watch his competitors' offers rocket skyward—Columbia's Clive Davis paid $200,000 to land Joplin and her band, while Capitol's Alan Livingston paid the Steve Miller Band an unbelievable $860,000, spaced over five years.

If they didn't actually say it to one another, they didn't need to: Smith and Ostin had glimpsed the future of the music industry before almost anyone else. Now they would not let their company be left behind again.

○

For more than a decade the music industrialists had no doubt that rock 'n' roll was just another fad, a sound that would rule the charts for a little while and then disappear without a trace. The teenyboppers would awake one morning grown up enough to realize that Sinatra really *was* where it was at, that all the smashing and wailing and yeah-yeah-ing was the sonic equivalent of toy cars and cowboy costumes: childish things to be put away. Except that was never going to happen.

This is what both Ostin and Smith knew. While the youthful rock 'n' roll audience certainly was growing up, they weren't going to abandon their favorite music. If anything, they'd just want smarter, more artistically evolved rock 'n' roll, music that spoke to its listeners' curiosities and expectations. They wanted new sounds, new ideas, new realities—the voice of the now.

Perhaps the idea came to Ostin during his San Francisco explorations in 1966. As he wandered the streets, he would walk past the hand-painted rainbows, the storefront incense holders, the street corner guitar strummers, the Uncle Sam hats; through incense, cigarette smoke, grass—all of it plumed together into a modern ether. The amplified music blared from everywhere at once, the waft and the bounce, this dizzy sense of infinite possibility. And when their new kind of rock 'n' roll played, these people listened closely, the way jazz fans absorbed their music, with serious regard and high expectations.

It stayed in his head for months, through the winter of 1967 and into spring. As the weather warmed into summer, Ostin traveled back to San Francisco briefly and then to the Monterey County Fairgrounds. The other record companies' race to lasso any and every unsigned act at the festival finally convinced Mike Maitland to surrender the last vestiges of his control over Warner/Reprise's artists and repertoire decisions to Smith and Ostin. What's more, they could sign all the rock 'n' rollers they wanted. Whatever opposition to the youth's music that remained in the first half of 1967 had now officially expired. Shortly afterward, maybe only a week or two, Ostin went to his A&R staff, then to the whole staff, with a new message. It was the most surprising request they'd ever heard from a top-rank record company executive. *Stop with the surefire singles and look for the artists who are going to make the best, most distinctive records.* That's how Norman Granz made Verve the jazz label of record in the 1950s, and the company was still profiting from the classic records it had put out back then. Really good music never fades away. *So, let's just make good records, and we'll turn those into hits.*

He knew it then and, more than half a century later, he's still sure of it. "I was into making quality records because if you do something good, good things follow," Ostin says. And maybe it didn't matter if the records were hits. "If we made good records by great artists, they didn't have to be commercial. Something good was always going to happen because you'd just made a great record."[6]

Things changed quickly after that. Soon came new executives, new staffers, and a slate of new artists, too. And the industry noticed. WARNER LABELS HUNTING FOR "NEW BREED OF MUSIC MAN" went the headline in a feature story printed in *Billboard*'s November 25, 1967, issue. "This new breed of creator is avant-gardish and very proud of his music," said marketing chief Joel Friedman, who went on to explain how the demand for the Grateful Dead on college campuses proved how popular the more serious-minded music was already becoming. The company's talent scouts were already fanning out across the Ivy League schools to track down the next big thing, the article noted before listing the company's most recent signings, including the First Edition, featuring Kenny Rogers; the Fugs; Jeremy and the Satyrs; Alan Watts, identified as a "far Eastern spiritualist"; Randy Newman (writer-singer); and Van Dyke Parks (writer-singer).

The last two came to the label through Lenny Waronker, the record producer and A&R man Joe Smith had hired in 1965. The son of a record company owner, Waronker, just past his twenty-third birthday, had been studying the record-making process since he was a young teenager. By the time he got to Warner/Reprise, he'd developed an ear for the songs and performers who could bring an idiosyncratic edge to pop music. The new hire spent his first couple of months in Burbank listening to demo tapes, then got his first real assignment when Smith sent him to the Autumn Records offices in San Francisco to figure out which of their acts would be worth bringing to Warner. Smith had bought the label mostly to get the Beau Brummels, whose pair of Top 20 hits ("Laugh, Laugh" and "Just a Little") seemed to promise more and perhaps bigger future hits. The executive also decided to snap up Bobby Freeman, whose hit "Do You Want to Dance?" had been a listener favorite when Smith spun it on his radio show in 1958. Waronker, as expected, focused more on the younger, more offbeat acts, adding the barroom rockers the Mojo Men and the harmony-singing surf band the Tikis. Both groups had limitations, mostly when it came to songwriting, but Waronker already had ideas about that, and his enthusiasm was intoxicating. "I remember thinking how slick he looked," said Ted Templeman, then the Tikis' lead singer, recalling the producer's gold ID bracelet and hand-draped suits. "But we got excited when he told us he'd make a record with us and use accordions."[7]

Ostin handed Waronker his next major assignment in late 1966, an open-ended appeal to light out to the pop scene's far horizons. *Find me the best new acts around,* he said. *I don't care if they have hit material.* All that mattered was how special the artists were. If they had the talent and drive to make records that were truly innovative, records that he and the rest of the Warner staff would be eager to play for their hippest and most sophisticated friends, it would be more than enough. Waronker knew exactly what Ostin was after. Better still, he knew where to find it.[8]

Gentle-natured and lightly haunted, the young Waronker first sturdied himself in his new job by coming into work in a suit and tie. Realizing that he was the only music staffer dressed so formally, he shifted down to stylish shirts and slacks set off with the gold ID bracelet flashing on his wrist. The son of Simon Waronker, cofounder and chairman of the successful independent label Liberty Records, Lenny grew up hearing tales of recording sessions, publishers, publicists, and the promoters who worked to make hits for the likes of jazz singer Julie London, late-fifties rocker Eddie Cochran, and the label's biggest stars, Alvin and the Chipmunks, the cartoon characters whose helium-voiced singing fueled smashes that included "The Chipmunk Song," which topped the pop charts in 1958.

Living in the Pacific Palisades neighborhood in West Los Angeles, the elder Waronkers were close to the family of Irving Newman, a doctor whose son Randy was two years younger than their Lenny. The boys befriended one another when they were still in diapers. "I don't remember not knowing him," says Randy Newman, who can still recall his grade school chum's bursts of bad temper and his pastime of inventing movie plots he'd describe beat by beat while his younger friend listened silently. "He was a leader type," Newman says.[9]

The young Waronker took after his dad, a bluff entrepreneur who burst into every room with the thunderous brio of a man accustomed to being the center of attention. Energetic and ambitious, Simon Waronker did his job at top speed, perpetually out the door to spend a week in Liberty's New York offices or to go on a scouting mission for the label's next big act. Lonely for his dad and intrigued by the music business, the teenage Lenny took to spending his summers at his father's elbow in Liberty's home offices and on the road, sitting in on meetings or sometimes wandering alone to the company's recording studios, where he could watch the staff producers and musicians turn raw songs into the fully produced records he heard on the radio. During his college years at the University of Southern California, Lenny spent his summers working in Liberty's promotions office in New York, then became a protégé of the label's chief producer, Snuff Garrett, who taught him the basics of music publishing and studio recording. Soon, Garrett tapped the younger Waronker to produce demonstration records for the company's songwriters. Waronker loved it so much that he'd abandon his classes at the slightest provocation—"Like if I couldn't find a parking place around campus"[10]—pull a U-turn, and head back to Garrett's studio for another day of study with the master.

Lenny shared his growing passion for music with his pal Randy, who had been drawn to the piano since before he could walk, and started studying the instrument seriously during grade school. Newman took naturally to both playing and songwriting. Both his uncles were prominent composers and orchestrators in the movie industry, and by the time they were in junior high school, Waronker could tell that his friend had a special talent. He encouraged Newman to write more, and as his songs took on greater musical and lyrical sophistication, Lenny made a point of comparing Newman to the young songwriting professionals he'd encountered in New York and Liberty's studios in Los Angeles. "You're better than these guys," he'd say, meaning it.[11] Even now, the memory of Newman's budding talent moves Waronker.

"It affected me," he says. "When you see an artist and they're getting better and better and better, and then they're great, what it gets you is like what you get out of love."

The memory is just as significant to Newman. "I didn't have much self-confidence, and if I wrote something, I'd like it at first, then fade on it. But when I'd play it for Lenny, and he liked it, he'd get excited. He was *really* into it. And his belief in me had an impact."[12]

●

Back in Burbank in late 1966, Waronker started with the Mojo Men, taking a song he'd fallen in love with when he heard its publishing demo a year earlier. The song, "Sit Down, I Think I Love You," was written by Stephen Stills just before he teamed up with Neil Young, Richie Furay, Dewey Martin, and Bruce Palmer to form the band they called Buffalo Springfield. Waronker's attempt to bring the new band to Warner/Reprise fell apart due to their managers' friendship with Atlantic Records' Ahmet Ertegun. But that didn't mean the producer couldn't do something with Stills's song once Buffalo Springfield put it out. After the band had had their go at the tune, Waronker called his new friend and not-quite-signed artist Van Dyke Parks to come up with an original arrangement. Parks came back with a baroque mélange of drums, electric bass, dobro, accordions, slide guitar, dulcimers, and multiple keyboards. With all the parts handled by studio musicians (including Waronker's pal and not-quite-signed artist Randy Newman), Parks on keyboards, and the Mojo Men (which now included Mojo woman Jan Errico on drums and vocals), the track came out sounding like a cross between a rock band, the Mamas and the Papas, and a stoned calliope. Released in the first weeks of 1967, the tune took the Mojos into the Top 40 (No. 36) for the first and last time.

Waronker's production of "Sit Down, I Think I Love You" served as a marker both for his musical imagination and for the future of the fast-evolving Warner/Reprise record company. Months before Ostin issued his no-more-hits proclamation, Waronker was on board. "The world was changing. I didn't want to go and cut singles," he says. "I told them that I didn't know shit about that." As if to emphasize the point, he convinced Ostin to secure Parks's services not just as a recording artist, but also as a studio musician, arranger, and co-producer. So intent was Waronker on having Parks to draw on that he added a clause to the deal guaranteeing that the musician be part of every recording session Waronker produced for as long as he remained a staff producer for the company.

True to his cantankerous soul, Parks wrinkled his nose at Waronker's next assignment: to write an arrangement for a cover of Simon and Garfunkel's "59th Street Bridge Song (Feelin' Groovy)" that he wanted to record as the Tikis' debut single for the label. The tune was too simple and silly for Parks's taste, a position he expressed by pointing to its title: "'Groovy,' huh?" Waronker wasn't going to noodge his new collaborator to do anything, but he also wasn't going to change his mind about recording the song, which he'd pegged as a hit the moment he first heard a snippet of it in a radio ad for the New York duo's 1966 album, Parsley, Sage, Rosemary and Thyme. In search of another offbeat arranger, he went to Leon Russell, a young Oklahoma-born keyboardist with bigger ideas than eighty-eight black and white keys had the power to express. Russell satisfied Waronker's request for something out of the ordinary by centering the arrangement on flutes, oboe, and bassoon and adding a kaleidoscopic a cappella breakdown that put the group's lush harmony singing front and center.

Despite his distaste for "Feelin' Groovy," Parks joined Waronker in the Tikis' album project, contributing a dizzying arrangement to his own psychedelic summer song "Come to the Sunshine," which would serve as the opening track, along with an array of backing vocals, instrumental parts, and production ideas. He and Waronker invented a new persona for the Tikis, too ("We saw them as pot-smoking choirboys," according to Waronker[13]), and helped develop the group's new name, Harpers Bizarre, a play on the fashion magazine *Harper's Bazaar*. Released in January 1967, the "59th Street Bridge Song (Feelin' Groovy)" single fell just short of the Top 10, at the No. 13 spot. The group's next single, "Come to the Sunshine," stalled at No. 43, and a campily orchestrated arrangement of Cole Porter's "Anything Goes" did only slightly better, which Ostin anticipated the moment Waronker first played it for him. "I don't know," he mused. "It's almost *too* good." Waronker wanted to give it a shot anyway, and Ostin told him to go right ahead. "It was pretty out there," Waronker says. "But Mo's support was unbelievable."[14]

At the same time, Waronker continued hunting down the fringe-y artists he'd been sent off to discover. Randy Newman was his first stop, but by the time he called his best pal to give him the good news, the pianist-songwriter was on the verge of signing a deal with Warner/Reprise competitor A&M Records. Waronker got Ostin to make a counteroffer, and though he fell short of A&M's numbers, the producer blew his top when Newman said he wanted to stick with the other company's richer deal. "How can you do that?" he demanded, hurling questions like fast pitches at a batter's head. *Who are you going to be working with there? Can you trust them, and I mean* really *trust them, with your career?* Newman was stunned. "There were all these things that I didn't even know were there," he says. When Newman brought up the bottom-line fact that A&M was offering more money than Warner/Reprise, Waronker waved his hand. "Don't *worry* about the money. The money will come."[15]

"It was a nice thought," Newman says. "And he did believe it. But money wasn't important to him. I think it was because of the way he, *we*, were brought up. We were already comfortable, so the coin of the realm wasn't money. It was being good at music, at what you do. At least trying to do your best. [Money] wasn't the primary thing."[16] Once again unable to resist Waronker's big brother style of authority, Newman scratched his name on the Warner/Reprise contract. Waronker co-produced his first album with Parks and produced or co-produced all but one of the ten albums that followed over the next fifty years.

●

Taking his mission to New York in early 1967, Ostin visited Ed Sanders, the radical poet, writer, and activist whose literary gazette *Fuck You: A Magazine of the Arts* was a central news source for the city's hippie-radical demimonde, to talk about his latest project, a folk-rock-protest band named the Fugs, after the word Norman Mailer invented to replace the verboten *fuck* in his World War II novel, *The Naked and the Dead*. As disciplined as he was ambitious, Sanders teamed with the poet/provocateur Tuli Kupferberg and with Ken Weaver, a former Russian interpreter for the U.S. Air Force, while also hiring a few experienced musicians to help wrap their antiauthoritarian lyrics in surprisingly sleek, pop-friendly tunes. The Fugs performed as often as they could, building an audience big enough to convince Atlantic Records' master producer Jerry Wexler to sign them to his vaunted label.

The group recorded its debut album, *The Fugs Eat It*, for Atlantic Records, but when Sanders went to the company's office to play the album for Wexler and a few of his compatriots, songs like "Wet Dream," "Coca-Cola Douche," and "Aphrodite Mass" spurred an executive freak-out convulsive enough to torpedo the Fugs' multi-album contract on the spot. Ostin, on the other hand, was struck by how Sanders and band blended poetry, rebellion, and bawdy humor into something like rock 'n' roll street literature.

Ostin also signed Woody Guthrie's twenty-year-old son Arlo, who projected his just-deceased father's folk ballads into the 1960s with an eighteen-minute anti–military draft song/story called "Alice's Restaurant Massacree." Based on a misbegotten Thanksgiving visit to friends in the Berkshire Mountains of Massachusetts in 1965, the song sprawled into a shaggy-dog tale about a brush with the law that wound up saving the singer-songwriter from the military draft. As pointed as it was funny, the song became a sensation when Guthrie started performing it in New York folk clubs. When he played it on Bob Fass's *Radio Unnameable* program, on the noncommercial WBAI-FM, the song became the most requested piece of music in the station's history. To raise money during WBAI's fund-raising week, Fass used "Alice's Restaurant Massacree" as a prize: when donors pledged a certain amount, he'd play the eighteen-minute version Guthrie had performed in their studios. Donations skyrocketed, and soon, as Guthrie recalls, they started raising cash from listeners who wanted them to *stop* playing it. "I think they made more money for that one," he says.[17]

Guthrie and "Alice's Restaurant" were the hits of the 1967 Newport Folk Festival in August, and though there was no way to edit the song down for radio play, Ostin had faith that the Warner/Reprise audience would not only find the album, but also buy it in quantity. He had similar faith when he encountered the performer known to nearly nobody as Herbert Buckingham Khaury, an oddly proportioned thirty-five-year-old longhair who performed as Tiny Tim. Khaury's Dickens-derived pseudonym proved as appropriate for the times as his offbeat interpretations of American Songbook standards, which he performed in a shaky falsetto to his own accompaniment on ukulele.

Back in Los Angeles, Waronker continued his hunt for more artists whose talents and interests took them as far away from Hitsville as possible. The arranger/producer Jack Nitzsche introduced him to Ry Cooder, a gifted blues guitarist from Santa Monica whose fascination with indigenous music from across the Americas, along with his ability to play virtually every stringed instrument set before him, made him a walking Smithsonian of roots music. Ostin offered the young musician a multi-album deal, much to the surprise of Cooder. "I figured I'd be that guy in *Shoot the Piano Player* who plays in a dive in Paris and every day goes back to his crap apartment and nobody knows his name or cares who he is. I didn't want to be anyone. I just wanted to play and be good."[18] Cooder, who played on albums by the Rolling Stones and other artists before getting around to making his self-titled debut album, stuck with the blues and folk music he loved rather than remaking himself to fit the times. He was everything Ostin wanted Warner/Reprise's signature artists to be.

So, too, was Frank Zappa, whose Mothers of Invention came to the company in a wide-ranging deal that included Dadaist bluesman Captain Beefheart, the all-groupie band Girls Together Outrageously (better known as the GTOs), and a psychiatrically troubled singer-songwriter named Wild Man Fischer, who at times accompanied himself on a cardboard cutout of a guitar.

Soon, Warner/Reprise came to resemble an old-fashioned cargo truck hurtling down a mountain road with its load shifting and straining in every direction. Jazz singers that way, folk singers down here, acid rockers cartwheeling across the roof, traditional pop singers over one wheel well, their pop-rock inheritors crowded above another. The Grateful Dead's self-titled debut album came acid-dipped with its electrified folk songs, apocalyptic ballads, and leering blues rave-ups. The Electric Prunes went on a psychedelic symphony trip with their *Mass in F Minor*. South African refugee Miriam Makeba sang her homeland's folk music in *Pata Pata*, while the Kinks flirted with concept albums. The Jimi Hendrix Experience made sounds from beyond this time-space continuum while nice, clean-cut kids the Association, Petula Clark, and Nancy Sinatra made life more comfortable for the older-gen likes of Frank Sinatra, Duke Ellington, Dean Martin, and Ella Fitzgerald. Then came Van Dyke Parks's *Song Cycle*, the Fugs' filthy-dirty *It Crawled into My Hand, Honest*, bluegrass heroes Flatt and Scruggs's deceptively cheery theme to the film *Bonnie and Clyde* ("Foggy Mountain Breakdown"), which kept pleasant company with global folkie Theo Bikel.

Anything was fair game. Someone would get a tip about a good act, and if the act had the right zing, they'd bring it to Ostin or Smith, work out an advance and royalty structure, then explain what it meant to record for such an artist-friendly organization. *Work with one of our staff producers or don't, but be assured that no one from Warner/Reprise will ever tell you how to make your records. And if your first album flops, don't worry too much.* It was never okay to turn in half-assed material, but as long as you were growing, taking chances, making interesting music, and building a core audience, you'd have a home at Warner/Reprise—mostly.

*Billboard* and other industry publications noticed the changes at the Burbank record company. First came the WARNER LABELS HUNTING FOR "NEW BREED OF MUSIC MAN"[19] piece in November; then *Variety* jumped in a few weeks later with a bigger feature, one pegged to the tenth anniversary of the original Warner Bros. Records. W-7 CREATES "NOW" POWER[20] paid tribute to the company's earlier breakthroughs before noting the litany of freaky acts that had set up at the company in recent months. The piece included Smith's reassurance that the company hadn't gone completely bonkers. "We're still in Establishment," he said, referring to label standbys like Sinatra, Petula Clark, and Dean Martin. "But we've managed to get a line of communication going with the young writers, artists and producers." The coverage was entirely positive, particularly given that the company was projected to gross $30 million in 1968, *thirty* times what it had done in its first year.*

●

We're back in Monterey now, back to that garden weekend when the young gods smiled on the crowd, when the children danced night and day to music that was born of love, all of it part of the religion coming into the world before our eyes and ears. This according to the British blues rocker turned sparkle-eyed hippie Eric Burdon, along with the Animals, on their post-festival single "Monterey," on which Burdon tells his version of that fateful weekend on California's northern shore. Three days of peace and love, he sings. So how peaceful and loving was it, Eric?

> *Even the cops grooved with us*
> *Do you believe me?*

Yes! Mostly!

Because there were hassles and misunderstandings, too, as when Joe Smith and his wife, with another couple in tow, discovered a bunch of hippies perched in their reserved seats. It was the big night for Warner/Reprise, the one that would end with the Jimi Hendrix Experience. And with the freakiness so thick in the air, the executive was a little on edge. He tapped the closest fellow on the shoulder, leaning into his gigantic puff of frizzed-up white boy Afro to point out that these were his reserved seats. *So sorry, but could you and your friends get up now?*

The guy didn't move, didn't even look up. Just snapped off a two-word response, in the vernacular:

---

* Though, of course, it now included two companies (three if you include the soul music affiliate Loma Records) and had significantly larger expenses, too.

*Fuck off.*

Smith, who had learned how to handle himself in the blue-collar suburb of his boyhood, was not prepared to fuck off. Instead, he grabbed the guy's frilly collar, hauled him halfway out of his chair, and spoke a little more firmly this time:

*Nope. These are our seats. Get the fuck out of here.*

This sent the hippies scuttling off, much to Smith's satisfaction—and eventual horror when he saw the same hippie taking the stage with Hendrix a few hours later and realized that the fellow he had all but punched in the face was the guitarist's drummer Mitch Mitchell. Oops.

If only things could ever really be that perfect.

But were they ever, really? You had to be pretty dull-nosed not to sniff the tang of commercialism mingling with the joss sticks and herbal cigarettes. And once the music faded, it was replaced by a chorus of unsettling questions about where all that money they had supposedly raised for charity had wound up going. Festival publicist Andy Wickham not only had anticipated it all, but had made it the point of the essay he wrote for the concert's official program. Not that anyone else ever saw it: once festival co-producer Lou Adler glimpsed the piece, he fired the twenty-two-year-old Brit on the spot, leaving him on the festival grounds jobless and with nothing to do but hang out backstage and chat with the likes of Mo Ostin, who picked up on Wickham's subtle but intoxicating hipness and knew instantly that the reed-thin, chain-smoking fellow belonged alongside him in Burbank.

## ONCE YOU GET USED TO IT,
## HIS VOICE IS REALLY SOMETHING

It's 8:30 p.m. on September 17, 1967, a warm Sunday in Los Angeles, and right up there in the sky, flowing through the airwaves on KRLA, at 1100 on the AM dial, comes a new voice, one with a British accent and a jaunty new philosophy of being.

"Good evening, hello! This is Derek Taylor, you see, so stay where you are on this channel and you'll have some fun! 'Cause fun's the thing this year, you see."

Taylor is the former publicist for the Beatles. He'd relocated to Los Angeles a year earlier to bring the Mop Top magic to the likes of the Byrds, the Beach Boys, the Monterey Pop Festival, and more. Now he's doing the same for KRLA-AM's Sunday evening programming, which is why the opening bars of Procol Harum's phantasmic "Whiter Shade of Pale" has become background music for Taylor's spin through the new consciousness.

It's the dawn of free-form radio in Los Angeles, and though a tiny scattering of specialized stations around the country has given their disc jockeys the freedom to spin whatever turns them on in the moment, most of those are strictly jazz stations or some way-left-of-the-dial outfit with wattage in the dozens. This thirty minutes on KRLA, thanks to Taylor and the moment he has helped create, feels like something else altogether: a broadcast from a society still aborning.

"All you need in life, apart from love, is some sort of skill or talent or drive. Not to be successful but to do the best you can. And winning isn't the thing. Digging things. Hippies, if I may use the term, say dig yourself, and that's the way to start, really. Does LBJ look as if he really digs himself? The amazing thing is that he actually believes that it's important that he gets reelected next year. So, don't turn off. I mean, turn ON. It's marvelous. It's getting better. And it'd better be—it's been terrible for far too long."

Taylor has more to say—about Hitler and Jesus both living within us, and how important it is to avoid angry thoughts so Adolf will starve and die. But Taylor keeps coming back to music. In a moment when God has come to seem ossified, or even dead, music is more alive than ever. It's the nexus of everything that matters. It's politics and culture, sex and sanctity. It's the line dividing the old and the young, short hair and long hair, tyranny and freedom. It's the central organizing principle of right and wrong, of good and bad.

"Frank Sinatra is fifty-one, I believe, and I'm wondering what he learned. I don't know him. I don't know people like him. He's not one of us now. We're trying to be very selective about who we know, which isn't arrogant. It's just that there's so much hassling these days, you see, that if we can't make the bad people good, they'll just have to stay outside the room. You see?"[1]

●

As Ostin had intuited on the Monterey County Fairgrounds that weekend, Andy Wickham was not only in the room, but standing at dead center. He didn't exactly look the part, with his short sandy hair and steel-rim glasses, to say nothing of his Etonian accent and tart views on politics, the antiwar movement, and Mexican immigrants. But Wickham also shared his Laurel Canyon house with left-wing folk singer Phil Ochs, and, most important, he had sharp antennae for the most vital new artists, often because he'd already seen them play, shared a joint with them, and heard enough of their demos to know what their first albums would sound like. So, if you were on a hunt for the most promising singer-songwriter-musicians in Los Angeles, Wickham was the man you wanted to talk to first.[2]

Some of it was happenstance: being the right expat at the right time; coming to Los Angeles in the Beatle-crazed 1960s with a British tongue, proper manners, and a line into the Rolling Stones that went back to when Wickham was an eighteen-year-old artist at London's Grey Advertising. He had been inking ads for ladies' shoes alongside Charlie Watts, who had started moonlighting as the Stones' drummer. When Watts quit the agency to follow his fortune into music, Wickham soon did the same. He was never going to stand in the spotlight, but then, that wasn't his style. And there were plenty of other jobs to be worked in the musical revolution.

Inspired by Stones manager Andrew Loog Oldham, Wickham moved to Los Angeles and took a job with manager/promoter Lou Adler. The relationship soured in the spring of 1967, when Wickham wrote his dyspeptic, and ultimately unpublished, essay for the concert program. When he got back to Los Angeles without a job, he took a few weeks off and then began to consider his prospects. One call had come in a few days after the festival, but Wickham had ignored it. But now that he needed work, he dug into his stack of messages to find the scrap of paper with Mo Ostin's number on it. It was not a call he was eager to make. The peevish Brit hadn't liked Ostin when they met in Monterey, getting the impression, surprisingly enough, that the Reprise Records director was too garrulous and loud for him to countenance. But a job's a job, so Wickham set up a meeting, and when he sat down he was surprised when Ostin ditched the usual job interview grilling to ask after his guest's life and ambitions. "Mo was the first [employer] who treated me as a person," Wickham told Stan Cornyn a dozen years later.[3] When the time came to discuss the specifics of an offer, Ostin let Wickham take the lead. What did he want?

*Two hundred dollars a week.*

Ostin nodded. *Great. What else?*

*A secretary.*

*No problem, anything else?*

*When do I start?*[4]

For lack of a better term, Wickham was declared the company's liaison to its younger (read: hippie) artists while also being its eyes and ears in the apartments, garages, and basements where the next wave of artists were honing their chops. Living among the bohemians in Laurel Canyon gave Wickham a significant advantage. The houses tucked along the eucalyptus-scented roads made up a hillside campus for young folk with guitars in their hands and songs in their ears. Go visit Frank Zappa on Lookout and you might catch a glimpse of Joni Mitchell, the Canadian singer-songwriter whom David Crosby had been talking up for the last few months. The ex–front man of Ireland's blues-rock combo Them was reinventing himself not so far away, and Jim Morrison's house was a whiskey bottle's throw from the Country Store's patio on Rothdell Trail. Mama Cass lived in the shop's basement before buying her own place on the hill, while an entire menagerie of Monkees, Byrds, Buffalo Springfielders, and future Eagles teemed within a short drive.

Wickham knew them all—knew who they were, where they were, and who their favorite up-and-comers were—and he reported back accordingly. *Check out these songs by Joni Mitchell. Van Morrison is on to something really interesting. You couldn't land Stephen Stills for a solo deal? His ex–Buffalo Springfield compatriot Neil Young is looking for a deal.* All became Warner/Reprise artists. And then Warner/Reprise became something else altogether.

○

The Last Tycoon.

That's what *Newsweek*[5] called Jack Warner in its 1966 profile of the grand old man of American movies. By then, he was the last standing member of the original Mayers, Cukors, Zukors, and Warners, the families who got into the industry back in the days of nickelodeons, relocating to Los Angeles to build vast film studios that became empires. But by late 1966 Warner was ready to call it quits. He was nearly seventy-five years old and wanted to get out of the movie business while there was still a business to get out of. Fifteen years since television arrived in American living rooms, the age of big studio pictures was fading into the western horizon. Still, Warner Bros. Pictures boasted its library of classic movies such as *The Jazz Singer*, *Casablanca*, and *Rebel Without a Cause*, along with a few other entertainment enterprises, including its pair of small but profitable record labels.

Jack Warner may have been eager to leave his throne, but Eliot Hyman, the chief of the small but growing media company Seven Arts

Associated Corporation, was just as eager to take his place. Hyman scraped together $31.7 million[6] in cash, made out a check to Warner, and received the keys to the studio's front gate. Soon, the trademark WB painted on the studio lot's famous water tower became a stylized W7. And in November 1966, Warner Bros. Records, the entity that owned both the Warner Bros. and Reprise labels, became Warner Bros.–Seven Arts Records Inc.[7]—or, according to its logo and journalists in search of a catchy abbreviation, W7.

The change in ownership didn't trouble Ostin at all. He never had much of a relationship with Warner, and Mike Maitland was doing a fine job of keeping the labels free from corporate intrusion. Which probably wasn't about to start no matter who owned the company, he says. "That was at the beginning of the years when we were exploding, making incredible signings, making incredible money," Ostin says. As long as they kept making money, he assumed, he'd be secure in his job. And he was.

Hyman was far more interested in the movie business. And like most of the Warner–Seven Arts top executives, he treated the company's music division as a necessary evil, a regrettable but increasingly efficient fount of cash that could keep the company's faltering movie studio in business. He didn't try to tell the Warner music companies what they could release, if only because he didn't like any of it and wanted as little to do with it as possible. But profits are profits, and once they had Warner Bros. Pictures and its music division in their grasp, Hyman and his Seven Arts compatriots aimed to expand even further. They set their sights on one of the nation's most prestigious independent record labels, Atlantic Records.

Atlantic had been founded in 1947 by Ahmet Ertegun and the husband-and-wife team of Herb and Miriam Abramson, all of them jazz fanatics with matching enthusiasms for gospel and early rhythm and blues. The young trio—Ertegun was twenty-four, the Abramsons in their early thirties—had set up shop in Midtown Manhattan in an office they also used as a recording studio, pushing their desks aside to make room for the musicians. From such humble beginnings came an astonishing parade of transformative artists and music: Ruth Brown, Ray Charles, the Coasters, Big Joe Turner, Bobby Darin, the Drifters, Wilson Pickett, Otis Redding, Percy Sledge, Aretha Franklin, and on and on. Years of internal changes had elevated Ahmet Ertegun to the fore of an ownership circle that included his brother, Nesuhi, and the label's key creative force, Jerry Wexler (who served simultaneously as talent scout, A&R chief, musical arranger, and record producer).

They'd generally made a good living for themselves, but they'd also weathered enough tough times to have developed a taste for the kind of security Hyman's multimillion-dollar offer could give them and their families. And it wasn't like they'd be abandoning ship, either. In fact, Hyman was eager to keep all three men exactly where they were. Hyman was willing to pay a premium not only for their services, but also to guarantee their independence from the Burbank labels. Their central charge? Just keep doing what you're already doing. The Erteguns and Wexler agreed to the deal, and by the end of 1967, the Warner Bros. Pictures music division included three record companies. Ahmet Ertegun also became part of the larger company's brain trust and an important New York–based ally to his compatriots at the Burbank music companies—all except for Warner Bros. Records (the entity that included Warner/Reprise) president Mike Maitland, who viewed Atlantic as an addition to his fiefdom. He could already count the millions the division could save each year by merging Atlantic's back-office workings (accounting, financial duties, etc.) with the existing Warner/Reprise setup.[8] But that was the last thing Ertegun wanted, and the opposite of what he'd been guaranteed in the buyout deal. Still, Maitland persisted. The Atlantic purchase was almost exactly like the Reprise deal from four years earlier, when the cost of the new company had gone onto the Warner Bros. Records books and its operations turned over to music division boss Maitland. *Why should this be any different?* Maitland wanted to know, especially given what he'd managed to do with the record companies?

Maitland had no reason to suspect that he'd come up short in his battle against the Turkish arriviste in New York. The sputtering, debt-ridden record label he'd taken over in 1961 had become immensely profitable. Plus, he'd become close to Jack Warner and never had to doubt that the Old Man would back him in any corporate disagreement. But when Seven Arts took over the corporation, its chief executive knew little about the history of Warner Bros. Records, let alone Maitland's role in it. And no matter what he'd done for the company, Hyman figured, Maitland would always be someone's employee, while Ertegun, along with his brother, Nesuhi, and Jerry Wexler, had started and owned Atlantic. This distinction mattered to Hyman,[9] and Ertegun came out on top. Atlantic would continue to operate as it always had. Maitland got a promotion to executive vice president of the music group of Warner–Seven Arts. He also got a permanent rival in Ertegun, whose star was just starting its climb in the Warner Bros. firmament.

The Seven Arts organization improved the lives of all the Warner staffers, most of whom had been underpaid by Jack Warner over the years, with a more generous salary scale and bonus ratios, a profit-sharing program, and benefits far more luxe than anything they'd ever imagined getting from the Last Tycoon. The Hymans also made a brilliant investment in Atlantic Records, buying out the Erteguns and Jerry Wexler when their label was on the verge of crossover smashes from roster acts Aretha Franklin, Otis Redding, and Wilson Pickett, among others, and even bigger hits from its new collection of rock 'n' roll acts: the Cream; the Rascals; Led Zeppelin; Crosby, Stills, Nash, and Young; Iron Butterfly; Vanilla Fudge; and more. Atlantic's sales in 1967 doubled its tally from the previous year. Revenue in 1968 would be 85 percent higher than that, and its run was just getting started.

Still, the companies overlapped in places, especially now that Atlantic had expanded into the rock 'n' roll business. When Ostin learned in 1968 that the former Yardbird and session guitarist Jimmy Page was forming a new band, the executive dialed England to talk to the new group's manager and told him he was willing to sign them to Warner/Reprise as soon as possible. Page and the manager, Peter Grant, zipped off to Los Angeles, and after a few meetings they shook hands on a deal. And just like that, the group that would be Led Zeppelin, one of the most monumental of all the late 1960s and 1970s rock bands, would be Warner/ Reprise artists.

Except, wait. When news of the impending deal reached Wexler, he launched a sneak attack to get Page and Grant to change their minds. *Just come and meet with us,* Wexler implored the Brits, who took him up on the offer to be flown to New York and pay a visit to the home of the record company whose artists had fueled Page's musical imagination more than those from any other label. Wexler amped up his charm, took them to visit the great Ahmet in his office, and by the time Ostin even had an inkling of what was going on Page and Grant had signed Led Zeppelin to Atlantic.[10]

Ostin was as aggrieved as you'd imagine, but he knew that was a fair move according to the company rules. The allied companies were free to compete with one another in every conceivable way *except* with money. So, sell your charm, sell the power of your promotions and publicity departments, sell all the artistic freedom you can offer. Just don't try to outbid each other, because they would all end up paying for that. And Ostin played that game, too. When the Rolling Stones' contract with Decca ended in 1969, Ertegun spent months on the case, wooing Jagger with everything he had: his history with rhythm and blues and some of the form's greatest musicians, his entrée in high society, and his eagerness to match the era's ultimate rock star drink for drink, toke for toke, and snort for snort all night long. As Ostin knew, the Stones, Ertegun, and Atlantic were close to a perfect match, but that didn't mean Ostin was going to abandon his shot at the storied British band.

Ostin was on his way to fly to London to meet with Jagger directly when he bumped into producer Richard Perry and his wife, Linda, who in the spirit of the times handed the executive two joints to take home for his later enjoyment. Ostin, who limited his smoking to parties and other social moments, slipped the reefer into his coat pocket and forgot all about it until he got off the airplane at Heathrow. While pulling his passport out of the same pocket, his fingertips brushed the illicit hemp and his heart sank. *Ooooh*, he thought, recalling that Tony Curtis had recently been busted for carrying the dreaded stuff through Heathrow.

Fortunately, the customs agent simply stamped the executive's passport and sent him on his way. At the Dorchester Hotel, Ostin nearly collided with Ertegun, whose face fell when he recognized his colleague. What, he wondered, was Ostin doing there? Meeting with Mick Jagger, of course. The Atlantic president spoke quickly: Could he sit in on the meeting? Ostin laughed. "Ahmet, are you out of your *mind*?" They were both trying to convince Jagger to bring the Stones to their label! There was no way Ertegun could sit in on Ostin's meeting! Ertegun surrendered that point, but could he come up when they were done talking business? Ostin sighed.

*Sure, fine. Call up in a couple of hours, and we'll see where we are.* Precisely two hours later the telephone in Jagger's room rang. Ertegun came knocking a minute or two later, and the sight of him made Jagger's face light up. "Ahmet! I'm so glad to see you!" he exclaimed. "I'm dying for a joint. Do you have one?" Ertegun grimaced. On this of all days, he wasn't carrying anything with him! What could they do now?

Ostin raised his hand. *Wait a minute, fellas,* he said, fishing into his coat pocket and coming out with the Perrys' joints.

*Fantastic!* Jagger cried.

Ertegun gazed over at Ostin, his supposedly square counterpart from California, looking completely baffled. *Ohhh,* he said weakly. *Wonderful.*

Ertegun wound up signing the Rolling Stones, but Ostin didn't have time to mourn the loss. His company was once again off on a tip no other record company was pursuing.

Did Eliot Hyman or anyone else at Seven Arts realize how unconventional the record company doing its business just across the street from their movie lot had become? And the wild-looking artists and bizarre-sounding records they made were only a part of it. Given his growing authority at Warner/Reprise, Ostin, with Smith at his shoulder, had set out to change nearly everything about their company.

Even the most uncommercial artists who signed contracts with Warner/Reprise could choose their own material and record it whenever and however they felt most comfortable. For Van Dyke Parks and Randy Newman, the point was moot because they had both been signed and produced by Lenny Waronker, who saw his role as something more like a co-conspirator than a company watchdog. And you didn't need to work with a staff producer to get the same treatment. Album covers were designed according to the artists' tastes and released with all the ballyhoo the company could muster. Making a debut album that becomes a smash hit was always a fine thing, but nothing close to necessary. Ostin and Smith were more focused on building long careers for their artists and, as they knew, that took time, money, and persistence.

○

The first thing that changed were his sideburns. What had been abrupt culs-de-sac ending at the wings of Ostin's eyeglasses sprouted into chin-length panhandles. The glasses were next, the traditional executive models blooming sportier wings and boxier lenses. It wasn't Ostin's style to chase the latest fashions, but he also wasn't immune to the changing times. The goatee came next, then the full beard he'd wear for the next fifteen years.

At home, Ostin was the same warm, if preoccupied, family man he'd always been. The Ostin place was a lot like the other well-to-do tract homes on the upper slopes of Encino: airy and modern, equipped with a swimming pool, a driveway spacious enough for half-court basketball, and windows that looked over a twinkling expanse of the San Fernando Valley. If you were a teenager in Encino during the late 1960s, the Ostin place was where you wanted to be. The three Ostin boys, Randy, Michael, and Kenny, were athletic, charismatic, warm, and generous to a fault. They had the most welcoming pool and patio and the sweetest dog, a romping Saint Bernard whose soft eyes and cuddlesome ways were a perfect match for her name, Luv. Evelyn Ostin welcomed her kids' friends like family, and when Mr. Ostin got home, things could get really interesting. Mo wasn't as outgoing as his wife, but everyone knew what he did for a living. He'd often walk in carting an armload of records, the latest releases from his and other labels, and sometimes advance pressings of Warner/Reprise's coming albums or even acetate discs from sessions that were still in progress. It'd be Hendrix one day, the Fugs the next, Arlo Guthrie, the Kinks, Frank Zappa.

Ostin's world spun faster now. He'd have to slip away after dinner to catch a set at the Troubadour or the Whisky, or to make an appearance backstage to cheer on a Reprise act at the Santa Monica Civic or the Forum in Inglewood. Then came the signing parties, the gold record parties, the industry banquets, awards shows, fund-raisers, presentations, testimonials, retirement parties, the whole music business schmear. Sometimes Mo would bring a colleague home for dinner—maybe an executive from New York; maybe the furtive Van Morrison, off-balance and aloof, but not unfriendly. Joni Mitchell couldn't keep her hands off the piano or her guitar, introducing songs with the pride of a new mom; while the great jazz musician, arranger, and record producer Quincy Jones liked to set up at the dinner table for hours, chatting about jazz, art, film—anything under the sun.

Or sometimes it'd be just Mom, Dad, the kids, and often their after-school tutor, David Berson, around the table, talking about the Lakers, the day's school assembly, or whatever was in the headlines. One night, Mo loaded his boys and Berson into his Cadillac after dinner and took them to a second-run theater to see Bruce Brown's surfing documentary *The Endless Summer* in a double feature with D. A. Pennebaker's Bob Dylan documentary, *Dont Look Back*. The Dylan movie, with its blistering footage of the singer's controversially electrified 1965 tour of England, got Mo especially fired up. Berson was overflowing with thoughts about Dylan, too, and they kept going on about him while they were tending to their cones at Wil Wright's old-fashioned ice-cream parlor. The Dylan talk continued in the front seat of the car during the drive home, and a few days later Berson came across Ostin between tutoring sessions with the boys.

"Have you ever thought about working with records?" Ostin asked him.

Berson had already decided to take the summer off from his college laboratory job, so he did have some free time coming up, now that Ostin mentioned it.

Ostin nodded. "Take some trips with me. You'll meet some interesting people."[11]

David Berson was a twenty-one-year-old biology major at UCLA when he first found his way to the Ostin house in Encino. Bright and personable, he had developed a small career as a tutor for high schoolers who needed a little one-on-one attention to gird themselves in their fight against algebra, *The Great Gatsby*, or the specifics of the Treaty of Versailles. The three Ostin sons were all energetic, rambunctious kids in their teens who enjoyed the company of a tutor who was as eager to shoot hoops as they were. Evelyn, who could never resist pulling people into her life, started setting a place for Berson at the family dinner table and made him know he was welcome whether he was working with the boys or not. Mo took an interest in his fellow UCLA Bruin, and when Berson's take on the Dylan movie opened his eyes, Ostin cleared a space next to himself and invited Berson to take a seat and prepare for action.

Ostin had business in England just when Berson was finishing an extended visit to the Shakespeare festival in Stratford-upon-Avon, and they set a time to meet in London. But when Berson got to Ostin's hotel, he learned that Mo had been hauled off to a hospital in St John's Wood with a ruptured ulcer. He would be fine but still required a couple of weeks to recover. Berson visited regularly, and as the patient regained his strength, he filled his visitor in on the latest developments at Warner/Reprise. Ostin had been to the Newport Folk Festival and caught Arlo Guthrie doing his "Alice's Restaurant." His connections at Pye Records and elsewhere were tipping him to the best of the United Kingdom's new acts; he was particularly high on the quirky blues band Fleetwood Mac and the British folk-rock band Jethro Tull, both of which had scored major hits in England and Europe while remaining unheard of in the United States. Berson, who had been working for an advanced degree in molecular biology, realized he'd had enough of studying the aging process in potato skin and took Ostin's offer to become his personal assistant at Warner/Reprise.

○

The Burbank offices filled with shaggier heads and hairier faces. Ostin, with his beard, increasingly bushy hair, and new collection of brightly patterned shirts he wore with a button or two undone to give him even more room to move, fit right in. His look telegraphed the feeling he wanted to permeate the company: relaxed, creative, a place where work and fun went arm in arm. He was particularly intent on the latter. Music was supposed to be fun, he liked to say. *If we don't have fun producing it for people, why would they want to listen to it?* And when Ostin talked about creative freedom, he wasn't thinking just about the artists.

The spirit of unbridled creativity, along with the new gang of staffers who were just as young, hip, and freaky as the artists, transformed the company offices into a clubhouse for Warner/Reprise musicians and employees alike. The new vibe was contagious. Joe Smith traded his horn-rims for hip steel-rimmed glasses and washed the oil from his hair and let it wander past his perpetually open collar. A staff photo taken in 1969 shows that of the nineteen men pictured—only two employees were women—nine were fully bearded, two others had bushy mustaches, and all save one sported hair that either touched their shoulders or was piled high atop their heads. Love beads, rope bracelets, and ankhs tangled and jangled; incense thickened the air in offices and conference rooms; while the parking lot collected at least as many smoked-down joints as it did Marlboro and Pall Mall butts. You didn't have to indulge in the sacraments of the era, and more than a few didn't, but you can see how it might have felt like a professional obligation. To get into the right headspace, you know. To drink of the wine and breathe of the smoke and see how things sounded when you were on the same wavelength as the artists and record buyers you were trying to reach.

Stan Cornyn, the veteran editorial director who had tuned in, if not turned on, during his visit to San Francisco in early 1966, was always eager to check out the groovier stops on the hippie underground. So, he'd tag along with the younger staffers on their lunchtime trips to Headquarters, a head shop near the UCLA campus in Westwood. They toured the shelves to explore the hand-carved pipes and jewelry, the psychedelic posters and books on Eastern religions and New Age spirituality, and the works of Jack Kerouac, Carlos Castaneda, and Timothy Leary. Cornyn made a habit of buying the underground newspapers and magazines Headquarters stocked and bringing them back to the office to soak up the attitude and language and sink as deeply into the vibe of the moment as he could from the safety of his Burbank office. Not that he was opposed to a certain amount of full-body immersion. When Van Dyke Parks offered to indoctrinate him in the ways of the modern hophead, Cornyn put the smoldering joint between his lips and sucked it in, getting so high that when Parks steered him into a movie theater, the executive could fixate only on the black bars framing each celluloid image in the film.

Meetings with artists played out like lightly purposeful hang-out sessions. A smattering of budgets, release schedules, tour dates—and then on to what really mattered: the latest records, the new issue of *Rolling Stone*, Eastern philosophy, what Copernicus learned about the universe by watching the vibration of zither strings. Van Dyke Parks spent a lot of his time hunkered down with Waronker and Ostin, and when Neil Young dropped by, he'd hole up in an office with whoever was around, smoke a joint or two, blast records, check out demos, and shoot the shit. Eventually, they'd get to the crucial stuff: *Where should we go to lunch? Are you headed to the Troubadour tonight? Want to go together?* When they all came rolling out into the evening, it was hard to tell the musicians from the staffers. They were all young, clad in the same rainbow clothes, headed to the same parties, enjoying the same drugs, and paired off to make like double-backed beasties with each other. And why not? These were the days of infinite turn-ons, and if you were part of the Warner/Reprise scene you were blessed.

When *Rolling Stone* sent L.A. correspondent Jerry Hopkins to file a report on the state of hip Los Angeles circa 1968, he dove deep into the city's paradoxes. It's "a relaxed and relaxing city," he wrote, "veined with canyons where musicians and artists live. It is also 'uptight plastic America,' crawling with buyers and peddlers of flesh and the masters of artificiality." In search of the city's hippest new faces and places, Hopkins made a beeline for Burbank and the appealingly dumpy Warner/Reprise HQ on Warner Boulevard.

"In Sinatra, the Association and Bill Cosby, they have some heavy breadwinners. However[,] the corporate thinking is headed down primrose lanes which include Tiny Tim, the Grateful Dead, Joni Mitchell, the Fugs and Jimi Hendrix. (It is a minor amazement that a collection like the Fugs, the Dead, Tim and Hendrix should all be one label!)" Hopkins also cast an approving eye on the company's executives, "a fairly solid group," he wrote, who ". . . know where they want to move their company, how and why. It is highly probable they will be a very major label in just a few years [*sic*] time."[12]

On the radio, the revolution came from the other side of the dial. FM broadcasting was developed in 1933 by an engineer named Edwin Armstrong, who discovered that radio signals traveling on the frequency modulation band delivered a much stronger, clearer, and dimensional sound than the crackly low-fi sound coming through the AM (amplitude modulation) signal. During the late 1930s, a handful of small outfits set up in the likes of Syracuse, New York; Paxton, Massachusetts; and as far west as Milwaukee, Wisconsin, but all were low-watt stations. Sensing the approach of formidable competition, the dominant broadcast networks on the AM dial did their best to keep the superior technology from taking root. But the spirit of innovation sweeping the United States into the 1960s, along with the launch of stereo broadcasts, spurred a scattering of new FM stations. Most of them came from nonprofit educational or community organizations, but a few focused on jazz, classical, and other specialized music. Virtually all the advertising money stuck with the AM dial, and particularly the Top 40 pop music stations that had dominated the airwaves since television put an end to radio dramas. But while it was both expensive and difficult to get a broadcasting license on that end of the dial, frequencies on the lightly populated FM dial were cheap and easy to find.

Meanwhile, in San Francisco, Warner/Reprise's favorite disc jockey and former Autumn Records owner Tom Donahue, itching for a new challenge, spent a January evening listening to the Doors' just-released debut album. Donahue flipped over what he heard, and being a radio guy, he went to his receiver and spun through the AM stations in search of one playing the record's lead single, "Break on Through (To the Other Side)." But the tune and the Doors were nowhere to be found. Intrigued by the FM dial, Donahue discovered that the Bay Area station KMPX, which played mostly canned foreign-language broadcasts for the region's ethnic populations, was so low budget that its owners didn't bother keeping a telephone line in the office. Donahue tracked down the owner and pitched him on letting him turn the station into a freewheeling, rock-based outfit with hip young disc jockeys playing whatever they felt like hearing themselves. They'd sell ads to the businesses that catered to the hippies and other young adults, and given their minuscule overhead they'd offer rates that were a tiny fraction of what the powerful AM stations charged for airtime. The new KMPX launched on February 12, 1967, with the new content at first played in the gaps between the foreign-language broadcasts and then becoming the station's only format in August. Donahue started programming KPPC-FM in Los Angeles, and the format, which had been bubbling up in a few smaller cities, too, soon swept across the country. The one thing these FM stations had in common was that they appealed directly to the freak-minded listeners most likely to dig Warner/Reprise's new generation of artists.

It couldn't have been a better-timed movement for Ostin and his record company. They could send promotional copies of new records to the stations with almost 100 percent certainty that they'd end up on the air. At the same time, the advertising rates were extraordinarily low, a virtue the stations shared with the counterculture-focused magazines such as *Rolling Stone*, *Cheetah*, and *Crawdaddy*, and the local underground newspapers and journals popping up across the country and in western Europe, too.

Stan Cornyn had been studying these rags intently. And even if he was a decade older than their intended readers, he knew how to speak to outsiders—especially the ones who yearned to be at the center of everything. Cornyn's lightly subversive style, what he liked to call his "sassy" way of writing, had been part of the Warner Bros. Records' persona since the bygone days of Ira Ironstrings and *Music for People with $3.98 Plus Tax (If Any)*. Musing on a recording session he'd seen for Sinatra's *September of My Years* album, Cornyn sculpted a tribute to a continually evolving artist to whom maturity had brought only new gifts:

"He has lived enough for two lives, and can sing now of September. Of the bruising days. Of the rouged lips and bourbon times. Of chill winds, of forgotten ladies who ride in limousines. . . ."[13]

Cornyn won a Grammy for that one in 1966, and took home a second trophy for his essay on the back of *Sinatra at the Sands* a year later. It felt like serious work to him, translating the passion in the music into words that built a bridge between the sounds and the people listening to them. And when it came to adopting the spirit of the counterculture to promote rock 'n' roll records to the freaky freaks who needed them the most, he blazed a trail many others would attempt, and almost always fail, to follow.

In 1968, Cornyn became Warner/Reprise's director of advertising. To anyone who knew the advertising game, it was a shockingly bad hire. He had no experience in advertising, and what's more, he was proud of it. Commercials chafed against his skin: all that shouting about the new, extra-strength variety, the fast-acting medicine, the greatest ever, the new and improved; all the exaggerating and flat-out lying. Not that he was opposed to selling things. But shouldn't it be possible to promote something honestly, with a modicum of creativity and even *wit*? The outgoing advertising director, Joel Friedman, who was taking a break to go to law school, certainly thought so, and Ostin, Joe Smith, and Mike Maitland had worked with Cornyn long enough to trust that he could write anything they asked him to put his pen to. Besides, record ads already sucked. It wasn't like he was going to make them *worse*.

And if they were ever going to hand the Warner/Reprise advertising department to a know-nothing, this was the perfect time to do it. Up until 1968, virtually all pop music ads were created for, and often by, the insider trade publications like *Billboard*, *Variety*, *Cash Box*, and *Record World*.

Designed to speak directly to the distributors, disc jockeys, radio program directors, and record store buyers, the ads focused almost entirely on the records' sales potential. It was an insiders' game, a system geared entirely for risk-averse pop industrialists. A few hundred bucks tucked into a disc jockey's front pocket didn't hurt a record's chances, either, but no amount of baksheesh was going to get Van Dyke Parks's musical hallucinations into the Top 40. And given that many pop music fans would surrender their allowances *not* to have to listen to the likes of Captain Beefheart and the fist- and penis-waving Fugs, Cornyn's new job required him to invent a new way to communicate with customers.

On the surface it seemed undoable. How can anyone advertise to an audience that hates advertising? How do you sell art that exists to counter the idea that art should be sold? It got even more complicated when it came to the Fugsian radicals, whose central purpose was to loft a middle finger into the eyes of traditional society. So, the ads would have to work on two levels, promoting the artists and their records while also establishing something about Warner/Reprise itself: that this record company was up to something different; that it was the music-for-music's-sake home for serious musicians, formalists, wild rockers, avant-garde adventurers, and every inspired artist between and beyond them.

Cornyn penciled out ideas for ads. His absurdist sense of humor would inevitably dominate the pieces, but when it came to style and tone, he found inspiration in another unlikely adman. Howard Luck Gossage was a San Franciscan whose lukewarm feelings about the advertising business gave him the confidence to create type-heavy ads that projected an unexpected ambivalence toward the consumer. Consider Gossage's full-page piece for FINA gas stations:

IF YOU'RE DRIVING DOWN THE ROAD AND SEE A FINA STATION
AND IT'S ON YOUR SIDE SO YOU DON'T HAVE TO MAKE A U-TURN
THROUGH TRAFFIC AND THERE AREN'T SIX CARS WAITING AND
YOU NEED GAS OR SOMETHING, PLEASE STOP IN.

The only gestures to the company's actual iconography came in the pink type that reflected the stations' signs and a tiny version of the company's logo, set in a clip-out coupon for a pink FINA gas cap.

Still, when Cornyn's first ad showed up in January 1969, you might have thought it was a joke of some sort. Jethro Tull, a hairy-faerie folk-rock band whose debut album, *This Was*, had jumped to the No. 5 slot on the British sales charts, had signed a deal with Warner/Reprise and was just then heading for the American concert circuit. Ordinarily, the launch of an act would have been an occasion for a breathless sales job, a celebration of conquering heroes and so on. Instead, Cornyn produced a full-page declaration of tough-loving skepticism. The headline, written strikingly in 24-point type across a plain white field that took up the top two thirds of the full page it occupied, was this:

**AN OPEN LETTER TO JETHRO TULL**

The bottom third of the page was taken up with a five-hundred-word mini-essay describing the challenge lying ahead for the aspiring band. "Sure, you're popular in England," it read. "But right now, the reaction of most of us Yanks is, 'Who in the merry hell is Jethro Tull?'"

Cornyn wove together descriptions of the group's progresso-folky-jazzy sound with its eccentric presentation—all four members aged themselves for the stage with whitened hair, beards, etc.—and included a juicy blurb from the United Kingdom's *Northern Review*, offset by a gentle needling ("But who in the merry hell is the *Northern Review*?"). He closed with a final wag of the finger ("So, Jethro Tull, you may be hot spit in England, but here you've got a ways to go") that set up a litany of dates in the group's Warner/Reprise–supported American tour.

Cornyn was only getting started. Randy Newman's first album, co-produced by Lenny Waronker and Van Dyke Parks, was released in the fall of 1968. The eponymously titled *Randy Newman* soared out of Burbank with the highest of hopes. Leading rock critics weighed in with strong praise ("One of the most stunning albums released thus far in 1968," wrote *Hullabaloo*), which was echoed by testimonials from the Olympian tongue of Beatle Paul McCartney. How could it fail? Sure, Newman's songs, ranging from darkly comic takes on God to a stark portrait of an abandoned parent to a cheerfully repellant pitch for a freak show attraction, could be challenging. And maybe even more so given the artist's voice, a slurry New Orleans drawl that reminded some listeners of Ray Charles after a shot of

Demerol. But the songs were terrific! The Warner/Reprise staff couldn't stop playing it on their in-house audio system! And did that matter at all? No, it didn't. When the W/R sales department issued the numbers a couple of months later, Newman's *Newman* had sold a total of 4,700 copies.

But the Warner/Reprise people still loved Randy Newman. Ostin, in particular, really loved Newman, so he kept the publicity money flowing. The art department recalled the existing albums and replaced the original, arguably cluttered cover with a new design featuring a close-up portrait of the artist. The sales force went after the distributors and record shop buyers with the fire of evangelists. And still no one would buy it. So, Cornyn rolled a piece of virgin paper into his typewriter and, after a time, emerged with a splashy ad for the thus far benighted *Newman*. This time the headline took on one of the artist's most vulnerable points: his burry, slurry singing.

**ONCE YOU GET USED TO IT,**
**HIS VOICE IS REALLY SOMETHING.**

"Apparently, it's taking longer than we thought to get used to that voice," the ad began. "Undaunted by the lack of rush to buy the album, we comforted ourselves with critical notices which, like they say, 'glowed.' We also wondered, 'Are we fooling ourselves?' No, we decided, because people whose judgment we respected, like Mr. McCartney and Miss Collins and Mr. Nilsson, told us *Randy Newman* was in the masterpiece category. Where had we gone wrong?"

When that first ad failed to light a fire under *Randy Newman*, Cornyn came back with another full-pager. This time the headline was even more striking.

**WANT A FREE ALBUM? OKAY.**
We'll give you a Randy Newman album. Free. Just write us. We'll send you one.
You don't believe us, do you.
Read on.

Cornyn dished more of Newman's praises, but from there the ad was entirely about Warner/Reprise and its employees' dented feelings. Because they had all worked so hard on this album and believed deeply in what they were doing. And not only had their work all come to naught, but they were still being scolded by all the "flower boppers" who put them down for being soulless greed-heads. What could they do to make you believe in their souls? Well, Cornyn had an answer: OUR FLOWER CHILD PUT-UP-OR-SHUT-UP FREE ALBUM OFFER.

> For this one brief shining moment, darlins, you're seeing Capital-ism crumble before your eyes.

As advertising pitches go, Cornyn's pieces were screwballs. They jumped, dropped, and quivered in their own velocity. The customary hard sell gave way to self-deprecation and confessions of failure and even self-doubt. And they were *funny*—not just about Warner/Reprise's artists and the company itself, but about the entire music business and the celebrity-commercial-industrial complex that existed around it. To promote the Grateful Dead's first two records, Cornyn came up with the Pigpen Look Alike Contest, charging readers to send in hand-drawn renderings of the band's album covers along with a photo of someone who resembled the group's hairiest, scariest-looking member. "Do not, please, send in the actual people," Cornyn added. "We got problems of our own."

When the Fugs released their first Warner/Reprise album, *It Crawled into my Hand, Honest,* Cornyn promoted a "Win a Fug Dream Date" competition, a perfectly cribbed variation on the *16* and *Teen Beat* magazine contests to meet the Monkees' Davy Jones, Herman's Hermit Peter Noone, and so on. But here, the dreamy boys were bearded radicals who sang gleefully filthy songs like the one that explains why the singer doesn't want to go to Vietnam: "I'd much rather stay home and screw your mom." The rules were simple, just send in your thoughts on the album, plus the name of your favorite Fug, but the responses were something else altogether. Cornyn was particularly fond of the entry sent in by a Barbara Cipolla of Reno, Nevada, who answered with high Fugsian brio: "Dear Sirs (Or whoever you are), I would like to go out with Tuli [Kupferberg] because I would like him to fuck me. PS: Even if I don't win I would still like it."

Whether Ms. Cipolla, or anyone, actually hit the town with Kupferberg or another favorite Fug is unclear. But the point of Cornyn's ads was that Warner/Reprise wasn't out to fleece its customers. Instead, it had thrown open its doors and windows and invited its customers to come in and have a look around; it had nothing to hide. When records flopped, Warner/Reprise admitted it. When it lost money, it said as much—and, seemingly, how much. For young but maturing pop music fans, Cornyn's ads were a revelation, and what happened next was even more stunning: the company began to get fan letters addressed to its advertising department.

"If no-one else has already done so, please relay a string of superlative compliments to your advertising agency for your latest series of quite extraordinary ads," wrote Mr. David Wild in 1969. "I feel that they should receive some kind of consumer-appreciation award."

Ronald Alden of Maplewood, New Jersey, responded to a Joni Mitchell poster offer by sending in his own handwritten letter so he could have an undamaged original " 'Cause the copy is so ingenious."

Amy Nechenie, a high schooler from West Caldwell, New Jersey, took her pen in hand to thank the advertising staff and everyone else at the company for being "unselfish, truthful, meaningful, reliable, never letting ya down, sticking to their words, always helpful people." Fifty years later, Nechenie, who is now a librarian in Connecticut and goes by the surname Bansak, can still remember finding the ad in the *Village Voice* when she was a fifteen-year-old sophomore in high school. "What hooked me was that offbeat image," she says. "I looked for their artists after that. Anything new or a little different, and that was their puddle."

Cornyn's ads played a central role in transforming Warner/Reprise's image, a reorientation that, along with its growing reputation for granting full creative control to its artists, made the company a magnet for the innovative musicians it most wanted to land. Whether the ads helped sell more copies of anyone's record is less clear. A lot of the self-effacement in the pieces came at the artists' expense, even while the ads drew attention to their work. Those "How We Lost $35,509" spreads that Cornyn wrote for Van Dyke Parks's *Song Cycle* left the touchy artist convinced that his record company was trying to destroy his career. Randy Newman was less ruffled by the ONCE YOU GET USED TO IT, HIS VOICE IS REALLY SOMETHING ad, but that didn't mean he liked it. "I didn't think they were funny," he says of Cornyn's ads. "And I don't think four people bought the record because of [the *Randy Newman* ad]. It drew a lot of attention, but mainly to itself."[14]

If one artist suffered the most from Cornyn's sassiness it was Joni Mitchell. The extravagantly talented singer, songwriter, and musician came to the company through Andy Wickham in 1967 and quickly established herself with songs that blended modern folk with probing lyrics and a sophisticated musical sensibility. Already accustomed to the condescension of less talented male artists, Mitchell was infuriated when Cornyn's ads for her work played almost entirely on her femininity, as viewed through the eyes of a paternalistic lech. When the singer-songwriter's debut album didn't sell well, Cornyn led an ad with JONI MITCHELL IS 90 PERCENT VIRGIN, which was only sort of about the small number of music listeners who had given her record a shot. When Mitchell was late delivering her second album, Cornyn promoted a free-but-for-a-quarter Joni poster with a sex joke: JONI MITCHELL TAKES FOREVER. The next ad, heralding the release of Mitchell's delayed album, reduced it to the terms of a frustrated swain who at long last gets what he's after: JONI FINALLY COMES ACROSS. Mitchell was rightfully furious. The new generation with the new explanation, as it turned out, was just as sexist as their parents. The man's man's man's world kept spinning, and it would be years before men were made to give it a second thought.

No matter. The readers of *Rolling Stone* and the rest of the underground media continued to marvel over the Warner/Reprise ads, which were often more engaging and funnier than the articles in the publications. That's what occurred to Peter Asher, who tracked the Warner/Reprise advertisements in London, where he had served as the head of A&R for the Beatles' Apple Records. Asher had been deposed by the group's new manager and was preparing to move to the United States to help American folk-rock artist James Taylor build his career in his homeland. In search of the best possible record label for the fast-budding singer-songwriter, Asher made a total of one telephone call: to Joe Smith at Warner Bros. Records. And why not anywhere else? Having Joni Mitchell, Neil Young, and singer-songwriter Eric Andersen on the label didn't hurt. "And, of course, they had Stan Cornyn's super-hip text ads," Asher told me in his gold-and-platinum-record-lined Santa Monica office. "We'd seen them all and kind of went, 'These people are *cool.*'"[15]

○

It was the damnedest thing. A few months after Cornyn's ads started popping up, you would swear he'd started writing his colleagues' memos and hallway conversations, too. Adjectives went technicolor. You wouldn't settle for describing the Fugs as controversial when you could call them an aggregate of bathless degenerates. You didn't refer to Mo Ostin as the chief of Reprise Records when Pixie Mogul was so much more descriptive, just as his charming counterpart at Warner Bros. Records had evolved into Smilin' Joe Smith. And the most surprising thing was that the top execs not only allowed such hijinks at their expense but *approved* of them, as Smilin' Joe said a few years later.[16] The reflexive iconoclasm, the skepticism of the tried and true, the emphasis on creativity, and all of it cushioned by droll wit and a light chuck of the cheek. It was fitting the way Cornyn ended each of his ads by declaring that so-and-such was on Warner/Reprise, "Where They Belong."

James Taylor wasn't the only sought-after artist who came to Burbank wanting to talk about how cool the Warner/Reprise ads were. Smith had worked with musicians and their managers for years and had never even heard of artists citing a company's advertising as a primary attraction, but they were doing so now. As Cornyn wrote in his memoir, he was working at his desk one day in 1969 when Ostin, showing a hotly pursued artist around the building, opened his office door and pointed in his direction. "*That*," he announced, "is Stan Cornyn!"

Other record companies tried to catch up. But Columbia's notorious BUT THE MAN CAN'T BUST OUR MUSIC ad, illustrated by a staged photo of a jail cell holding a half-dozen longhairs, scattered protest signs (WAKE UP! MUSIC IS LOVE!), a functioning hi-fi, and attitudes of boredom and contempt, earned the company little more than ridicule. Cornyn also had a sharp eye for writers who understood his sensibility and knew how to adapt it into their own work. Like most record companies, Warner/Reprise produced a regular newsletter promoting new artist signings, release dates, sales figures, and executive comings, goings, and promotions. *Callboard* was as flavorless as its name, and that had to change. Cornyn hired two journalists, a freelancer named Judith Sims and the *Los Angeles Times* rock critic Pete Johnson, to create and run a new magazine, and the thing launched during the summer of 1969.

They called it *Circular*, one word that described both the shape of the company's products (if not the publication itself, which was square and the size of a 45 rpm record sleeve) and, in a slightly archaic variation, the dictionary definition of what such a publication was: a pamphlet, handbill, flyer, mailer, etc. And if that wasn't clear enough, the logo on the front described itself as WARNER/REPRISE'S WEEKLY NEWS THING.

Its first issue appearing in the middle of August, *Circular* started tentatively, the most notable piece being a pretend classified ad seeking "Qualified Girls" to file paternity suits in order to draw attention to "some of our less fortunate artists." The second issue led with a profile of the Fugs, including the description of the group as "bathless degenerates" and, in a second burst, "dirty perverts and general no-goodniks." The same issue included a set of paparazzi-style photos taken at a company party for the Kinks, where the RKO radio conglomerate's top programming executive was identified as "Bill Drake, who does something for a chain of radio stations." Another photograph described its subject as "Miss Priscilla Plunge, Miss Galaxy, 1962." In one group shot, a stylish young man posing next to Ostin and Ray Davies was identified, inaccurately, as "Ullia Della Ferragnio," an accountant. The Ostin-centered group in the photo below it included a handsome young man in a fashionable suit identified as "teen idol Harry Kleen," while the man in the background was dentist "Prince Rupert Volnupechki." The odd thing here, other than that there was never a singing star named Harry Kleen, is that the man identified as Prince Rupert was also the accountant Della Ferragnio, seen above.

Available to the usual industry outposts around the country, *Circular* could also be had by anyone requesting a free subscription. Thousands did, and what they received each week was something never seen before or since: an in-house promotional newsletter that doubled as an insider's portrait of a record company, tripled as a fan's one-stop source for news on their favorite Warner/Reprise artists, and quadrupled as a humor magazine.

None of it played as expected. The artist interviews often featured snide and/or absurd questions. The news breaks, most frequently seen in the Ruby Tuesday column written by Alison Wickwire, included jibes at other companies ("Rumor has it that Capitol Records will replace no top executives this week"), insults launched at Warner/Reprise's own executives (Cornyn's high-profile speech to an international record convention was, according to *Circular*, subtitled "Confessions of a Child Molester"), and occasional plugs for particularly good records on other labels. Cover stories and other major features took on potentially embarrassing subjects, such as the time when the lousy sales figures of one wave of releases prompted the company to put a hold on all the next month's records until the promotions staff could ignite more interest in the ignored albums. There were clear-eyed explanations for why the company had deleted failed albums from its catalogue and what became of the stock that remained. (It was sold to clearinghouses that retailed it for a dollar or less per copy.) Another cover story, headlined THIS REALLY SUCKS, collected some of the angriest letters from dissatisfied customers, including one who so hated a radio ad that included the nerve-grating sound of a phonograph needle being *scraaaaaaaatched* across the surface of a record that he promised to boycott all Warner/Reprise releases for six months if they didn't, in his words, "get the goddamn, fucking piece of shit off the air."

You win some and you lose some. And at Warner/Reprise, you took the bad with the good and put it all out there for everyone to see, because . . . why not? Because nobody's perfect, and trying to pretend otherwise was just another shuck. Plus, it was fun. And as Derek Taylor proclaimed to the new generation tuned in to KRLA, "Fun's the thing, you see."

# HOW CAN WE BREAK
# THE RULES TODAY?

**B**etween 1967 and 1970, Ostin and Smith added no fewer than *ninety* new acts to Warner/Reprise, an A&R spree that was breathtaking not just for its immensity but also for the riches of talent, cultural impact, and commercial power they would unleash upon the company. To examine the list now is to see much of the foundation of the popular music of the last fifty years. Joni Mitchell, Neil Young, Van Morrison, James Taylor, Randy Newman, Van Dyke Parks, Ry Cooder, Fleetwood Mac (from which would also come solo hits by Stevie Nicks, Lindsey Buckingham, Christine McVie, and earlier member Bob Welch), Jethro Tull, Frank Zappa, Charles Wright and the Watts 103rd Street Rhythm Band, America, Alice Cooper, Deep Purple, the Fugs, Black Sabbath, Gordon Lightfoot—the list goes on and on.

They signed their share of lesser lights, too, including the Los Angeles witch Louise Huebner, whose *Seduction Through Witchcraft* didn't get to first base with much of anyone. A group called Nikita the K and the Friends of Ed Labunski went nowhere with their *Go, Go Radio Moscow*, while the Marvelows, the Johnnys, the Invincibles, the Next Exit, Fabulous Farquahr, the West Coast Pop Art Experimental Band, and Luke Warm went the same way as Wilderness Road, whose *Sold for the Prevention of*

*Disease Only* sold exactly 7,388 copies. While they were at it, the Warner/ Reprise crew also turned away an array of artists who went on to make hits and sometimes became superstars for other companies. Both the Doors and Jackson Browne were shown the door, as was John Denver, Iron Butterfly, and the Rhodes scholar turned modern country favorite Kris Kristofferson.[1] But in an industry that considers a 5 percent hit rate a triumph, Warner/Reprise's late 1960s haul was a long way off the map of typical results. As Cornyn figured it, they locked in twenty-four artists whose work held musical and cultural significance, sixteen of whom were already selling or would soon sell records by the millions. It's a level of success that no other record company had (or still has) come close to matching.[2]

The most immediately significant signing in the late 1960s turned out to be James Taylor, the American singer-songwriter whose self-titled 1968 debut album had floundered on the Beatles' Apple Records. Born in Massachusetts and raised largely in North Carolina, Taylor moved to London in early 1968 and was quickly signed to Apple by the new company's A&R chief, Peter Asher. The record they made together, with Asher producing, included standout tracks "Something in the Way She Moves," "Carolina in My Mind," and "Rainy Day Man," but it fell through the cracks when it came out that December, even given largely positive reviews. Back in the United States in 1969, in part to fight off his latest wave of drug problems, Taylor was soon joined by Asher, who had left Apple and come to America to continue his work with the promising singer-songwriter.

Cornyn's ads had piqued Asher's interest in Warner/Reprise, and Taylor's set at the Newport Folk Festival in July won the artist the interest of both Smith and Ostin. Sent to the Warner Bros. Records chief by the record producer Joe Boyd, Asher negotiated a forty-thousand-dollar advance for Taylor's first album over breakfast at the Hyatt House hotel on Sunset Boulevard, with half up front and the other half coming when they delivered the completed record. Recorded in December 1969 and released in February 1970, *Sweet Baby James* sold well from the start and then took off in the fall, when its second single, "Fire and Rain," hit No. 3 on *Billboard*'s Hot 100, carrying its album to the same slot on the album chart a week later. By the end of the year, *Sweet Baby James* had sold 1.5 million copies, and that was just the start of a run that would help turn

Warner/Reprise into a very different record company than it had been just a few years before.

○

The Grateful Dead wanted to be heard. They also wanted to make money, buy fancy cars, live in nice houses with plenty of land, and indulge their appetites for good food, oceans of alcohol, the best drugs, and the most profligate women. In this they were as traditionally American as Joe Smith, even if his chief indulgence was his growing wine collection. But they didn't see it that way. From the night Smilin' Joe met them backstage at the Avalon Ballroom in 1966, only to hear bassist Phil Lesh declare that his grandmother had warned him about men like Smith, the executive's relationship with the band had been strained, to say the least. When he wrote to manager Danny Rifkin, imploring him to get his band together enough to finish their next album, the musicians mailed the letter back to him with corrected spelling and punctuation and a big FUCK YOU scrawled across the front. And even when they were being chummy, offering Smith a beer or a soda when he came to see their shows, he knew that only meant they were trying to dose him with their intensely potent LSD. "There was always a mischief maker in the band, or someone like Phil Lesh, who would try to fuck up your life," Smith told me. "I told them I was never going to eat or drink anything around them, no matter what. I said, 'Look, I'm a Jewish guy who went to Yale. I'm not going to start taking dope now.'"[3]

Smith did try to meet them halfway, agreeing to take a hit of laughing gas from one of the industrial-size nitrous oxide tanks the band kept with them. And they returned the favor when he asked them to add a song to their first album that might appeal to radio programmers, coming up with "The Golden Road (to Unlimited Devotion)," a tuneful rocker with a chorus inviting listeners to "join the party every day." Top 40 radio wanted nothing to do with the tune, but the group's self-titled debut album became a favorite on free-form stations, and the exposure, along with the group's expanding tour schedule, pushed the record to No. 73 on the *Billboard* charts. Not an inauspicious start for a hippie band focused so ardently on creating sounds for, and perhaps *from*, another time-space continuum.

But Warner/Reprise's commitment to the Grateful Dead was about something more than the number of records they sold or even how good their music was. As one of the counterculture's most admired bands, the Dead pushed the company's image that much further from its Frank, Dean, and Sammy days. Other counterculture artists would be that much more eager to sign deals with the company that had the Dead on its roster, and some of them may have been even more likely to make hit records of their own. Just like Cornyn's outlandish ads, the Grateful Dead were selling Warner/Reprise as hard as the company was selling them. And even if all that came to nothing, they were still one of the most innovative bands out there—and as Ostin insisted, it was important for the company to support the artists whose work advanced the art that supplied them all with their livings.

Warner/Reprise's staffers, from Ostin and Smith on down, tried to approach their jobs just like the counterculture artists pursued theirs: to follow a vision; to be creative and unafraid to experiment; to keep in mind that lasting success requires risk, and risk often ends in failure; and to remember that failure isn't necessarily a bad thing, if only because learning what you shouldn't do is such an important part of learning what you *should* do. "You could take all the chances you needed to take," says Carl Scott, who spent three decades working in and around the Warner/Reprise offices. "You had to do it honestly, steadfastly, and get the job done. If you fucked up, okay. As long as you owned up to it and were forthright, you'd probably get a pat on the back for having the guts to step up and try something."[4]

Even given the traditional corporate structure—presidents and vice presidents managing department heads and lower-level staffers—the atmosphere at 3701 Warner Boulevard felt open and egalitarian. The layout of the building, with its U-shaped design, cheap plastic wood paneling, and limited office space, compelled staffers of all ranks to work in one another's pockets. Some staffers, including division chiefs, worked from desks stationed in the hallway. Ostin and Smith's presidential offices were just a touch larger than the ones occupied by entry-level staffers. You didn't need an appointment to get the attention of one of the labels' presidents. Whether you were a vice president or a mail room clerk, you needed only poke your head through Ostin's or Smith's door to get a word in. And if that kid from the mail room felt strongly about an act or a record, the top executives took his feelings seriously: as they knew, their company's core audience had a lot more in common with Warner's junior staffers than they did with its chief executives.

To push through the glass doors of the Warner building during the workday was like strolling into a purposeful commune. Most office doors stood open, a necessity given the building's indifferent ventilation system, but it also encouraged impromptu visits and hang-out sessions, which often turned into serious discussions of record culture and promotional strategy, ideas flowing from every direction as everyone pitched in to get their artists' music into the ears of the people. They knew it was all a business, this making and selling of commercial products, but it felt like so much more than that. By putting out records by the Dead, the Fugs, Jimi Hendrix, Captain Beefheart, Frank Zappa, Arlo Guthrie, and all the other freaky acts they'd swept into the company, they were at the forefront of the revolution, sending bulletins to young people across the nation, all of them eager to hear the latest on where it was at and what needed to happen next.

That was the vibe, anyway, and in those days, it was as irresistible as it was intoxicating. Everyone pulled in the same direction, from the mail room clerks to the artists, and all of them, or at least most of them, were determined to make a difference. So, when word came that someone was in a pinch—needing enough hands, say, to get a thousand mailers into the post by 4 p.m.—you'd find staffers, executives, and even a musician or two rolling up their sleeves and stuffing envelopes. It was a business, a revolution, and also a family, because it was still a small crew in there. They all knew one another's names and faces, and they were all in it together.

●

And yet there were promotions men, salesmen, and distributors who still didn't get it. When Cornyn began to suspect that the company's salesmen, along with record store buyers and disc jockeys, were too overwhelmed by the variety of offbeat records coming out of Burbank to actually listen to them, he came up with the idea of printing sampler albums, isolating the best tracks from the month's lesser-known releases and compiling them into a twelve-track anthology, with one song from each new or lesser-known artist. The first release, titled *Some of Our Best Friends* (a reference to the freakiness of the new acts), worked just as Cornyn had hoped: interest in the new acts blossomed among the sales and promotion reps. This turnabout gave the advertising chief an even more dramatic notion: sampler albums for the general public.

No other company had tried it before, which made it all the more irresistible a challenge. So, Cornyn came up with a plan for a series of double-record sets that would include the work of all the company's artists, including its most popular acts, organized into elaborately designed gatefold covers with detailed liner notes. And because the samplers could be categorized as promotional releases, and thus not subject to songwriter and performance royalties, they could sell them for a cool two dollars apiece. To launch the series, Cornyn compiled *The 1969 Warner/Reprise Songbook*, featuring the work of artists ranging from the loony singer-songwriter Wild Man Fischer to Miriam Makeba to British folkies Pentangle to Jimi Hendrix, Arlo Guthrie, the Kinks, the Electric Prunes, the Everly Brothers, and the Fugs.

The Loss Leaders, as Cornyn dubbed the series, became another cornerstone in the Warner/Reprise persona, due both to the extraordinary music on the vinyl and to Cornyn's typically absurdist way of pitching them to the public. Cornyn's ads and liner notes, printed in the usual underground papers and on the inner dust covers of almost all the company's albums, rode the same balance between cheery hype and even cheerier transparency. These records were cooperative affairs, he wrote. Despite the premium packaging, top artists, and songs that were actual top-grade material, the double albums cost a fraction of their real value because the artists and what Cornyn called "this benevolent record company" had agreed that it was better to have their music heard by as wide an audience as possible. "If our accounting department were running this company they'd charge you $9.96 for each double album. But they're not. Yet."

Still, even the good folks at Warner/Reprise weren't entirely benevolent, Cornyn admitted. What they really hoped was that everyone who bought a two-dollar Loss Leader would run to a record store with a pocket full of cash to buy their just-discovered faves' albums at full market rates. But for now, they were happy to bring the music to the people. And the people were happy to receive it, mailing in for more than forty thousand

Mo Ostin didn't set out to be a record man but became one of the most successful and beloved executives in the music industry.

Joe Smith was a popular Boston disc jockey before moving to Los Angeles to get into the record business.

Untrammeled, Unfettered, Unconfined: Frank Sinatra declares his independence with Reprise Records in 1961.

Stan Cornyn (far right) cuts up at a 1964 sales convention, with Joel Friedman (center) and Ed Thrasher (left).

An unlikely member of the Rat Pack, Ostin, posing with Dean Martin, Sammy Davis Jr., and Sinatra, earned the trust and friendship of the whole gang.

Mike Maitland (center, with football) captains WBR's 1965 team, including a front row of soon-to-be key players (from left to right) Stan Cornyn, Joel Friedman, Joe Smith, and a very young Lenny Waronker.

Stan Cornyn's groundbreaking series of ads projected Warner/Reprise's new identity into the counterculture and beyond.

Van Dyke Parks was convinced that Cornyn's ads for *Song Cycle* would destroy his career.

By the start of the 1970s the Warner/Reprise executives looked as freaky as their artists. Back row, left to right: Tom Ruffino, Don Schmitzerle, Clyde Bakkemo, Ed West, Bob Regehr, David Herscher, Hal Halverstadt, Ed Thrasher, Adam Somers. Front row, left to right: David Berson, Stan Cornyn, Murray Gitlin, Ed Rosenblatt, Mo Ostin, Joe Smith, Lenny Waronker, Pete Johnson, Walt Calloway.

From *Song Cycle* to Gordon Lightfoot, Maria Muldaur and beyond, Lenny Waronker was the primary architect of the Burbank sound.

The Grateful Dead (Keith Godchaux, Phil Lesh, Bob Weir, Jerry Garcia, Pigpen) ridiculed Joe Smith for his commercial ambitions, but were delighted when their self-titled live album struck gold in 1971.

*Circular* teases Jerry "Captain Trips" Garcia for investing his new riches into a luxury car.

**Good Old Bentley** — Jerry Garcia, saintly guitarist with the Grateful Dead, was cruising Santa Rosa, California, one day when he spied an old Bentley with a For Sale sign. Garcia, never one to be impressed with material possessions, was impressed with the Bentley. He bought it and drives it very slowly.

Stan Cornyn, the king of Creative Services, explains the company's position on music industry traditions.

Lenny Waronker, Andy Wickham, Ted Templeman, Russ Titelman, and John Cale. Dubbed Warner Bros.' newest supergroup by Cornyn, the company's ace record producers pose for their own ad in 1972.

Ain't nothin' but a Warner Bros. party. When the artists on WBR's 1975 package tour through Europe turned a Graham Central Station song into a celebration of their record label, they invited Joe Smith to sing it with them onstage.

When the WEA network gave the company's record labels full control of the production, promotion, and distribution process, Stan Cornyn dubbed the system the Big Button and drafted Ostin, and all the Warner companies' chief executives, to tell their rivals all about it.

WHY ARE THESE MEN SMILING?

BECAUSE THEY'VE JUST HEARD SOME GREAT NEW ALBUMS.

SEALS & CROFTS
TOWER OF POWER
DEEP PURPLE
DOOBIE BROTHERS
VAN MORRISON
ON
WARNER BROS. RECORDS

At the height of Warners' mid-seventies success Cornyn bought a billboard on Sunset Boulevard to let all the other executives know how much better it was in Burbank.

When Ostin landed ex-Beatle George Harrison, Warner's star-besotted CEO Steve Ross joined the celebration. Left to right: Nesuhi Ertegun, Ross, Harrison, and Ostin.

Mo Ostin (second from left) celebrates the mega-success of *Rumours* with Fleetwood Mac (John McVie, Stevie Nicks, Christine McVie, Mick Fleetwood, and Lindsey Buckingham) in 1977.

Ostin greets Prince Nelson, the teenage singer-songwriter/ multi-instrumentalist who soon became one of the company's defining artists of the 1980s and beyond.

Ted Templeman (standing to Ostin's right) discovered Van Halen (left to right: Michael Anthony, David Lee Roth, Eddie Van Halen, Alex Van Halen) and produced most of the pop metal group's multi-platinum albums.

Installed as WBR's president in 1983, Waronker made a perfect partner for company chairman Ostin.

In the late 1970s the Ostin family (Kenny, Evelyn, Randy, Mo, and Michael) was a vision of happiness and success. Trouble loomed in the future.

copies of the *Songbook*, the first in a long series of samplers that would continue into the 1980s.

○

In the summer of 1969, three-day music festivals were everywhere. Hit the American highway with a tank full of gas and a glove box full of maps, and you could find a different rock festival virtually every weekend, and sometimes two or more. From the Northern California Folk-Rock Festival on Memorial Day weekend to the Denver Pop Festival in late June, to the Atlanta International Pop Festival over the Fourth of July weekend to the Laurel Pop Festival a week later in Maryland, to the Midwest Rock Festival the weekend after that to the Atlantic City Pop Festival, the Vancouver Pop Festival, the Seattle Pop Festival, the Texas International Pop Festival, the Toronto Rock and Roll Revival—you could just keep rolling and rolling. If you were in a really peripatetic mood, you could jet over the Atlantic to catch more festivals in Bath and on the Isle of Wight.

A certain sameness prevailed. Nearly all the affairs were outdoor gatherings at stadiums, raceways, or pastoral settings expansive enough to handle one hundred thousand–plus attendees, plus their cars and tents and youthful abandon. The entertainment came out of the same pool of freak-approved acts: Jimi Hendrix, Janis Joplin, Santana, Jefferson Airplane, Creedence Clearwater Revival, Canned Heat, Al Kooper, the Grateful Dead, Led Zeppelin, Joni Mitchell, Country Joe and the Fish, Joan Baez, and so on. They also shared the same promise of cultural transcendence: that for these few days, you could be among your own kind. And for as long as you were all together, you could live the future: peaceful, unhassled, free to smoke, drink, and drop whatever you felt like without fear of a cop swooping in to unleash the bummer you had come to escape. You could even argue that the music was just a part of what the throngs were after, and not the most important part, either.

The organizers of the Woodstock Music and Art Fair made this a central part of the promotional campaign for their event. The long list of acts (all those just listed save for Led Zeppelin and Al Kooper, plus a battalion of others) was secondary to the event itself: Three Days of Peace and Music that would also be, in astrological terms, an Aquarian Exposition, a bridge to a new age of social consciousness, of vision, of progressive values, of collaboration, humanitarianism, and a level of grooviness that rivaled your most hallucinogenic dreams. Between that and the lush green hills of upstate New York, it just had this glow about it, a sense of impending magic, of generational portent.

Still, it takes a lot of work, and workers, to get that kind of magic off the ground, and as the spring turned to summer, the festival's organizers—young, ambitious, and inexperienced—ran out of money. With tens of thousands of tickets sold and the weekend fast approaching, there was not nearly enough dough to pay for the supplies and workers needed to construct the stage, let alone to pay the artists to perform. So, producers Michael Lang and Artie Kornfeld went to studio president Ted Ashley at Warner Bros. Pictures to sell the rights to the documentary they were already making with filmmaker Michael Wadleigh. Ashley, who had run his own talent agency before jumping to the WB studios, cut the deal for one hundred thousand dollars, thereby saving the Woodstock festival and, though this wouldn't be evident for another year, acquiring the first smash hit movie Warner Bros. Pictures would release in years.

When the music filled the sky that weekend, it often came on a breeze from Burbank, from Arlo Guthrie on Friday to John Sebastian and the Grateful Dead on Saturday. Neil Young played with Crosby, Stills and Nash on Sunday; and Jimi Hendrix gave the climactic performance at dawn on Monday morning. When the three-hour documentary of the concert swept across the world in mid-1970, it climaxed with Crosby, Stills, Nash and Young's driving cover of Joni Mitchell's "Woodstock," a retrospective account that described the festival (from a distance, given that Mitchell had missed her set at the festival in order to perform on *The Dick Cavett Show* in New York City, per her manager David Geffen's suggestion) as a religious awakening.

○

In the late summer of 1969, not long after David Berson ended his graduate school studies and started working as Ostin's executive assistant, his boss invited him to accompany him on a business trip to the East Coast. Berson didn't have particular duties; mostly Ostin wanted his new charge to watch him perform the diverse rites of a music executive and soak up the atmosphere in the skyscrapers, swank Midtown restaurants, and bunker-like underground clubs where it all took place. Observing quietly from a few feet away, Berson marveled at how easily Ostin moved through every situation. He could marshal sales statistics and corporate management theory with shinily shod businessmen, or he could talk songwriting and Los Angeles recording studios with a stoned James Taylor on the lawn of the Newport Folk Festival. Straight from there, he could spend the night rapping philosophy with musician/cult leader Mel Lyman in the crumbling house he and his followers occupied deep in the Boston slums of Roxbury.

Ostin knew how to hang with the freaky folks. The jazz players he'd worked with at Verve were pretty edgy themselves, and the gang at Reprise, including those super-straight nightclub entertainers, chased their art through a firmament defined by the muse and the pursuit of vision and expression. Artists ran hot, cold, and in curlicues. As Ostin saw it, the executive's job was to work according to their expectations. He knew the value both of the good hang and of the line dividing friendly enthusiasm from grating sycophancy. He had an ability to project so much belief in an artist and her vision that his enthusiasm would reflect back onto the artist, nurturing her artistry and fostering more and better creation, to the point where even the looniest propositions could flourish into something truly special.

Still, Mel Lyman presented a special case. A gifted musician who had played banjo and harmonica for Jim Kweskin and the Jug Band (a hotbed of future Warner acts that included Kweskin, Geoff and Maria Muldaur, and Lyman), Lyman was also a charismatic leader and writer whose first book, *Autobiography of a World Saviour*, cast him as a Superman figure, come down from a distant planet to liberate the human race from the folly of society's illusions. Another book, *The Mirror at the End of the Road*, collected Lyman's musings on philosophy, astrology, sexual submission, and more, with an industrial-grade messiah complex tying it all together. Even then, it sounded like hooey, but Lyman had these bottomless eyes, a rich store of psychedelic drugs, and personal magnetism that made some people *believe*. Kweskin himself, who tapped Lyman to play banjo and blow a little harp for his popular Jug Band in 1963, eventually found himself so enamored of his sideman that he made room for him at the front of the stage and encouraged the rest of the bandmates to treat Lyman as their spiritual leader. Kweskin stepped away from his music for several years, and when he returned as a solo artist in 1969, the album he called *Richard D. Herbruck Presents Jim Kweskin's America, Co-starring Mel Lyman and the Lyman Family* turned out to be a musical tract centered on the teachings of his former banjo/harmonica player. "I am singing America to you and it is Mel Lyman," Kweskin wrote in the liner notes. "He is the new soul of the world."

And while that would seem to be an all-consuming position, Lyman had plenty of time to pursue both Kweskin's and his own music. In time, Mo Ostin heard that the guy wrote ear-catching songs, could play a variety of instruments, and had enticed enough good musicians into his cult of followers to make him seem like a decent prospect. So, what the hell, Ostin signed Mel Lyman to a recording contract.* Told that Ostin would be in Boston, Lyman invited the president of his record company to preview the Lyman Family's first album in the very commune where it was hatched. Ostin took him up on the offer, and there they came, the record company president and Berson, his young aide-de-camp, up the fractured steps of the house at the center of the family's spread of tumbledown buildings near Fort Hill Park. Every room in the place, Berson noticed, featured a framed portrait of Lyman. They gathered in one room to hear the album, all eyes on Ostin, who nodded and tapped his foot approvingly. Also present were the actors Mark Frechette and Daria Halprin, two gorgeous young humans who had just been invited to star in Michelangelo Antonioni's film *Zabriskie Point*; the two were excited to take the parts but were still waiting for Lyman's okay.† When the music was over, Lyman asked Ostin to see something else: the final draft of the liner notes he'd written for the back cover. Did Ostin think they could use it without making any changes? It was a loaded question. What Lyman really wanted to know was if the president of a corporate record company would actually allow his

---

* Ostin had been offered the same opportunity with an L.A.-based musician and cult/family leader near the same time, but despite Beach Boy drummer Dennis Wilson's sponsorship and Neil Young's recommendation, he had chosen not to get into business with Charles Manson. This rejection infuriated Manson so much that he sent some of his family members to pay a visit to the home of record producer Terry Melcher, in the Hollywood Hills. Melcher had moved by then, renting his place to Roman Polanski and Polanski's wife, Sharon Tate, and I don't have to tell you what happened next.

† He approved.

company to be a tool in the cultural, social, and musical revolution. Lyman handed over a sheet of paper and gazed expectantly while Ostin read.

This, the manifesto declared, was *contemporary* music, created for an age in which the old forms must be destroyed in order for new sounds to emerge. "Music is neat and clean and void of real life," it went on. "We say fuck those people, we just want to blow. Folk music is dead, it got too fond of itself. Jazz is dead, it got too lost in itself. Rock is screaming its brains out trying to make up for the loss."[5] On and on, all of it tooled to diminish every note of every record Warner/Reprise had ever released. And what did Ostin think of that? The executive scanned the page, read the words closely, then looked right at Lyman.

"Oh my God," he said. "This says *everything*. It's perfect. Don't change a word."

The musician/cult leader smiled. Ostin and Berson spent the rest of the evening talking music and record making, and then were free to rejoin ordinary society—not that Lyman or anyone else had made it seem like things might not turn out that way. But it was September 1969, less than two months after the Manson horrors in L.A., and paranoia hung thick in the air, just not around Ostin. He'd spent his entire career in the company of artists, tycoons, and cockeyed visionaries from the loftiest executive suites, the freakiest backstage scenes, and even the mail room in his own building. Normal was fine for ordinary businesses. But pop music, like every other form of art, required something a little more extraordinary.

○

Crosby, Stills, Nash and Young, the surprise hit of Woodstock, were only the latest, if by far the most successful, example of the phenomenon in late 1960s rock 'n' roll: the supergroup. The trend began in England in 1966, with the launch of Cream, the power trio that joined ex-Yardbird guitarist Eric Clapton with Jack Bruce and Ginger Baker, the bassist and drummer, respectively, of the Graham Bond Organisation. That same year, an American soul music counterpart, the Soul Clan, joined Otis Redding, Wilson Pickett, Solomon Burke, Don Covay, and Joe Tex in a kind of all-star Temptations, to lesser effect. No new all-star groups formed in 1967, but the next year produced a bumper crop, including the original three-some of Crosby, Stills and Nash (from the Byrds, Buffalo Springfield, and the Hollies); Led Zeppelin, which unified another ex-Yardbird guitarist, Jimmy Page, with singer Robert Plant and drummer John Bonham, both from the Band of Joy, with leading session bassist John Paul Jones; and the so-called *Super Session* albums, built from in-studio jams by Stills, famed Bob Dylan sideman Al Kooper, and blues guitar hero Mike Bloomfield. Cream's breakup in 1968 was just a prelude to the launch of Blind Faith, in which Clapton and Baker joined forces with Traffic's Steve Winwood and Ric Grech from the Family. And it didn't stop there. Just imagine poor Greil Marcus, chief record critic for *Rolling Stone*, getting avalanched by this stuff. One day in the late summer of 1969, he threw up his hands and . . . *Gah! Enough!*

Fed up with the hype and the gimcrackery, Marcus sat down with fellow *Rolling Stone* writer Bruce Miroff, and together they imagined what the ultimate supergroup would look like. You'd need Beatles, of course, so how about John Lennon, Paul McCartney, and George Harrison? Bob Dylan would be there, too, as would the Stones' Mick Jagger. Just imagine what kind of gold-plated mess those godliest of the young gods would produce, to say nothing of the legal entanglements their many contractual obligations would create. So, what do you call a group so super it can't acknowledge its own existence? Somewhere between them, a name presented itself: the Masked Marauders.

Working together, Marcus and Miroff crafted a breathless review of the nonexistent album, describing the imaginary creation of a Beatles-Dylan-Stones summit, along with details of the top-secret recording sessions. Gathering in a town near the site of the original Hudson's Bay Colony in Canada, where they could hide in plain view of the Eskimos and fur traders, Lennon, McCartney, Harrison, Dylan, and Jagger would spend three days working with star producer (and *Super Sessions* costar) Al Kooper to create, among other brilliances, an eighteen-minute cover version of the UK folk singer Donovan's "Season of the Witch," a McCartney-led take on Al Jolson's minstrel tune "Mammy" ("And they say a white boy can't sing the blues!"), Lennon's cover of James Brown's "Prisoner of Love" ("Complete with a full 10-minute false ending"), an original Dylan instrumental called "Cow Pie," Jagger's "instant classic" called "Can't Get No Nookie," and a Jagger-McCartney a cappella cover of Dylan's "Masters of War" that would, as the review paraphrased Dylan's famous lyric, make a listener "truly wish . . . that they could stand over their graves until you're sure they're dead." None of this sounded all that promising, even as the review's kicker crowed "[T]his album is more than a way of life, it *is* life." Marcus and Miroff credited the bogus review to "T. M. Christian," a name adapted from the title of Terry Southern's satirical novel *The Magic Christian*, which is, fittingly, about an eccentric billionaire who pulls elaborate pranks to fool people into believing ridiculous things. Marcus showed the manuscript to *Rolling Stone* editor Jann Wenner, who loved the idea of spoofing his magazine's more gullible readers, and approved it for the magazine's October 18, 1969, issue.

If anyone else got the joke, their words were lost in the roar of voices insisting that it must be, that it *had* to be, true. The start of the sixties had been so full of promise and hope. But by the end of the decade, that spirit had been ripped apart by bullets, war, fire, and rage. The disillusionment and heartbreak that had swept through the decade couldn't stand as its legacy; even in 1969, the children of Camelot still yearned for hope. For many of them, the likes of the Beatles, Bob Dylan, and the Rolling Stones seemed to be the only magical things left alive. And as unlikely as it was that the three would end the decade by uniting into an Olympian conglomeration, the need for it to be true, for a stone-cold miracle to occur at long last, was palpable. So much had been taken away over the previous ten years, the universe owed us the Masked Marauders. And within a matter of days, they came to exist, sort of.

Langdon Winner, a *Rolling Stone* writer and UC Berkeley student who hung out with the members of a folkie Berkeley band called the Cleanliness and Godliness Skiffle Band, also cohosted a weekly music discussion show on the free-form San Francisco radio station KSAN-FM.* Tickled by Marcus's bogus review, he corralled some of his friends to help him write and record songs to match the descriptions Marcus and Miroff had written for their *Rolling Stone* piece. Winner also knew a guy with a recording studio in his garage, so they all gathered there, along with a case of beer and a handful of freshly rolled joints. Marcus came in to help write the Jaggerian lyrics to "Can't Get No Nookie." A singer/musician named Brian Voorheis rolled out his Dylan and Jagger impressions. A neighborhood

---

* Most of Tom Donahue's original staff from KMPX-FM had helped found KSAN following a conflict with the original station's owner.

dobro player put the twang of Dylan's *Nashville Skyline* into "Cow Pie," and Winner himself added some piano tracks. When they finished recording a few hours later, the Masked Marauders of Marcus and Miroff's imagination had a sound, of sorts.

Next, Winner called WBR's *Circular* coeditor Pete Johnson, whom he knew from music writer circles, to see if the world's leading counterculture record company might be interested in pursuing the project as a full-length album. Johnson took the prospect to Cornyn, who was interested enough to track Ostin to the Warner studio commissary where he was eating lunch. Partway through Cornyn's pitch, Ostin interrupted to ask how much it might cost to make the record. Stuck for an answer, Cornyn guessed. Thirty thousand dollars? Ostin waved a hand. "For that amount of money don't even call me," he said. "Just do it."[6] Cornyn put his telephone receiver down, grabbed a pen and paper, and dove into his first A&R assignment, secure in the outlandishness of his own imagination.

Back in Ira Ironstrings territory, Cornyn had Johnson write a press release that announced the Masked Marauders signing, without admitting or denying anything else. "Our official position on this group should be as follows," one in-house memo declared. "We do not know the names of the people comprising the group, and the only thing we know about it is what we read in *Rolling Stone.*" It was a perfect balance of truth and absurdity, and Cornyn was most pleased.[7]

You had to be a little off-kilter to work in the advertising/promotional division Cornyn had dubbed Creative Services. When he needed to fill jobs, he often opted for candidates with no experience in the music industry, preferring smart, interesting people with a good sense of humor. A diploma from Pomona College didn't hurt, either. His first hire, Hal Halverstadt, was a classmate; Johnson graduated a few years later. Even more important than their alma mater, both had a rebellious spirit that aligned with Cornyn's favorite workplace motto: How can we break the rules today?

Winner and his KSAN cohost John Morthland, still another *Rolling Stone* writer–slash–Berkeley grad student, played the tunes on their next broadcast, and most of the listeners who called in to talk about the music seemed to grasp that they were playing along with an elaborate joke. But when Winner, feeling ever more swept up in the prank, passed dubs of the Masked Marauders songs to a few other radio stations, and those disc jockeys dubbed copies for their friends at other stations, the story spread across the country, only without the ironic asides that had shown through the original Marcus/Miroff review and Winner/Morthland's presentation of the songs on KMPX. Winner, whose name was associated with the original tapes, started getting calls, first from reporters out of underground newspapers and then from an executive at Motown Records in Detroit, who offered a fifty-thousand-dollar contract, but only if the Masked Marauders were truly Lennon, McCartney, Harrison, Dylan, and Jagger. Marcus, at his desk in the *Rolling Stone* offices, took a call from Albert Grossman, the actual manager of the actual Bob Dylan, who apparently hadn't heard from his client in some time: Soooo . . . is that really Bob with all those guys?[8] Not as far as Marcus knew, but you never knew where Dylan would turn up next, so who could say for sure? Al Kooper, the long-time Dylan intimate and partial target of Marcus and Miroff's review (as one third and producer of the original *Super Session* album), played along by dismissing one reporter with a terse "No comment!"

Given a fifteen-thousand-dollar budget and a month of production time, Winner and his gang got to work in Berkeley. Meanwhile, Cornyn fired off a memo to promotions director Bill Casady, who alerted his staff on October 22 that "Our official position on this group should be as follows: We do not know the names of the people comprising this group and the only thing we know about them is what we read in *Rolling Stone*." A directive from sales manager Dick Sherman instructed the company's distributors and sales team to look for shipments of window streamers reading MASKED MARAUDERS NOW IN STOCK and prepare themselves for an album "that could well be our biggest this year." Meanwhile, Johnson sent out a press release that was so convincing that both *Cashbox* and *Record World* gave the debut single "Cow Pie" their Pick Hit designation. *Billboard* and *Record World* printed Johnson's press release word for word, as if it were a reported story by their own staff members.[9] And as the excitement built, Cornyn and Johnson, the latter writing as "Solomon Penthaus," an occasional *Circular* contributor now identified as the president of the Marauders' Deity Records imprint, teased the release of the Marauders' first single by placing an ad in the trades. That ad sought to spin the web even denser; it made the false accusation that Capitol Records (identified only as "a certain large record company, one with seven letters in its name, which begins with the third letter of the alphabet and ends with the twelfth letter") was scheming to release its own Masked Marauders album. "I don't know why all this fuss has started over them," Penthaus/Johnson declaimed, "but I do know that the other record company, the one I didn't name, can only be recording imposters."[10]

The legitimate—if that's the word for them—Masked Marauders were still hunkered down in their South Berkeley garage, now realizing that their songs would be released, promoted, and heard all around the world. Given a clear shot at the big time, they started to take the music more seriously, spending hour upon hour working out arrangements, getting every part that much more perfect. And this took time, more than the four weeks Cornyn and the rest of Warner/Reprise had given them. "That's when the fun-loving atmosphere ended," Winner recalls. The sessions devolved into debates about arrangements, mixes, and how the harmonies should sound. Winner fielded increasingly cranky calls from Cornyn wondering where his album was and how it could possibly take so long to record a bunch of silly songs satirizing a group that didn't exist. "You're nickel-and-diming me," Cornyn grumbled, which made as much sense as Winner's assertion in the liner notes that some of the tracks took only one take to record "and some took even less than that."[11]

Thinking reasonable thoughts about journalistic integrity, Jann Wenner and his crew at *Rolling Stone* printed a story confessing to the hoax in the magazine's November 15 issue, right about the time the Marauders album hit the record stores. The album's reviews toggled between gentle debunking, as in the *Los Angeles Times* column by Robert Hilburn, who called it "a remarkably good comedy album,"[12] and a sarcastic rave in *Circus* that seemed to be written by T. M. Christian's less intelligent younger brother.[13] *The Masked Marauders* fell short of being Warner/Reprise's best-selling album of 1969, but it did rise as high as No. 123 on the *Billboard* album charts—due in part, Winner says, to at least one distributor who exaggerated his sales figures to see how high he could propel it onto the hit parade. Nevertheless, the album sold forty thousand copies, enough to make a neat profit for the company's trouble. The musicians made do with their happy memories of being, at least for a short while, the hottest supergroup on the planet.

# THE GOLD DUST TWINS

In an industry where you're exactly as hot as the last thing you did, Ostin and Smith's run through the late 1960s gave them the light and velocity of twin comets racing across a moonless sky. How had they figured out the future so soon? What else had the others failed to recognize? How many mountains of cash could you earn if you put one of them in charge of your record company? By the time Eliot Hyman started to think about selling the company in 1969, both his record company chiefs were getting calls: friendly greetings from top executives and record company owners from all over Los Angeles and New York, just passing along their congratulations on all their success and letting them know how much they admired what they were doing. And if they ever wanted to have lunch and get to know each other a little better, well . . .

Then came the straight-up propositions. "Mo had an offer from [Elektra's] Jac Holzman that would get him a piece of the company," Joe Smith told me. "I had one from RCA. We were very desirable executives. And we really were the [hottest] record company [at Warner Bros]."[1] But neither man wanted to leave the company, especially now that their work was beginning to pay off. And their work at Warner wasn't close to finished. They'd made a daring turnaround, and their numbers were still heading skyward; anyone could see that. But they'd set out to do more than simply succeed. They wanted to redefine the meaning of success in the commercial arts. They still wanted to be paid what they were worth, but all Warner Bros. had to do to hang on to them was acknowledge their achievements with appropriate salaries, year-end bonuses, and so on, with all of it guaranteed for the length of a five-year contract. Rather than provoke a confrontation with the already beleaguered Maitland, the label chiefs went to Mickey Rudin, the Verve and Sinatra lawyer whom Ostin had also retained as his counsel. Sinatra, who had received one-third control of Warner Bros. Records' available stock in his Reprise/movie contract deal in 1963, stood to gain or lose depending on the record companies' successes, so Rudin took the message to Maitland along with Sinatra's strong suggestion that he give Ostin and Smith what they wanted, and fast.

And yet Maitland dragged his feet. It took a while to get the new contracts written. It took longer to get the papers to Ostin and Smith, and even longer to get them to sign and hand them back. Who knows why? Maitland certainly had a lot of other things on his mind in 1969. Along with his duties at Warner Bros., he had started a pair of high-profile jobs in industry organizations, serving as the president of the Recording Industry Association of America and as a board member of the publishing organization ASCAP. And he was just about to board an airplane for a European business trip when he was called to an airport courtesy phone, over which he heard the discourteous voice of Jack Warner, still wielding power as a stockholder and the company's president emeritus: *Do not board that airplane until you've got those contracts signed.* Maitland hightailed it back to Burbank and did as he was told.

Feeling more appreciated and secure in their long-term contracts, Ostin and Smith dug into their jobs for the long haul.

○

By the start of 1969, his record companies were thriving, but Eliot Hyman still wasn't happy. When he added Warner Bros. Pictures to his burgeoning media empire, he had thought he was getting into the movie business, joining the grand parade of Goldwyns, Mayers, Cukors, and Warners who had built their fortunes on the great masterpieces of twentieth-century American cinema: *Gone with the Wind, The Wizard of Oz, Casablanca,* and a hundred others. But the Warner Bros. Pictures he wound up with had faded, producing movies few people wanted to see, spewing cash to the point of being forced to contemplate auctioning off its fabled studio lot to property developers, and unloading its library to the highest bidder. The company's music division kept the entire enterprise's lights on, bringing in nearly 80 percent of the Warner corporation's revenue in 1968. But Hyman didn't trust the record business. As he saw it, following the caprices of children did not feel like a reliable business model. By early 1969, the word filtered into the investment community: Warner Bros. Pictures was back on the block.[2]

Meanwhile, Steve Ross, the chief executive of Kinney National Service Inc., best known for its funeral homes, limousine services, and parking lots, was eager to add a movie and/or television company to his holdings. His first choices, ABC and MGM, proved beyond his grasp, but the floundering Warner–Seven Arts was an easier reach. At least two other companies were circling it,[3] but Ross, a hotly ambitious forty-two-year-old, was determined to move into the center of the entertainment business. The son of a businessman who had lost his money in the Wall Street crash of 1929, Ross grew up in a tough section of Flatbush in Brooklyn, determined to work himself into the monied classes. This aspiration had defined him since he was a boy. As Connie Bruck reported in her 1994 biography, *Master of the Game*, the grade school–age Steve tracked winter weather reports carefully, and when the forecast called for snow, he'd set his alarm for 4 a.m. and spend four hours before class shoveling driveways for the well-to-do homeowners a few blocks away. After school, he sold magazines and delivered groceries and dry cleaning.[4] Married at twenty-six to the daughter of the Riverside Chapels funeral home company, Ross joined his father-in-law's funeral home company and spurred his in-laws to expand into limousine services and parking lots. Next, he convinced them to take the company public to raise capital, then set to growing the business. Looking past the new parking lot and limousine business, Ross steered the redubbed Kinney Service Corporation into printing, periodicals, and then, in his biggest play yet, the Hollywood-based Ashley Famous talent agency.

Still, Ross and Kinney made an unlikely suitor to Warner–Seven Arts. Ahmet Ertegun was particularly skeptical of Ross's comprehension of the music business. How could he work for someone who had built his business by selling coffins? Ross didn't need Ertegun's approval to make the deal, but he went out of his way to charm him. He managed to win the Atlantic president's heart by vowing that he had no intention of interfering with how he ran his company. He extended the same promise to the other record label chiefs. *I leave you alone,* he explained. *Once a year, we'll talk about numbers, and if that goes well, we don't have to talk for another year.*

He meant it, too, and then some. Thoroughly besotted by show business, the chief executive treated his entertainment executives as if they were just as magical as the famous artists at the center of their businesses. Being starstruck served Ross and his company quite well. The most important skill they had, their ability to choose hit artists from among throngs of others, was as mysterious to him as the thickening streams of income were promising. Absent any Old World notions about the shadiness of rock 'n' roll, Ross embraced the music and called for more. He'd figured it out once he saw the last few years of Warner's annual reports. He wasn't buying a struggling movie studio with a glorious past; he was buying a thriving music company with a limitless future.

Ross's passion for Warner's record labels benefited Ostin and Smith even before he got the keys to the corporation. The real reason Jack Warner was so aggressive about ordering Maitland to produce the five-year contracts for his label presidents was to satisfy Ross's insistence that Warner's most profitable businesses would continue to be run by the men who had made them successful. Both Ostin and Smith scored a minor windfall in those deals, but once Ross took over the company the skies cracked wide open.

Ross followed a three-step recipe for keeping his top executives happy: get the best people, stay out of their way, and make them so happy they'll never leave. And so, in early 1970, it began. All the Warner/Reprise executives got raises. The ones judged particularly important to the company got dealt into Ross's bonus system, through which he would, after an especially profitable year, increase their annual salary by more than 100 percent. Soon, they were making significantly more than their peers at other companies. Eventually, a few of his employees would actually earn more than even Ross, but how else could he reward the men who made his record companies the most successful labels during the most profitable era in the history of the American entertainment industry?

Only one barrier stood between Ostin and Smith and the full, unfettered launch of the Steve Ross era in the Warner Bros. music division, and its name, sadly enough, was Mike Maitland. It was painful to think of him as an obstacle. Maitland's efforts had kept Warner Bros. Records alive when so many of Jack Warner's top lieutenants were crying out for its destruction. He understood the need to invest in rock 'n' roll and didn't question the contracts offered for the likes of Hendrix, the Grateful Dead, the Fugs, and many other untested artists who were exactly the type of wild-eyed rockers his bosses had once ordered him never, ever to sign. But Maitland chose the wrong adversary in Ahmet Ertegun. Based in New York, the Atlantic president had constant access to Ross, who was already besotted with the record man's exotic urbanity. And when Ertegun worried that his increasingly hot counterparts in Burbank might get tired of reporting to Maitland, he noted his own financial stake in Warner/Reprise's success—the Atlantic buyout deal included a sizable chunk of Warner Bros. stock—and urged Ross to make sure they felt appreciated enough to stay in place for a good long while.

Not long afterward, Ertegun, accompanied by Ross's top executive, Ted Ashley, went to Ostin offering to promote him into Maitland's position as president of Warner Bros. Records, the larger entity that included the Warner Bros. and Reprise labels. Aghast at the thought of pushing Maitland out of his job, Ostin refused. Maitland had been too good an ally for too long. "Then they said, look, he's gonna get fired no matter what," Ostin recalls. "So, if you don't take this job, someone else will." Still, Ostin spent a torturous night talking it over with Evelyn, worrying over how unfairly Maitland was being treated. "But I wasn't responsible. That was Ahmet's doing. And I really wanted it, so I accepted the job and negotiated a very strong contract."[5]

Maitland got the bad news on January 25, 1970. Ostin called the same evening to tell him how sorry he was. As he recalls it, Maitland accepted his words graciously and gave him his blessing.*

Then came Joe Smith. He and Ostin had worked as equals for half a

---

* The defenestrated executive took a new job with MCA Records and promptly signed a young but balding singer-songwriter-pianist who called himself Elton John. Maitland also scored Lynyrd Skynyrd and the smash hit soundtrack to the hit 1976 movie *Car Wash*, among other hits.

dozen years. But there could be only one president of their joint company, and Ross, with Ertegun's counsel, had chosen Ostin. Smith was just as qualified to run a record company, and had a drawerful of offers from other companies to prove the point. But while Smith was disappointed to be passed over, Ross had offered him a new contract, too. And when he realized that Ross was offering him far more to stay as Ostin's number two than he would have asked for to be the top man, it didn't seem so bad to be second chair. Ostin and Smith had tickets to see the Lakers play the Houston Rockets the night after Maitland's firing and spent the evening whispering to each other. *Oh my God, what just happened? How are we going to do this?* "It was a small company then, and Daddy was going away," Smith told Stan Cornyn a decade later.

The news of Maitland's departure and Ostin and Smith's ascension broke across the industry, as expected. But with so few details available, it fell to the company's in-house magazine, *Circular*, to set things straight in its next issue. The headline was dramatic: THE SCANDAL AT WARNER/ REPRISE. And yet even that barely described the story just below. "Guerrilla bands swept through the corridors of the Warner/Reprise Burbank headquarters, raping accountants and knifing and shooting officials of the dying regime," it began. The guerrillas, who had apparently emerged from the jungle canopy, wore rustic shoes that couldn't grip the building's modern linoleum floors. Nevertheless, they slaughtered their opponents during a fierce battle on the stairs, and once they gained access to the building's central power source it was all over. "Lights flickered, record players slowed, and died. By the time emergency power was restored, the foreign crew had taken the President's office and proclaimed a new chief executive for the record company: Mo Ostin . . . The coup (pronounced coo) had succeeded."

○

The headline on *Stereo Review*'s December 1970 cover described Warner/Reprise Records' progress through the last few years in vivid terms: THE GOLD DUST TWINS IN BEAUTIFUL DOWNTOWN BURBANK: A SUCCESS STORY.

*Stereo Review*, founded in 1958 as a hi-fi hobbyist's publication, had by the late 1960s evolved into an outlet for serious writing about every aspect of music, from deeply informed record reviews to *New York Times Magazine*–caliber profiles of artists and industry figures. Its readership, while never enormous, was both elite and savvy. And when they dug into author Martin Gottfried's* piece, they found a story that seemed almost too utopian to be true. "Extraordinarily successful," he wrote of the Burbank record company. "Genuinely interested in art" . . . "Music with a special quality" . . . "A mystique . . . a sense of something magical." And all of it was grounded in "a *philosophical* attitude that goes beyond temporary fads in taste."

The reigning exemplars of that attitude, Gottfried continued, were two of the least popular artists on its increasingly hot roster: Randy Newman and Van Dyke Parks. "These two composers, probably the most glittering in all contemporary popular music, are its platinum twins," Gottfried wrote. "They make everyone, from Ostin on down, proud to be identified with Warner/Reprise and certain that they are involved in something more important than just 'the music business.'" And not despite their poor sales records, either. In fact, the company's adoration of the two artists seemed to be in some part *because* their work eluded the comprehension of the Ordinary Joe and Nancy Normals of the record-buying world. "The aura that surrounds them, the purity of their music, and their sheer spirit have taken Warner and Reprise a giant step beyond mere music-making."

Three years past Ostin's directive to stop trying to make hits, the Warner/Reprise labels were regularly sending records into the highest reaches of the sales charts. Even the freakiest of the freaks were breaking through. Tiny Tim's 1968 debut, *God Bless Tiny Tim*, climbed the *Billboard* charts to the No. 7 slot, elevated by his cover of Al Dubin and Joe Burke's 1929 song "Tip-Toe Thru the Tulips with Me," which dandied its way to the No. 17 slot in the Hot 100. Arlo Guthrie's *Alice's Restaurant*, the album built around the eighteen-minute title track, hit No. 29 in 1968 and stayed on the best-seller charts for more than fifteen months, including a run back to No. 63 in the wake of the 1969 release of the acclaimed *Alice's Restaurant* movie, which racked up an Academy Award nomination for director Arthur Penn.

---

* Gottfried was best known then as the drama critic for the *New York Post*.

At the same time, Joni Mitchell, Neil Young, Van Morrison, and the Kinks all sent albums and/or singles into the Top 10. The newly signed singer-songwriter James Taylor's *Sweet Baby James* launched like a rocket, and singer-songwriter Gordon Lightfoot, another one of the company's new artists, did nearly as well with his hit single "If You Could Read My Mind" and its album, *Sit Down Young Stranger*. And as if that weren't enough, the Grateful Dead, of all bands, released a successful concert album, *Live/Dead*, in 1969, setting up a pair of 1970 studio records, *Workingman's Dead* and *American Beauty*, that climbed into the Top 30 on the album charts, both records selling more than 700,000 copies, more than enough to be certified gold by the end of the year.

As Ostin had intuited, the audience for Warner/Reprise's brand of idiosyncratic music already existed in 1967 and grew by bounds over the next three years. As *Stereo Review*'s Martin Gottfried noted, the new generation of young adults was uniquely aware of and connected to the one record company that shared their tastes and worldview. Charlie Springer, then a clerk working behind the counter of Hear Here records, near Northwestern University in Evanston, Illinois, noticed that when his regular customers came in looking for something new, their curiosity had a sudden focus. *What's new this week?* was now *What's new on Warner/Reprise?*[6] Music critic turned cultural observer and author Greil Marcus felt the same way. "[Warner/Reprise] had the most inventive producers, took chances on all kinds of people, and issued marvelous records, and surprising records. It was clear to people that Warner's was the label where idiosyncratic people could go."[7]

And though the label's music became increasingly eclectic, taking in everything from the evolved soul of Charles Wright and the Watts 103rd Street Rhythm Band to the folk-based story songs of Gordon Lightfoot and James Taylor, it was still possible to identify a consistent aesthetic— what *Stereo Review* dubbed "the Burbank Sound." Writing in *Vogue* in early 1970,[8] the critic Richard Goldstein described it as a "commitment to understatement"[9] shared by A&R/production chief Lenny Waronker and colleagues Andy Wickham, Richard Perry, and Sonny Burke. No matter whom they were producing at the time, the Warner/Reprise records had a vibe that felt somehow *organic*. Wooden instruments set the tone, the electric ones mixed in without drowning out the more delicate nuances coming from the other players. Hands squeaked on guitar necks, the strings so close you could feel the scrape of horsehair against violin strings. Filigree, to the extent they used it, came from unexpected sources: the jangling strings of a bouzouki, a synthesizer hoot, or the worrying of an oboe. Waronker had made that feeling a hallmark of his productions, and his influence could be heard far beyond Warner/Reprise.

○

Now with full control over both the labels operating within the Warner Bros. Records company, Ostin accelerated his campaign to transform the way the company did business, encouraging each staff member to look at how his job had always been done, smash that model to pieces, and rebuild it in smarter, better ways. To rid the company of standard thinking, Ostin made a point of hiring people who had never before worked for record companies, filling offices with school teachers, writers, musicians, and anyone else who seemed smart, creative, and daring. Unpolluted by experience, the new hires went at their tasks with fresh eyes and no sense of what was supposed to be impossible.

Anything new and innovative was celebrated, even if it ended up not working out. Hey, at least you had the guts and imagination to try, and that's what Ostin was after: a way of doing business that was as daring and unprecedented as the records they were making and, believe it or not, turning into hits. And when it all started working, when the ex–machine shop in Burbank became the epicenter of the spirit of the younger generation, when the upper notches on the *Billboard* charts were chockablock with Warner/Reprise artists and the Hollywood music industry experts came parading up the 101 to find out what secret Mo Ostin and Co. had cracked open over in Burbank, Stan Cornyn would shrug and tell them it was easy. The secret of the company's immense growth and success, he said time and again, boiled down to three words: *Let's try it!*

Cornyn's department was a central vector for the company's rebels and freethinkers. In 1971, looking for someone who could bring an imaginative touch to the company's promotional campaigns, Cornyn set his sights on Bob Regehr, a towering forty-year-old Hollywood publicist—not what you'd call an *ordinary* publicist, however. Called in for an interview, Regehr entered Cornyn's office carrying two things: a résumé and a deck of cards. The former wasn't entirely necessary, as he'd already worked on a few smaller projects for Cornyn. The cards said more about Regehr's character. A charming rogue with a mysterious past and a sharp nose for what was going to happen next, he had the heart of a riverboat gambler. Cornyn hired him on the spot and put him in charge of what would soon become the Artist Development department.

What that would be wasn't clear. But it was fueled by one of Ostin's central charges: to build the company around artists with the talent and ambition to hold an audience's interest for years or even decades. You couldn't create that by signing one-hit wonders or expecting overnight success from artists who worked painstakingly to find their voices. And as Ostin had made clear to Ross and his financial team, it takes time and money to create a company that's built to last. And that's where Regehr came in.

Six foot three and constructed as if by a brickmason, Regehr draped his jack-o'-lantern head in strands of long brown hair and cigarette smoke, the latter an animation of the internal seething that fired his carnival imaginings. Regehr's background was a bit mysterious, even to his closest friends. He had been raised in Salina, Kansas, without ever knowing his father, who died in an accident soon after Bob was born in 1931. His mother supported them with a career that elevated her to JCPenney's first female executive. Young Robert joined the U.S. Army at eighteen, then went to college in Mexico City, possibly because the city was so rich in his two favorite drugs, marijuana and psychedelic mushrooms. After college he headed to Los Angeles, where he settled in the bohemian groves of Laurel Canyon and befriended sculptor Ed Kienholz, among other bohemians. A budding writer, Regehr published a Western[10] and sold a handful of television screenplays before switching to public relations, where his brains, wit, and offbeat charm served him well as he shepherded Ann-Margret and her glittery kind through press junkets, screenings, and other spotlit setups. Regehr was just as adept at playing pranks on his colleagues. When one of his compatriots was on the verge of marrying his third wife, Regehr called for an office celebration featuring a wedding cake he'd prepared with the traditional bride and groom on top—only, this groom was accompanied by three brides,[11] each of them with the same hopeful smile drawn across her unsuspecting plastic face.

Regehr continued his antics in Burbank, scrawling mustaches on publicity posters and making prank phone calls to his colleagues to see if he could convince them to deliver strange messages to higher-ups, such as the time he put on a scratchy falsetto and instructed Ted Templeman's secretary to tell him his mother had called to say the drums on the Doobie Brothers' new single had too much echo in the right channel. You know, normal stuff like that. Fortunately, his first triumph came early, when Shep Gordon, the young and hotly ambitious manager for the shock-rock group Alice Cooper, came in to prod the company into doing something to draw attention to his guys.

Alice Cooper, a five-piece hard rock band known for its cross-dressing, horror movie villain–style front man (who later took the band's name as his own), had been a tough sell for its first couple of years in the Warner/Reprise family. Signed by Frank Zappa for his Warner-distributed Bizarre/Straight label, the band's first two albums bombed, due in part to Zappa's disinterest in them. The band didn't help itself the night Gordon corralled a group of Warner/Reprise executives to their show at the Whisky a Go Go and, amid the band's lackluster set, the drummer managed to fall off the stage. A terrible show.

But Gordon, all of twenty-two, was convinced his group was bound for stardom, so when they were offered an opening spot on a national package tour in the summer of 1970 only to be denied the tour support money they would need by Zappa's partners at Bizarre/Straight, the manager decided to take his case to the central office on Warner Blvd. Gordon gathered the group, bought a few sacks of tacos on the way to Burbank, waited until Joe Smith had gone out to lunch, then rallied his troops to invade the label president's office, where, with their large and odoriferous lunch in hand, they stretched out on his chairs and sofas to wait. When the executive got back, Gordon greeted him at his door and introduced himself. He and his entire group were staying put, he promised, until Smith came through with the cash they needed to go on their summer tour. Or else, Gordon continued, Smith could always call the police and have them thrown out. But then the matter would be in the public record, and did Smith really want to read news stories about how he'd had one of his own bands tossed out of the building? Smith gave this some thought and then nodded. "You've got balls," he told Gordon, with new respect in his voice. "Come with me." Smith led the manager down to the finance office and told them to cut the check.

The tour went well, and given the dough to produce a new single, the band came up with the rocking but tuneful "I'm Eighteen," a tale of adolescent frustration that scraped against the Top 20 on *Billboard*'s singles chart. Reassigned from Bizarre/Straight to Warner/Reprise, the group saw their third album, *Love It to Death*, climb to No. 35 in March 1971. In it, the band traded its psychedelic influences for a crunchy hard rock sound that, along with its comic book horror, satire, and some distinctive sexual transgression, put them at the fore of the blossoming glam rock genre. It was a potent combination, but how could Warner/Reprise distill its essence into a promotional campaign that would grab the media by the ear? This was a problem Bob Regehr was uniquely equipped to tackle.

Hunkered together in his office, Regehr and Gordon fell into a brainstorming session that began with the idea of throwing a debutante ball for the Alice Cooper character at the elegant Ambassador Hotel, where all the best Los Angeles families celebrated the launch of their daughters' social lives. The Ambassador's managers would never allow it if they knew what the event was actually about, so Regehr asked his assistant, Shelley Cooper, who had the most proper voice and attitude in the building, to deal directly with the hotel. No one was to give any hint that the debutante in question was actually one of the freakiest rock 'n' roll bands currently in existence. To make certain that Mo Ostin and Joe Smith attended, Regehr scheduled the affair for the evening of July 14, so it could double as a fete for Evelyn Ostin's birthday. Did they know July 14 was also Bastille Day in France? They didn't, but they tossed that in, too, because why not? Then, with all that figured out, they got to work on the details. And this was where things got interesting, and expensive. After the bills topped seven grand, a massive amount for a single event in 1971, a very concerned Smith came to ask what the hell they were up to. Regehr gave him some kind of reasonable explanation, then told Shelley Cooper to stop sending the invoices to the finance office until after the party was over. "If it's a success, they won't care," he explained to her. "If it's not, then we'll all be fired anyway."[12]

They hired a traditional dance band to play standards, procured an oversize wedding cake designed to have someone pop out of it, rented a pair of gorilla suits, and hired, among other entertainers, a dog trained to do things dogs don't do, a three-hundred-pound singer/stripper named TV Mama, and an entire troupe of dancing drag performers from San Francisco known as the Cockettes. They then sent engraved invitations to hundreds of industry and media figures, asking that they dress formally, or "appropriately," which could, and did, mean many things to the many people in the Warner/Reprise sphere. Regehr had specified that their debutante, young Miss Cooper, would prefer a room bedecked with chandeliers, so the Ambassador's managers put the affair into the regal Venetian Room. When the evening arrived, some guests arrived clad in tuxedos and gowns, others in suits or cocktail dresses, and still others in worn denim cutoffs and midriff-baring halters. The actor Richard Chamberlain was there, along with the pop poet and Warner Bros. recording artist Rod McKuen, Randy Newman, Gordon Lightfoot, Steppenwolf's John Kay, Donovan, Cynthia Plaster Caster,* and a handful of the company's other acts, along with dozens of writers, reporters, critics, and industry figures.

The gorilla suits were assigned to two waiters, greeting the guests with silver trays of hors d'oeuvres, which some nibbled as they found their way to one of the many open bars scattered around the room. The Edward Gould Orchestra played sprightly versions of "Moonglow," "Somewhere My Love," and other dance favorites as couples gamboled before them. When the appointed time arrived, the entire crowd gathered in the main lobby, much to the astonishment of the chiffon-clad society dames and tuxedoed gentlemen bound for other affairs. Gould's band struck up "Pomp and Circumstance" to kick off the procession. First came the Cockettes, a dozen heavily made-up men in spangled dresses and plus-size high heels. One was dressed as a nightclub cigarette girl with a shoulder-strapped tray bearing cigars, cigarettes, and tubes of Vaseline. Next came the dog walking on its hind legs and pushing a baby stroller with its front feet. He might have been wearing a party hat; memories differ. TV Mama, the three-hundred-pound singer/stripper, came next, in a silky, white fur–lined black gown cut to feature her prodigious assets.† Finally came Alice Cooper, the five band members clad in tuxedoes, one set off by his caked-on mascara, streaks of rouge, and heavily powdered cheeks, grasping one of the long-stemmed roses being scattered in front of and over him.

---

\* A member of the Plaster Casters, artistic-minded groupies who crafted sculptures of their famous lovers' erect members for the joint purposes of history and sexual weirdness.

† When Ms. Mama's husband was explaining her fee structure to Regehr, he said she got $150 for singing and $200 for stripping. She was happy to do either, so which did they want? Regehr: "Um . . . maybe both?"

Then the real revelries began, fueled by the sloshing open bars and whatever was causing all that snorfling and snuffling in the bathrooms. Mo and Evelyn Ostin arrived along with Joe and Donnie Smith, Ahmet Ertegun, and whomever he was dating in Los Angeles at the moment. Evelyn's arrival triggered a chorus of "Happy Birthday," led by TV Mama, who pressed in to sing, shake, and shimmy her assets as close to the birthday girl's personal space as possible.

When that ordeal was over, Evelyn grabbed Joe Smith's shoulder and shouted in his ear, "Are we supposed to be here!?"

Smith shouted back, "Where else in the world would you *rather* be!?"

Whatever Evelyn said in response was lost when the oversize birthday cake at center stage blew its top. Miss Mercy, the GTO band member they'd installed in the cake's inner compartment, had gotten sick of waiting for her cue and came exploding upward wondering, at the top of her lungs, what the *fuck* she was doing in there. Then she started scooping up handfuls of frosting and hurling it at the guests, many of whom hurled it right back at her. Alice Cooper played a short set, and as the clock spun to midnight and beyond, a laughing mayhem prevailed. The poet McKuen, a tumble of silver hair, aquiline nose, and bespoke tuxedo, climbed onto a table and started dismantling one of the chandeliers piece by crystalline piece, while the Cockette cigarette girls returned with trays overflowing with multicolor dildos, many of which were carted away by frisky couples eager to take a test drive. And somewhere out of sight, a Cockette had traded her gown for one of the gorilla suits, in which she scampered out of the hotel's main entrance and was last seen on the Sunset Strip galloping into the dawn.

When Regehr got back to the office late the next morning, his desk fluttered with angry messages from the manager of the Ambassador Hotel (*You broke our chandelier!*), from the costume rental company (*You stole our gorilla suit!*), from the hotel manager's boss (*You shattered our dignity!*), and a few others. But these were overwhelmed by messages about the avalanche of Alice Cooper coverage the party was spurring. The *Los Angeles Times* planned an A-1 feature for the next Sunday. The wire services spread the story into newspapers all across the country, while industry magazines cranked out their own party tales, all celebrating how Warner/Reprise had launched another hit act. The tsunami of publicity swept the three-month-old *Love It to Death* album back up the charts, where it remained for the rest of the year on its way to selling 1.2 million copies. *Killer*, released around Thanksgiving, climbed to No. 21 on the album charts. The group's next single, "School's Out," jumped into the Top 10 in May, tugging its album, also named *School's Out*, released a month later, to No. 2 on the album charts and more than a million copies sold. As Regehr predicted, no one ever asked how much the party cost.

◉

Former Artist Development executive Carl Scott comes to the door in a monk's habit. He is over six feet tall and also wide, like an eight-hundred-year-old redwood is wide. Scott is in his eighties now, and significantly slimmed down following a scary few years of being way, way too heavy for even his build. A few health crises set him on a different course, and now Scott, who carries a walking stick as big as the trunk of the redwood's adolescent son, keeps his appetites in check.

But as a guy who spent the bulk of his life pushing the buttons, pulling the strings, and kicking the asses necessary to bring pop musicians to the world's attention, he still can't resist the temptation to make things happen for folks. *I can be your rabbi on this*, he said after we'd talked about the book I wanted to write. I know what a rabbi is, of course, but I didn't know the term's significance at Warner/Reprise. The building was full of rabbis, but Scott was one of the best: a great ally and an enemy you really didn't want to have. When another executive wouldn't stop badgering him for tour support for an artist Scott had already written off, he slammed his office door on him with enough force to send the mounted posters and photographs on his walls crashing to the floor. "That was Carl sending a message," the guy said. It had been thirty years, and the *blam* of Scott's door still echoed in his ears. "He's really a lovely guy, but just don't piss him off."

Scott grew up in a small Pennsylvania town focusing his brain and energies on training his purebred Afghan show dog. Scott did particularly well at the Bucks County Kennel Club match show in 1955, where Tom Donahue, the star disc jockey at WIBG-AM in Philadelphia, served as a celebrity judge. Impressed by the kid's poise and similarly oversize build, Donahue introduced himself, and the pair hit it off. When the disc jockey moved to San Francisco, Scott followed, taking a job Donahue helped him get in a record warehouse. And as Donahue's kingdom expanded, so did Scott's horizons. He became a key part of the disc jockey's team as Donahue started producing rock 'n' roll package shows. And when Donahue and his radio partner, Bob Mitchell, launched Autumn Records, Scott joined in. Soon, he moved into managing Autumn artists, specifically the Beau Brummels and the Tikis (later Harpers Bizarre), which put him into the Warner/Reprise orbit. After the Beau Brummels broke up, Lenny Waronker steered Scott to Warner's Artist Relations Office, which eased the way for artists to come perform or record in Los Angeles.

Scott began to notice how Warner/Reprise's younger acts were handicapped by their similarly young and offbeat managers. Many of them had no idea how to get their groups, crew, and gear from one city to the next. And even if they could do that, they had no idea how to set up the events and interviews that would maximize local interest just as the band got to town. But knowing how to do all that in multiple cities required time, experience, and a Rolodex full of contacts. So, Scott figured, now that it was growing obvious that performing was the best way to build an audience, the company needed to create an in-house artist management department: a group of staffers who could work with the groups' managers to grow their careers. Scott sold Waronker on the idea, and the A&R chief took it to Joe Smith, who agreed to let Scott set up a package tour that would pair two of the company's rootsy hippie artists, Captain Beefheart and Ry Cooder. Traveling with the show, Scott worked as a combination road manager and promotions man, filling the groups' nonperforming hours with record store signings and radio, TV, and newspaper interviews before getting them to the venue with plenty of time to do a sound check and square themselves before hitting the stage. He handled everything, from grumpy hotel managers and crooked club owners to disc jockeys and record store event planners to suspicious police officers and homesick drummers. The tour lost money on ticket sales, but both acts' record sales jumped for months afterward, and their next tours drew bigger and more enthusiastic audiences all across the nation.

The company-managed tours took full form when Scott set up a summerlong swing that paired the seasoned blues-rock band Mother Earth with the freshly signed Doobie Brothers, a boogie-rock band from San Mateo, a few dozen miles south of San Francisco. The long-haired foursome of Doobies had met while attending San Jose State College and were a bit more sophisticated than the average aspiring rock band, but they still didn't know how to navigate the currents of the pop music industry. In fact, they'd been manipulated and ripped off from the start. Their first manager made off with most of the hundred-thousand-dollar advance he got out of Warner, then sat by while the band's chief songwriters, Tom Johnston and Patrick Simmons, got hoodwinked into signing away the publishing rights for the songs they wrote. After which, he stepped back and appointed a friend's younger brother, untroubled by experience of any kind, to be their day-to-day manager. Simultaneously on the verge of an enormous breakthrough and complete disaster, the Doobie Brothers made perfect subjects for Carl Scott's grand experiment in company-produced concert tours.

"Our lives were kind of a blur then," Johnston recalls. "So, Warner Bros. became our manager."[13] And a good one, too, even if the bargain $2.50 rate for tickets guaranteed the venture would be a money loser. No matter. Scott saw to it that the entire touring party stayed in decent hotels each night and had enough cash in their pockets to eat good meals while also earning a weekly salary, so they'd have something to show for their labor when they got back home. And to make sure they all had homes to go back to, another office in Burbank made certain all the group's rent and utility bills were paid. At the same time, the more experienced members of Mother Earth taught the younger musicians how to function in the midst of such a demanding and surreal undertaking, from having extra guitar strings at every show, to giving the reporters what they needed to write good stories, to charming record store managers, to making sure the band members paced themselves for the long haul.

The Mothers/Brothers tour put a $250,000 dent into the year's profit-and-loss statement, but the investment paid enormous dividends over the years. The Doobies' self-named debut album did next to no business when it was released, and the tour that followed didn't change that. But it did turn the band into a tight, rollicking unit, and with Johnston and Simmons's songwriting improving at the same clip, their 1972 follow-up, *Toulouse Street*, launched two hit singles ("Listen to the Music" and "Jesus Is Just Alright"), which drove the album to more than a million copies sold by the end of the year. And that was just the first step in a decade-long run of hit singles and albums, some of which would sell enough copies in a single day to pay for that 1971 package tour several times over.

Scott didn't have a job when he got back from the tour, but he kept coming in to the Burbank offices every morning. He figured he stood a better chance of landing a full-time job if all the executives assumed someone else had already hired him. Still, he didn't want to tip his hand to Ostin or Smith, so when he saw either heading his way, the big man scuttled into a hiding place he'd found behind a column beneath the staircase. One day, Smith walked by and, without looking up, called out to him, "I see you, Carl!" As Smith told me, it wasn't all that difficult a discovery. "Carl's this huge guy. It was like trying to hide an elephant."[14] Rather than throw him out of the building, Smith asked Scott to drop by his office, where the executive informed him that he and Ostin had decided to make his in-house management program a permanent part of Regehr's Artist Development department. Did he want to run it? He did. "So, Carl got busted," Smith said, "then stayed for thirty years."[15]

A more surprising addition to Warner/Reprise's office staff at the start of the 1970s was Van Dyke Parks. Still riding low in the wake of the public nonresponse to his *Song Cycle*, Ostin's favorite Warner/Reprise artist opted for a lower profile, producing albums for Ry Cooder, Arlo Guthrie, and Randy Newman and mastering the new and ever-changing Moog synthesizer (a computer that made music!), which he used to write rubbery instrumental music for TV ads promoting Datsun cars and the Ice Capades. Parks also entertained his new preoccupation with calypso steel drum music, which became the core of his long-awaited follow-up to *Song Cycle*, the all-Calypso 1971 release *Discover America*.

The record was still in production when Parks visited Ostin with an idea that drew as much from his experiences as a child actor as from his career in music. The fast-developing technology of video cameras, VHS cartridges, and editing stations made shooting short-form movies and artist performances surprisingly cheap and easy to do. So, why didn't they buy some equipment and create short films, videos, and advertisements to promote the company's artists on television and in movie theaters? The pieces would range from staged performances of individual tunes to short documentaries about the artists and their music, with an emphasis on what was new and available at your nearest record store. And who knew where it would end? Maybe they'd even sell Warner/Reprise music videos directly to consumers one day.

Ostin got it on every level, approved the proposal immediately, and named Parks the director of what became Warner/Reprise's audio and visual services department. Parks got a salary, an executive office, a job for his artist wife, Durrie, and loose instructions from Ostin to go forth and do cool things. With that, they were off, shooting a ten-minute featurette about the life, music, and tastes of ace guitarist/roots musician Ry Cooder and similar docu-shorts about Joni Mitchell, the quirky blues-rock outfit Little Feat, and others. A handful of shorter, performance-based videos followed, with many others planned. Parks refused Ostin's request to get involved in Frank Zappa's scripted performance film *200 Motels*. "Frank Zappa represents all that is ugly," Parks wrote on company memo stationery. "An inarticulate nihilist . . . I'll do nothing bizarre," the final word a play on Zappa's record label.

Even so, Warner/Reprise's most memorable foray into video was just that: bizarre. Parks wasn't involved in its production, but he supported it nonetheless. The storied sixty-second television commercial for Captain Beefheart's fourth album, *Lick My Decals Off, Baby*, must really be seen in order to be believed. Shot in black-and-white, the ad begins with a hand, cigarette butt clutched between thumb and forefinger, extended into a black, empty frame. A snippet of Beefheart's "Woe-Is-Uh-Me-Bop" plays for the 1.25 seconds it takes the hand to flick the cigarette against an unseen barrier in the blackness. The butt hits with a disheartening thud. The music stops, and the shot switches to a blur of what might be the side of a basket or frozen visual distortion. An unseen narrator speaks, invoking the names (or pseudonyms, anyway) of the men who put the magic in the Magic Band: "In Tustin, it's Rockette Morton." The same hand flips the cigarette butt again, and the unidentifiable blur returns with the narrator's voice: "At Santa Anita, it's Ed Marimba." The cigarette butt sequence repeats: "In Whittier, it's Zoot Horn Rollo." The hand, the butt, the split second of "Woe-Is-Uh-Me-Bop": "In Echo Park, it's Winged Eel Fingerling." Again: "In Bel Air, it's Drumbo." Finally, a new shot appears; a straight-ahead view of a long-haired, clean-shaven man in a dark blazer with a fierce gleam in his eyes and a fez posted on his head. "And in plain sight, it's Captain Beefheart." He makes an obscure dance move, extending his right foot and gesturing toward it with a taut right hand. The next shot shows a man with a hood draped over his face working an egg beater as he stalks across the frame. When he pops up again, he's holding some other implement close to his chest, seemingly playing it with a glass guitar slide. The silence holds as the scene shifts to a tight shot of Beefheart's foot tipping a bowl of mush onto the center line of a road. When that dissolves, we see a photo of Beefheart and his band posed on an elegant stairway, dressed in tuxedos. At this, the narrator switches into his smoothest, sellingest baritone: "New, on Reprise! It's *Lick My Decals Off, Baby*."

Mystifying, jarring, and either hilarious or horrifying, depending on your worldview, the TV spot met with immediate and overwhelming disapproval from the owners and managers of the TV stations asked to air the ad. There was nothing even remotely profane in the piece, but its aggressive strangeness so infuriated Charles Young, the station manager for Los Angeles' KTTV-TV, that he refused to allow the record company to put its Beefheart business anywhere near his television station.

"I just don't like it," Young told a reporter for *Jazz & Pop* magazine. Pressed for specifics, he could only say that he found the album title obscene, as though the mere mention of lickable decals would make Potter Stewart reach for his smelling salts.

Whatever, it rattled the kinky chimes of the curators at the Museum of Modern Art in New York, who eventually added it to the institution's permanent film/video collection. And in some places, the album sold. *Lick My Decals Off, Baby*, with its atonal songs, shifting time signatures, and snarl-gnarl vocals, found its audience, particularly in England, where it spent eleven weeks on the charts, rising as high as No. 20.

The brush with the British Top 20 turned out to be a fluke. But Beefheart, who had grown up as Don Van Vliet in the sunny Los Angeles suburb of Glendale, was touched by something. When writer Langdon Winner (last seen in the midst of the Masked Marauders episode) was interviewing Beefheart in his living room for a *Rolling Stone* story in 1970, the musician jumped up at one point and walked across the room saying he had to take a call from a friend. He then stood next to the silent telephone until it rang, and the friend was on the other end.

Beefheart and his band were well beyond the fringe, but as Warner/Reprise executive Hal Halverstadt described in the memo he sent back from the Beefheart/Cooder tour, the lunar bluesman was magnetic to a certain kind of music fan. Hundreds of them would crowd the theaters and take in his surrealistic blues in an ecstatic thrall. His records didn't sell a lot of copies in America, but the ones they did sell were bought by the right people: critics, tastemakers, current musicians, and musicians of the future. Any other commercial record label would have dropped him, would have *had* to drop him once they figured out who he was, *how* he was, and how commercial his music would never, ever be. Everything that made Captain Beefheart special made him incomprehensible to the general public, and ultimately the financial story of his recording career would be written in red ink.

But was that the full story? Because what if one of those Beefheart records found its way to the bedroom turntable of a fifteen-year-old high schooler in small-town Georgia? And what if that high-schooler took special notice of the company logo stamped on the label of *Safe as Milk* and realized it was the same Warner/Reprise he'd already seen on the James Taylor, Van Dyke Parks, and Joni Mitchell albums he'd already bought and loved?

"That," Peter Buck says, "was my first realization that record labels could have a philosophy. Not that all of them did, but Warner's definitely did."[16]

Buck liked the way that philosophy sounded. And it made an impression that was still with him twenty years later when his own band, R.E.M., was both on the threshold of mammoth success and looking for a major record company they could trust to get them there with their philosophy intact.

# THE ROCK MORALITY

W hen the members of the National Association of Recording
Merchandisers gathered for their annual convention in Los
Angeles in February 1971, the group invited Stan Cornyn, the most public
face from inside the surging Warner/Reprise record company, to deliver
the keynote address. Cornyn accepted the offer happily, and not just so he
could spend an hour cracking jokes and boasting about the extraordinary
streak of hits his company had been riding for the last few years. He had
a serious message he wanted to deliver.

Part scolding and part call to arms, the speech Cornyn gave, titled
"The Rock Morality," took measure of the popular music industry and
found it stodgy, out of step, and so wedded to old-fashioned standards
and practices that it was headed for the brink of nonexistence. For all they
kept talking about Warner/Reprise's great roster and its staff's unmatched
ability to find the winners among the freakiest hippie bands, the rest of
the industry had failed to recognize the most important parts of the Burbank company's success: trusting and investing in its artists, taking the
music seriously, and honoring the intelligence and taste of its customers.
And here they all were, more than a year into the 1970s, and nothing was
changing. Most of the executives still dismissed the younger generation

as stupid longhairs with lousy taste. But wasn't it obvious by now that average rock 'n' roll fans circa 1971 were, in Cornyn's words, "affluent, well-educated young people—the true elite of our society, its taste-makers and opinion-makers"?

At the same time, old-line companies like Columbia, Decca, Capitol, and their ilk refused to treat most of their artists and the music they made as anything more than numbers on their annual profit-and-loss statements. Record sales had skyrocketed, growing by a double-digit rate year after year. Just in the last three years of the 1960s, annual sales leaped from $1.17 billion to $1.68 billion. But most record companies continued to treat their artists as widgets, interchangeable pretties whose work amounted to little more than momentary distractions for high school kids looking for something to do with their weekly allowance. It was a volume business with no budget for sentiment, let alone the pursuit of art. *Just keep the product line flowing while minimizing expenses and maximizing profits.*

But Cornyn was here to say that the world was changing, so their way of doing business had better change along with it. Simply put: invest in your artists and their music. Give them the time and tools they need to be creative. Let them follow their muses. Take for granted that the next big thing might sound nothing like what came before. Because modern music wasn't for the merchandisers; it was for customers, who were half their age. "This is *their* art," Cornyn said of their customers. "They're demanding respect for it. And we'd better start giving it."

He then introduced a series of what he called "easy reforms," all of them drawn from the Warner/Reprise playbook. Start, he proposed, by respecting the audience enough to give them more value for their money: quality albums by inspired artists, packaged in artfully designed covers, all of it constructed from quality materials to make sure the products met the highest standards. Ease up on the corporate rigidity and have a little *fun* with what you're doing. Get involved with the music. Go to shows, hang out with the folks, get a feel for who they are and what really matters to them. Keep your mind and heart open and accept that artists don't, and shouldn't, behave like executives.

The time had come, Cornyn concluded, to launch the Age of the Creative Executive. And not just because it was the right thing to do, but because the new generation, the current and future generation, would accept no less. "Our business is their lifestyle," he said. "And they're not about to let us screw it up."

"The shit is about to hit our fan."

As a representative of Warner/Reprise, he didn't really mean the *our* part. His company, as Cornyn obviously saw it, was the paragon of this new morality. And the merchandisers clearly agreed: they had summoned Cornyn as the most visible face in the one corporate record company that had not only anticipated the cultural shift, but moved into it so quickly and confidently that the other record companies could only blink and wonder how they could possibly catch up.

○

As envisioned by Ostin, the company worked more like a for-profit arts collective than a traditional commercial enterprise. Selling vast quantities of vinyl and reaping the windfall they created might have been its prime directive, but it wasn't the only thing it felt obligated to do. Sometimes the bottom line for signing an act came down to how unique the artists were—or, as Waronker would say when he wanted to sign a profoundly uncommercial artist whose work was too good to pass by: *They deserve to have a record contract.* And it really did work like that. When new A&R man Russ Titelman brought Little Feat's Lowell George and Bill Payne in to play two or three of their eccentric blues-art-rock songs for Lenny Waronker, the A&R chief was so impressed by what he heard that he signed them on the spot. "That's great! Go upstairs [to Ostin's office] and make a deal." No audition necessary.

During the first years of the 1970s, the crew revolving around Lenny Waronker was at the height of its collective powers. Working separately or in two-man teams, they built a roster studded with artists whose work was as popular with critics as it was with everyday record buyers. Andy Wickham, who had been bringing in great artists since he walked into his office in the fall of 1967, was as productive as ever, wrangling Gram Parsons, Emmylou Harris, and the veteran country singer-songwriter Buck Owens. And when he wasn't collecting top-drawer talent for the company, Wickham produced albums for artists ranging from Nancy Sinatra to Van

Dyke Parks to the Everly Brothers. Former Harpers Bizarre singer Ted Templeman turned his pop-savvy ear to the work of the Doobie Brothers, Van Morrison, Captain Beefheart, and many more, while Van Dyke Parks enhanced the work of Arlo Guthrie, Ry Cooder, and Phil Ochs (though the latter recorded for A&M). Richard Perry, a twenty-five-year-old producer from New York when he came west to produce Tiny Tim's first album in 1967, proved himself a virtuoso of many styles, producing records for Captain Beefheart, Ella Fitzgerald, and Carly Simon. Waronker also hired the guitarist, songwriter, and Phil Spector apprentice Russ Titelman, and in time the Waronker-Titelman production partnership would produce dozens of successful albums, some of them among the most artistically and commercially significant releases in the company's history.

One of the most powerful tools in the Warner/Reprise strategy was simple patience. Liberated from the hamster wheel of living from one hit single to the next, it could give its artists time to hone their craft while also building their audience. The perpetually troubled British blues out-fit Fleetwood Mac made for a particularly challenging case. The group's second album sold fewer copies than their American debut, and though their third album did a bit better, the group's lead guitarist, singer and songwriter Peter Green, quit the band mid-tour, and his successor, Jeremy Spencer, did the same not long after, leaving drummer Mick Fleetwood, bassist John McVie, and their remaining bandmates to scramble for yet another lead singer/songwriter/guitarist. At that point, any other label worth its profit-and-loss statement would have sent the luckless band packing. But no matter who was fronting them, Fleetwood Mac's records always came out sounding cool. They also didn't lose *too* much of the company's money, and as long as there were enough other acts raking in the dough, that was enough to guarantee Fleetwood Mac a home on the label.

It wasn't always easy, especially with the likes of the Grateful Dead, whose members seemed to revel in making their music as strange and inaccessible as possible. But Smith held on to that feeling he'd had about them the night he first saw them play at the Avalon Ballroom in 1966, and when he dropped the needle on a near-final mix of *Workingman's Dead* in early 1970 and was greeted by the gentle strums and sweet harmonies of "Uncle John's Band," he realized his faith in the band was about to pay off.

*Well, the first days are the hardest days, don't you worry anymore*
*'Cause when life looks like easy street there is danger at your door . . .*

The music was tuneful, the lyrics plainspoken and direct, thoughtful and witty. For a moment, Smith, listening in a conference room packed with the Dead and their managers, wondered if he was getting pranked. The Dead were like that, you know, always with the practical jokes and surprise doses of LSD and whatever they could pull out of *A Boy's First Book of Dirty Tricks*. But this time they were serious; the music was real, and really accessible, even to listeners who never wanted to take a journey behind anyone's looking glass.

How could he have guessed? Through the first three years of the Grateful Dead's career at Warner, they had made records that limned the farthest reaches of sonic psychedelia, from the shape-shifting blues of their self-titled debut to the surreal weave of live and studio tracks in the careening *Anthem of the Sun*, from the only slightly more grounded *Aoxomoxoa* to the deep-space improvs on the double LP *Live/Dead*. Only the live record had sold well enough to gain a foothold on the sales charts,* granting a twinkle of hope to Smith's quest to propel the group to a mainstream audience.

And while the Dead certainly enjoyed twitting Smith for being the voice of corporate concern, making fun of his execu-casual clothes and his demands for some semblance of professional behavior, they weren't necessarily opposed to his efforts to build them a bigger audience. The band had produced *Live/Dead* with the specific goal of selling enough copies to pay down their hundred-grand-plus debt to the company. And like all artists, Jerry Garcia, Phil Lesh, Bob Weir, and everyone else in the Grateful Dead *wanted* people to hear their music. So, when they tired of outer space and came back down to earth, it was an easy move for the former jug band to head for the country. And when Smith got to the final notes of the wry, rat-a-tat-catchy "Casey Jones," the last song on the second side, he was so excited he went prancing down the halls, crying out in exultation, "We got a single! We got a Grateful Dead single!"

---

* It peaked at No. 64 in *Billboard*, spending a total of eight weeks on the magazine's album chart.

"Uncle John's Band" peaked at No. 69 on *Billboard*'s Hot 100 in September 1970, but *Workingman's Dead* had climbed to No. 27 on the album list by July, and remained among the best sellers for more than six months. Released just a few months later, the even more polished *American Beauty* launched "Truckin'" and "Sugar Magnolia" into the Hot 100, then hit No. 30 on the album chart in January 1971 and stayed on the list for nearly five months.

Warner/Reprise got an even bigger boost when James Taylor's next album, *Mud Slide Slim and the Blue Horizon*, came out in February, just weeks after *American Beauty* hit its peak. More than a follow-up to the surprise hit that *Sweet Baby James* had been a year earlier, the new collection was celebrated on the cover of *Time* magazine as the herald of the new decade. The nation's most prominent newsweekly rarely featured musicians, let alone rock stars, so the portrait on the cover, a lightly psychedelic portrayal of Taylor, his brown eyes shimmering and long, dark hair tumbling over his shoulders, symbolized an extraordinary amount of cultural impact. The cover line above his head hailed the moody songwriter as the leading edge of a fresh sensibility in popular music. THE NEW ROCK: BITTERSWEET AND LOW, it proclaimed, setting up a feature article that spoke frankly about Taylor's psychologically fraught past, including his two stays at psychiatric hospitals, and his stubborn appetite for heroin. Combined with his pretty, if emotionally desolate, songs, his undeniably smoldering sex appeal, the article declared, made him all but irresistible. "Taylor physically projects a blend of Heathcliffian inner fire with a melancholy look that can strike to the female heart—at any age."[1] It was a portrait of the moment's definitive pop star, and an enormous breakthrough for both Taylor and Warner/Reprise.

Landing an artist on the cover of *Time* was a major event, the stuff of record company ad/publicity executives' dreams. But Stan Cornyn's delight was shot through with dread. For all the years he'd worked there, he'd only ever known Warner/Reprise as an underdog company, the scrappy small-timers who had to hustle extra hard just to be noticed. But you can't say that about a company whose artists can command the cover of *Time*. "I said, 'Oh, I guess it's over now,'" Cornyn told company biographer Warren Zanes in 2008. "I said, 'That's not the *L.A. Free Press* anymore, is it?'"

Not that Cornyn, or anyone, was complaining. Once the Grateful

Dead got their first taste of mainstream acceptance, they grew to appreci-
ate the benefits of selling records in quantity. After first insisting that their
follow-up to *American Beauty*, a double live album of songs drawn almost
entirely from their country-rock repertoire, be titled *Skull Fuck*, the group
listened to Smith explain that so many chains of stores would refuse to
stock an album of that name that its sales would be reduced by at least 50
percent, and promptly reversed themselves. Suddenly, titling the package
*Grateful Dead* turned out to be a perfectly acceptable alternative. And they
were glad they did it, too. The live album rose to No. 25 and sold quickly
enough to hit gold status three weeks after its release later that fall. Soon,
*Circular* ran a photo of Garcia posing next to his newly purchased Bentley.

Times changed and people did, too, especially when they found themselves earning more money than they'd ever imagined possible. No surprise, then, that Cornyn was a whole new Cornyn by 1971. Four years
into Warner/Reprise's climb to major labelhood, during which his own
work had been singled out as the best of its kind in that, or any, era, he
had acquired a new wardrobe of mod clothes, a shoulder-brushing mane
with a just-bushy-enough beard, and a big, open-mouthed laugh. He was
a guy with a top-end Cadillac, a sprawling hillside house, and a pretty
blond wife to accompany him to the banquets and parties and weeklong
European junkets befitting a music executive of his time, place, and ver-
tiginous tax bracket.

All the leading executives got raises, bonuses, and stock options, along
with new perceptions of who they were and what their just deserts ought
to be. Ostin wasn't all that ostentatious, but he did like fancy cars, especially convertibles, and traded them out as often as he liked. The Ostin
home in Encino, while definitely in the style of the successful corporate
executive, revealed little of its owners' expanding fortune. But company-
booked travel accommodation was another matter, and when Mo took his
father on a business trip to New York, the older man was so taken aback by
the opulence of the hotel that he took his son aside and, in a tense whisper,
asked him what he *really* did for a living—as if his boy had become a capo
in Bugsy Siegel's mob.

Mr. Ostrofsky might not have believed that the pop music industry
could provide a living quite that extravagant, but Warner's breakthrough

came just as the entire music business began its ascent from the $600 million industry it had been in 1965 to the $2.4 billion one it would be ten years later. In Burbank, the endlessly inflating sales, revenue, and profit numbers seemed surreal, a stoned reverie that had somehow come to life. After all, Warner Bros. Records and its pair of constituent labels had been also-rans since their earliest days in the late 1950s. And the company's new persona, as conceived by Cornyn, felt like a grown-up, tuned-in hippie era iteration of Warner's beloved Bugs Bunny: the smart-ass street kid yanking on capes and inserting exploding cigars beneath every stuck-up nose it could find. Puff, puff . . . *kablammo*! And it wasn't even that they had beaten the others at their own game. The Burbank gang just invented their own game, reducing their rivals to hapless Elmer Fudds, sputtering and stumbling and shooting themselves in the feet with both barrels.

○

The cover of *Circular*'s September 13, 1971, issue put it about three different ways. Printed on currency-green paper, Warner Bros. Records' in-house journal presented a pastiche of play money—singles, fives, a few thousands, and a couple of hundred thousands—all surrounding the real American dollar bill at its center, an exact replica, except that George Washington's queasy alabaster mug has been replaced by a hale and happy Mo Ostin, his bushy face split wide by a high-beam smile. The undersize headline revealed what had put the grin on his face: PEAK WEEK FOR WARNERS. Inside, more detail: "Warner/Reprise last week enjoyed the Biggest Week in the Biggest Month of the Biggest Year in its history."

Most often in the record biz, abrupt increases in sales are spurred by a highly touted release by one superstar act. But this tsunami consisted entirely of reorders for records that had been building for months. The top five sellers, Black Sabbath's *Master of Reality*, James Taylor's *Mud Slide Slim*, Jethro Tull's *Aqualung*, Deep Purple's *Fireball*, and the Beach Boys' *Surf's Up*, moved 650,000 copies in five days, including 100,000 apiece for Black Sabbath and Deep Purple. Frank Zappa and the Mothers' *Live at Fillmore East* had also sold more copies than any previous Zappa work, and Randy Newman's *Randy Newman—Live*, originally produced as a radio-only promo release, got such a big reorder from the New York office, 5,000 copies, that sales director Eddie Rosenblatt made a long-distance call to figure out why they would have done such a crazy thing. "Because it's selling," he was told. *Randy Newman selling?* What else could go right? The Beach Boys' record, printed cautiously due to the dismal sales of the group's 1970 Warner/Reprise debut *Sunflower*, required the production department to rush-print nearly 60,000 jackets to cover the stacks of vinyl waiting to be shipped across the country. And remember Peter, Paul and Mary from the early sixties? Now they had broken up, but the solo records released by the latter *P* and *M* in early 1971 sold half a million copies between them, with both still going strong in the fall. It was that kind of week, month, and year. And it wasn't by chance. Of all the releases coming from the unified Warner/Reprise, Atlantic, and Elektra labels in 1971, the most successful by far was the global distribution network that in one stroke eliminated every barrier that had ever held them back.

The roots of Warner Bros.' distribution network go back to 1967, when Eliot Hyman and the rest of the Seven Arts gang not only took over Warner/Reprise from Jack Warner, but also bought up Ahmet and Nesuhi Ertegun and Jerry Wexler's Atlantic Records. It proved a brilliant investment for Warner and a regrettable deal for Atlantic's owners, who sold their hallowed R&B-based label just as their collective genius for finding the right artist at the right time was about to launch the label into the top tier of the nation's record companies. And when Eliot Hyman flipped the Warner companies to Steve Ross's Kinney National Services less than three years later, it was only a matter of time before the ambitious mogul started annexing other music industry companies into his thriving corporation.

It took only a few months for Ross to work a deal with Jac Holzman to buy Elektra Records, the company he and a friend started out of Holzman's dormitory room at St. John's College in 1950. Launched as a folk label, Elektra grew more diverse in the 1960s as Holzman added a budget classical music imprint he named Nonesuch Records and then began adding pop artists to its roster. Holzman's ear for psychedelic music was just as sharp as it was for folk and classical, and within a year or two he'd signed hit acts that included the Doors, soft rock hitmakers Bread, the proto-punk Iggy and the Stooges, Detroit's radical rockers MC5, folk-pop singer Judy Collins, and the beautiful, doomed singer-songwriter Tim Buckley.

Still, Holzman grew bored with running an independent record company, and by 1970 he was ready to sell. Steve Ross was happy to open his wallet, and the deal was finished within a few weeks.

Now, with a third record label joining the company—or a fourth, if you counted Warner and Reprise as separate labels, which they only sort of were—the Warner Bros. music operation hit a new threshold. Like all but the largest record companies, the Warner labels had to depend on a network of other companies to press, package, promote, and ship their products to the record shops, department stores, and anywhere else music products could be sold. The region-by-region system, pioneered in the days when local radio stations and record stores had an outsize role in determining which records would be heard and sold in their regions, was also the only affordable way for a smaller record company like the Warner/Reprise of the 1960s to do business. But it also left your company vulnerable, since the distributors had dozens of accounts with other companies, which could make you a second or third priority when you were back-ordered and needed ten thousand units shipped as quickly as possible. Joe Smith had been reminded of this all too pointedly during the surge that elevated the Grateful Dead's 1970 albums into the midtwenties on the album charts. That push could have been a lot more powerful if the distributors had stocked enough copies of *Workingman's Dead* and *American Beauty* to satisfy the demand coming out of the record stores. But the distributors were old-school guys, connoisseurs of the tried-and-true. Just because Warner Bros. Records believed in this group of scroungy San Francisco hippies it didn't mean their records would sell any copies in their region. And so it went. You could do okay with independent distributors, but you were never going to control your fate when you had to depend on outsiders to get your wares into the marketplace.

So, Ostin decided it was time for a Warner-controlled distribution network. He had been sketching out possibilities since the company's sales took their first major leap in the late 1960s. Holzman came into the company wielding the same vision in 1970, and as the aggregate sales of Warner/Reprise and Atlantic records started rivaling Columbia's it became obvious. As Ostin told Ross, it wouldn't be cheap to create and staff dozens of offices around the country while also setting up distribution warehouses and hiring all their managers and crew members. It would also take time to figure out how to work smoothly with one another while implementing the strategies coming down from the headquarters in Burbank and New York. No matter, Ross loved the idea. Anything they could do to enhance his corporation's piece of the marketplace was exactly what he wanted to do, start-up costs be damned.

And as Ross reassured all his record company presidents, having a common distribution network in no way meant that the separate companies had to sacrifice any of the independence he'd always granted them. No matter how large and powerful the distribution organization became, it would never overwhelm the leadership of the individual labels. Instead, they would all have the best of both worlds: the creative freedom of independent labels backed by the money and power of a large corporation. All the Warner label presidents signed on, and in 1971, Kinney Distribution (soon to be redubbed the Warner/Elektra/Atlantic distribution group) opened for business.

Now they could take a record into the marketplace with the force of a bulldozer, every move coordinated to come off at precisely the right moment. The recording, mixing, and mastering sessions could wrap up in time for the pressing plants to punch out the discs, place them into freshly printed covers, and truck them off to distribution houses. There, teams of salesmen, regional promotions staffers, drivers, and delivery folks could jump into action, and on the same day the promo copies landed at radio stations and the full-page NOW AVAILABLE ads hit across the country. If the Beach Boys' *Surf's Up*, or any other album, took off unexpectedly, the whole organization could pivot instantly, filling orders within a matter of days.

The Kinney-owned labels' combined share of the record-buying market, once an asterisk-size dot next to Columbia's towering sales, edged out the larger company by 18.4 to 15.3 percent in 1970, then dwarfed them in 1971, taking 22.6 percent of the industry's total sales compared to Columbia's 15.0. The company's rivers of cash all but jumped their banks, too. Kinney-wide sales added up to $144 million in 1971, then leaped to $170 million in 1972, with no sign of letting up. With the entire music industry erupting, it was almost impossible to lose money in that kind of market. But the record companies owned by what Ross in 1972 redubbed Warner Communications Inc. eclipsed all the others. And even if they were all on the same team, Atlantic's Ahmet Ertegun and Elektra's Jac Holzman knew which company set the standard for the group.

Still, for all the joy Ostin felt when San Cornyn showed him the *Billboard* annual market share study revealing the Kinney corporation's 7.6 percent lead over Columbia's parent corporation, CBS, in 1971, he was less delighted to see that the trade publication broke the Warner and Reprise numbers into separate entries. If Warner Bros.' 5.50 percent of the market and Reprise's 4.75 percent were added together into 10.25 percent, Warner/ Reprise would have been a close second to Columbia's industry-leading 11.92 percent. And given that they really were the same company now, with everything but the label designs in common, Ostin figured the time had come to unite Warner and Reprise in name, too. Most of the artists already issued their records on the Warner label, so it wouldn't be that difficult to migrate the Reprise artists over, too. He started to make the push in the coming years. Neither Reprise founder Sinatra nor Neil Young would agree to switch, but by 1977, the Reprise imprint would all but cease to exist—for a while, at least.

Some Reprise artists might have felt a twinge as their label started to vanish, but as the March 18, 1972, issue of *Billboard* made clear, it was difficult for anyone in Burbank to hold on to a sense of loss for very long. That was the week the top two slots of both the singles and album charts were occupied by Warner acts. And such was the equanimity of the moment that the No. 1 artist on both charts was Neil Young, with his *Harvest* album and "Heart of Gold" single; while the dual No. 2 holders turned out to be America, with their self-titled debut album and first single, "Horse with No Name."* Young's single spent only a week at the top, with "Horse" replacing it and staying there for five weeks, while *Harvest* held the top album spot for two weeks and *America* crowned the list for five. Young's quadruple-platinum *Harvest* would become the top-selling album of the year, with *America* just seven slots behind.

It was a hell of a thing, a quadruple-gold-starred triumph without precedent. But when *Circular* devoted two pages to covering the event,

---

* Which sounded so much like a Neil Young song, from its spare backing to the expressively quavering vocal, that when Young first heard it, he spent a few minutes trying to remember when he'd recorded it.

the story came with the title THE MISERIES OF RANKING #1 AND #2 IN LPS AND SINGLES IN THE SAME WEEK, WHICH WARNERS JUST DID. After first comparing the company's top executives to Gen. Sherman's bloody Civil War march from Atlanta to the ocean ("razing farms and raping widows . . . [but] getting to the top of the charts has, for WB execs, turned out to be nowhere near as much fun as burning Georgia"), the piece went on to include a list of every bad outcome that such overwhelming success can cause, and it was a long one—from renegotiating the hit artists' contracts, to dealing with envious label mates suddenly needing to know why *their* records weren't selling like that, to creating a false sense of instant wealth ("profitless prosperity," according to the accounting department) that inspires executives to toss their WBR credit cards farther and higher than ever before. And it didn't even mention the pressure not just to repeat the stunt, but to succeed bigger and better than before. Thus, the story concluded, the Warner execs had resolved never, ever to occupy the top two slots on *Billboard*'s charts again. So, if next week's charts showed another company's artists leading the pack, "count that slip as one more triumph for those heady execs repping the Big Bunny."

"'Mo' spelled backward is 'Om.'"

They'd say that around the Warner/Reprise HQ and giggle, like it was a joke about Ostin's untrimmed hair, flowery beard, and the way he could do all his big-dollar chief executry without ever resorting to the screaming and chest thumping that other power wielders considered a privilege of the executive suite. Such displays of dominance weren't necessary for Ostin, given the success he'd already racked up and the strength of his relationship with corporate chief Steve Ross. They also weren't his style; he wanted to build up his people to do their best, not shred their egos until they doubted themselves too much to tie their own shoes. Even if someone or something had gone wrong enough to warrant a closed-door session in his office, Ostin kept his voice down and his tone conversational. *How did this happen? How can we fix it? What should we do to keep this from happening again?*

Not that Ostin went around hugging folks and telling them how special they were. He was too reserved for such displays, which made his wife, Evelyn, all the more important to the company. She was the Ostin who knew the names of all the company's staffers and, most often, the names of their spouses and children, too. No birth, death, or family calamity escaped Evelyn's attention. When Carl Scott's mother died, Evelyn came over immediately to comfort and help him and his grandmother grieve. She befriended employees' spouses, particularly if they were new to Los Angeles, drawing them into her social circle to help them adjust to the city. When Evelyn suffered a bout of breast cancer in the early seventies, she called all the company's female employees to a meeting in the conference room and arranged for them to have regular mammograms and learn how to monitor their bodies for suspicious lumps or growths. Sometimes she'd spend an afternoon in the building making the rounds to check on folks, asking after their families and making sure her husband wasn't overwhelming them. *How's Little Mosie treating you?* she'd ask. *Are you getting what you need?* A seeker with an abiding fascination for spirituality, Evelyn saw to it that the company had an appropriately furnished and lit room set aside for employee meditation. She encouraged, and had the company pay for, employees to get acupuncture treatments, and brought in gurus and alternative healers to share their theories on physical and spiritual health. And she worried about Little Mosie's spiritual health, too. When Carl Scott snuck up behind his boss at a party and wrapped him in one of his larger-than-a-bear hugs, Evelyn nodded happily while her husband squirmed. "Don't ever stop, Carl," she said. "He really needs it."[2]

Many Warner/Reprise veterans describe the company's Ostin years, without irony, as utopian. "People cared about each other, for the most part," says Carl Scott. "The people in my division were really, really family-like. Everybody got together." After six decades of working in the entertainment industry, he sees no reason to rein in his description. "I make it sound like paradise, and it wasn't far from that, because it was the closest to being the greatest experience I ever had. I can't tell you what a pleasure it was to sit down with an artist and say, 'Okay, what do you want to do?' and then help them do it."

Others have more nuanced memories. "Don't let anyone tell you that it was all 'Kumbaya,'" one longtime executive cautioned me. People speak of fiefdoms, of maneuverings and manipulations. The weekly gathering of the company's vice presidents and other top executives was so long and ornery, so customary in the shouting and finger waving, that promotions executive Russ Thyret took to calling it "Korea," referring to the bitter, bloody, and never-resolved Korean War, and it became the gathering's generally accepted name.

○

For all his calm and understanding, the way he moved without troubling the water, Ostin was also a notoriously dogged negotiator. When it came to contracts—with artists, with vendors, with Ross and his team of seconds, with anyone trying to extract money from his company—he would take a position and stick to it. If you squeezed a little more out of him, it was probably because he had already decided to give it to you but wanted you to have to earn it, then go away feeling like you'd beaten him. David Geffen, renowned for his own killer instinct at the bargaining table, did everything he could to avoid sitting across from Ostin. Randy Newman still shudders when he recalls his attempts to get a better deal out of him. "It was like dealing with mortgage bankers," he told Warren Zanes. Ted Templeman, the successful producer and A&R man, had his own contracts with Ostin, and he saw artists he wanted to bring into the company take their beatings, too. "I think he'd make his mind up on a certain number and wouldn't budge." What made it so impossible to move him? "I don't think I understand it myself, but Mo was so articulate, he can remember everything, and he's such a fuckin' monster brain it's intimidating." Still, as tough as he could be, Ostin always told the truth. He didn't come up with elaborate stories to justify his position; he didn't pull bait and switches. But as Templeman told me, "When he dug in, that was it, the bottom line. No bullshitting."

It was the part of him that reminded people of how much he'd learned from Frank Sinatra and Mickey Rudin back in the early Reprise days, when the singer was, in Gay Talese's words, the only truly emancipated man in America. *This is how it's gonna be, fellas. Take it or leave it.* And if someone tried to cut a corner and stomp on your toes, well, you dealt with that, too. Maybe not immediately or obviously, but soon enough, and distinctly. When one of the independent distributors they dealt with in the pre-Warner/Elektra/Atlantic days short-circuited a telephone negotiation by threatening to back his position with some form of street vengeance, Ostin rang up Sinatra at home. "What do I *do* about this?" he asked. You don't worry about it, Sinatra replied. At which point he hung up, presumably made another telephone call, and, indeed, that was the last Ostin heard of the matter.[3]

Once the contracts were signed, Ostin reverted to Medici mode, and the artists ascended to their customary place in the Warner firmament. When Randy Newman wanted a full forty-piece orchestra for a recording session, he would get it, no questions asked, and with no muttering about how much his last record did or didn't sell. When Van Dyke Parks fell hard for steel drum music in 1970, he summoned the entire Esso Trinidad Steel Band, nearly thirty members, from their Caribbean home to record with him in Los Angeles, then convinced Ostin to sign them as artists in their own right. The prospects of steel band music breaking through to the mainstream were slim at best, but Ostin liked the music and believed in Parks too much to doubt his taste.

Parks, however, was one of the few artists who, in time, soured on the chief executive. His disillusionment with Ostin began when the artist turned executive launched the company's audiovisual services department in late 1970. A constitutionally offbeat fellow whose beliefs on art and commerce were as fiercely held as they were mercurial, Parks was equal parts brilliant, demanding, gentle-natured, and easy to offend. When he got angry, he lashed out, and Ostin's files include more than one memo from Parks, apologizing for what he'd done during his most recent blowup. In particular, Parks's work with Esso Trinidad bristled with misunderstandings, bureaucratic mix-ups, and Parksian indignation. When the twenty-eight-man band flew to Los Angeles for recording sessions, the company neglected to hand over a promised check for living expenses, leaving the group for more than a day without anything to eat. When news of the musicians' plight reached Parks, he stalked into the office of staff accountant Joan Taylor to unleash a torrent of rage, then dashed off to Ostin's office, where he erupted into angry tears. Resolutely calm behind his desk, Ostin told Parks to get himself together. "I have since been amused that I had to cry about the group's destitute condition and you had to say 'brace yourself,'" Parks wrote him the next day.[4] He wrote a similar letter to Taylor ("my direct apologies for the eccentricities I presented during your busy accounting procedures"[5]), and all was forgiven—by them, at least.

But Parks had other beefs, too. He reported directly to Ostin, a level of authority he shared with the company's vice presidents. Still, Parks says, he was paid a secretary's salary that was quite a ways short of high coin. This only increased his aggravation at how the terms of recording contracts always favored the corporation, often to the point of absurdity. Consider the breakage clause. When records were made from wax, back in the early days of recorded sound, a significant percentage of the discs would break on their way from the pressing plant to the shops. To make up for the loss, the companies inserted a clause into artist contracts that called for royalties to be figured on only 90 percent of sales, thus making up for the lost 10 percent. Fair enough, but then decades passed. The hardier vinyl replaced wax and reduced the number of broken discs to a small fraction of what it had once been. And yet the breakage clause remained, simply because the record companies, including Warner, had grown used to keeping the extra 10 percent and had no interest in giving it back.

Looking around the building in the fall of 1971 and seeing the same corporate screw at work, Parks pounded out a resignation memo that included digs at Cornyn and a conclusion borrowed from the Founding Fathers: "Hang together, then, or hang separately." When news of his leaving hit the pages of *Rolling Stone* a couple of weeks later, Cornyn and Ostin replied in their typical fashion: "It's the policy of Creative Services to get everyone mad at us at one time or another," Cornyn said. For his part, Ostin located the silver lining and buffed it to a high sheen. "An office is too limiting and confining for an artist of Van Dyke's talents," he said, adding that they were still very proud to have Parks as an artist, and that he looked forward to releasing his long-awaited second album in January. "I think Van Dyke has taken a positive step." Parks was out of his office well before the end of the year.

*Discover America*, his Calypso-accented portrait of American pop culture, was released on March 1, 1972. As with *Song Cycle*, it was rapturously received by critics and all but ignored by record buyers. In fact, the Esso Trinidad Steel Band's self-titled Warner/Reprise debut, a Parks production released in the fall of 1971, was more successful. It earned a Grammy nomination in the Best Ethnic or Traditional Recording category. The drummers eventually lost out to Muddy Waters, but the nomination once again affirmed Parks's ear for the transcendent. And when *Los Angeles Times* music critic John Rockwell wrote a profile of the band

and somehow neglected to mention Parks's role in their career, the writer received a stern upbraiding from Ostin, who knew a thing or two about the man's fierce support of the group. "Not only is Van Dyke responsible for bringing the Steel Band to Warner/Reprise Records, but he is also the Band's producer and constant advocate," he wrote. "In fact, the intensity of Van Dyke's commitment and dedication to his work in connection with the Band never ceases to amaze all of us at Warner Bros."

And Parks's run at Warner Bros. Records wasn't finished, not by a long shot.

●

When Parks left the team for Warner's audiovisual services department in 1970, Ostin rang up the American-born, London-based producer, promoter, and ex–Pink Floyd manager Joe Boyd, then working as a music coordinator for Warner Bros. Pictures, to see if he had any recommendations for a replacement. Boyd sent him to the ex–Velvet Underground songwriter, bassist/violist, and occasional singer John Cale. Tall, moon-faced, and stoic, Cale started out in Wales as a classical musician whose interest in composition theory led him to avant-garde projects and then to the artier fringe of rock 'n' roll. Relocated to New York City in 1963, he formed the Velvet Underground in 1965 with songwriter/guitarist Lou Reed, guitarist Sterling Morrison, and the mallet-wielding drummer Moe Tucker. Cale's aesthetic sophistication was a key part of the outfit's dark minimalism, but when his differences with the caustic Reed became intolerable, he split the band after its *White Light/White Heat* album in 1968. The musician took a job making quadrophonic mixes for Columbia Records, but he was exhausted by the New York scene and the louche habits that defined his life there. So, when Ostin offered to sign him up as both an artist and a staff producer, he jumped a westbound jet and soared into the cheerfully bourgeois life of the entertainment industry salaryman.

As he wrote in his memoir, *What's Welsh for Zen*, Cale's attempt to live the straight life was doomed from the start. He did his best, renting an apartment overlooking the San Fernando Valley and getting a dog he named Iolo Morganwg, after the eighteenth- and nineteenth-century Welsh antiquarian. He bought (and learned how to drive) a new Mustang Cobra and then settled into the daily grind at Warner's offices. In the morning, he'd spend a few hours listening to demos and writing up what he heard on the company's A&R forms, which graded aspiring acts on their material and performance abilities. The office setup reminded Cale of spaces for prep school teachers, with Waronker's larger executive warren serving as the faculty lounge. Some days most of them would be working in the recording studio, but anyone who was around would usually end their workday perched in one of Waronker's chairs trading gossip, shop talk, studio techniques, and more. Parks's new offices were close by, and he was likely to pop in and tell more of his stories about Brian Wilson and *Smile*, the lost psychedelic Beach Boys album they had worked on together for much of 1966.

Artists and managers walked through most days for meetings or just to say hi, and once a week or so, they'd have A&R meetings with the top executives, to talk about artists they wanted to sign, the state of ongoing recording sessions, release schedules, and the like. They were a convivial bunch, and Cale might have settled into the rhythm of it—if the rest of his life hadn't fallen so quickly into chaos. Women and surprise visits from former Velvet Underground singer Nico kept him distracted. Then there was the cocaine and even more cocaine, which he discovered he could pay for with his apparently bottomless expense account. When the tumult kept him away from the office for weeks at a time, Waronker either didn't notice or was too shy to complain about it. In fact, the only time Cale recalled Waronker saying anything remotely negative to him was at a company dinner, when he announced that he had just become engaged to marry his current girlfriend, former-GTOs member Miss Cindy, aka Cynthia Sue Wells. While everyone else shook Cale's hand, slapped his back, and called for champagne toasts, Waronker shook his head. "You're gonna be sorry," he told Cale. He wasn't wrong.

Near the end of 1972, Cornyn wrote a full-page ad to promote the company's A&R/record production crew at the expense of every hand-wringing button counter in the record company. To capture the spirit of the Crosby, Stills, Nash and Young–style all-star groups, Cornyn led the piece with a typically brash headline: WARNERS' NEWEST SUPERGROUP, it read, just above a deck explaining that the company's latest lineup of producers, known for these purposes as "Waronker, Wickham, Templeman, Titelman, and Cale," answered to no one beyond the company's artists and their own sense of what sounded good. After a brief recap of the hit albums the team had produced in the last few months, Cornyn focused on Waronker's recent work with Arlo Guthrie, which dragged on for so long that the lead A&R man had been made to fend off merchandising execs who, in Cornyn's words, "bitched about 'losing momentum' (as they put it) because 'Arlo's been off the market for so long.' And Lenny would listen and nod gravely and say yes, that certainly is so and what a shame, but Arlo just hasn't felt like it til recently, fellas." Then what happened? "Out of that album smashed Arlo's *City of New Orleans*," a hit single. And all thanks to Arlo, of course, but also to the supergroup, who keeps making Burbank sound better and better. "Even if it takes longer. Even if it costs more."

**11**

# IT AIN'T NOTHIN'
# BUT A WARNER BROS. PARTY

The first chimp came tearing down the hallway on a red tricycle. It was a few ticks before 4 p.m. and if you happened to look up from your desk when he came by your office door, you probably rubbed your eyes, assuming your rods and cones had misfired in some strange new way. But then came another chimp. And another, and then another after that. More than a dozen of them, and all on their own tricycles, going full tilt through offices, into conference rooms, bathrooms, any open door.

It had been a dark and chilly morning, another in a chain of unseasonably cold days that struck the Southland in the winter of 1972. To Artist Development staffer Shelley Cooper, it began to feel like the gloom had leached into her soul, dimming her eyes and stealing her hope for warmer days ahead. Surely, she couldn't be the only one who felt that way, and determined to fight back against the chill, Cooper pushed through the glass doors and marched straight to her boss's office. "I feel like dancing dogs," she announced. Given that her boss was Bob Regehr, no other explanation was needed. *Do whatever you've got to do*, he replied. A few telephone calls and one quick redirection later—no dancing dog acts were available—Cooper told Regehr that everything was set for 4 p.m. To make sure they got maximum bang for their circus act buck, he sent out a company-wide memo announcing a party to celebrate office accountant Joan Taylor for her many years of excellent service to the company. And indeed, Joan was a fantastic person and definitely worth celebrating, so calls were rescheduled, meetings shifted around, no big deal. Good old Joan!

When directed by their handler, the chimps abandoned their tricycles and galloped down the stairs and out to the parking lot, where two portable jungle gyms awaited. The Warner/Reprise gang gave chase and, quick as a flash, the all-simian troupe set to an astonishing display of gymnastic virtuosity, leaping, jumping, and spinning—midair somersaults, trapezerie, and more. The chimps all wore T-shirts, plain-fronted with their names stenciled on the back, and when someone noticed that among the Bills and Bobs and Suzies cavorted both a Mo and a Joe, the joy amped to an even higher level. Ostin and Smith weren't nearly as amused as their employees, but they didn't mind too much. And when it was over and everyone had munched the cookies and washed them down with the apple cider and headed back to their offices, the light in the building *did* seem sunnier than it had for the last week or two. The bill for the chimps came to three hundred dollars, which Regehr shifted to Neil Young's production account, noting it as a piano rental.

Sometimes Adam Somers's telephone would ring and he'd pick up and hear an officious voice bleating out of his earpiece. His beard would bristle, his sunny eyes would steel over, and the blood would sluice into the corpuscles around his cheeks. Ordinarily, Somers was a cool character. As director of Warner Bros. Records' merchandising department, he ran the company's toy department, coming up with fun ways to get people excited about the artists and music everyone was working so hard to bring into the world. You want a free Grateful Dead T-shirt or some Neil Young bumper stickers? If you were extra nice, he might even toss one of those official OL' BLUE EYES IS BACK shirts they made for Frank Sinatra's comeback album. Somers got a lot of calls for that one, and sometimes they came from men who weren't in the industry, exactly, but who still needed *one uh dose Sinatra shoits* to such a degree that anything less than a "Yes, of course, where should I send it?" might create some unpleasant consequences.

But even the mobsters weren't as bad as the accounting executives calling from the Warner Bros. corporate HQ in New York: *Hey, Adam, do ya have a minute? I was just looking at some numbers from last year's budget, and I've got some ideas for how you can cut expenditures for the current—*

Often that would be as far as the guy would get before Somers slammed his handset back into its cradle, *Blam!* Or he'd use a trick Russ Thyret taught him, breaking into the guy's rap and telling him that someone who really wanted to talk to him just happened to be standing there, *so, hang on* and—*blam!*—good-bye. When the phone rang again ten or twenty minutes later, it'd be Cornyn calling from down the hall to complain that now that New York guy was hassling *him* because of what you just did, and *I know he's an idiot, and don't ever do what he says, but can you at least pretend to listen so he doesn't fuck up my afternoon?*

Cornyn wasn't angry. He knew as well as Somers that the corporate guys in New York had no idea how the record business worked, let alone how the crew in Burbank was remaking it. Their perspective was entirely backward, always trying to extrapolate what would happen with this year's releases from last year's statistics, but with absolutely no comprehension of what factors governed the popular music market: the other new records in the shops; the moment's hit movies, television shows; whatever was going on in Washington, DC; the winter weather in the Midwest. And then there were the things you couldn't describe as much as *feel*: the shared subconscious; the winds on Mars; the aching place inside that people didn't even know was empty before they heard the music that filled it so perfectly. And how do you explain that to a guy whose sense of truth, beauty, and transcendent experience came out of the Wharton School of Business?

It took a special kind of corporate boss to understand how much he didn't understand about how his employees did their jobs, and Mo Ostin was one of them. So, if Somers or Cornyn was aggrieved enough to mention the latest annoying phone call to Warner Bros. Records' chairman, Ostin was likely to march right back to his own office and dial the offender himself to tell him exactly how unwelcome his advice was in Burbank. *Never talk to any of my people without clearing it with me first, do you understand?* Or if there had been a spate of these intrusions, Ostin would dial Ross directly and give *him* an earful about how the corporate guys were overstepping. And Ross would listen and agree that, yes, this was unacceptable, and he'd send a memo that very afternoon—and by the way, congratulations on the gold records you guys got last month.

Doing things in their own unique fashion had become a central part of the Warner Bros. Records DNA. It came through most clearly in Ostin's hands-off policy with his executives, allowing each department head to run his office and staff with no risk of being second-guessed or overruled from above. Was some band's manager freaking out because they weren't getting enough tour support for their winter swing down the East Coast? Ostin would pick up the phone and hear the usual rap about how unacceptable it was, how much their last record had sold, and how much better they'd all do if they could break open New York and Philly and Boston, and surely he could tell his man to squeeze another twenty Gs out of his budget and . . .

Ostin would listen, patiently as ever, until it was his turn to talk: *I get it, but that's Stan's department, and so it's his decision.* Would there be sputtering, incredulity, outrage, threats to go sign with A&M Records across town? Of course. But that's how they did business at Warner, and it wasn't going to change every time someone didn't get what he wanted.

○

Business at the Warner Bros. music division continued to get better and better. In 1973, Ross made a deal with talent manager David Geffen to buy his Asylum Records, the company Geffen had cofounded in 1971 with his business partner Elliott Roberts. The place was a gold mine, simply by virtue of the clients whom Geffen and Roberts represented. Asylum was home to budding superstars the Eagles, Jackson Browne, and Linda Ronstadt, soon to be joined by Joni Mitchell (who had chosen to follow her manager to his record company) just in time for her 1974 smash, *Court and Spark*, and its best-selling live follow-up, *Miles of Aisles*. Meanwhile, Warner Bros. Records' artists were riding the commercial jet stream, too. Sinatra's 1973 comeback album, *Ol' Blue Eyes Is Back*, took him to the upper reaches of the Hot 200, and the bearded pop duo Seals and Crofts launched a years-long hit streak with "Summer Breeze" and "Diamond Girl." Meanwhile, the band America continued to score gold and platinum albums and singles.

Still, the best illustration of the Burbank company's early 1970s success came with its February 1973 releases. Of the sixteen albums Warner Bros. Records uncorked that month, ten of them had climbed onto *Billboard*'s best-selling album charts by April.[1] The rest of the year was nearly as hot, but even that was eclipsed by sales during 1974. While the rest of the music industry fell back a tick from the previous year's record-setting pace, revenue for Warner Bros. Records soared *250* percent over the best-ever numbers from the previous year. The dimensions of the entire Warner Bros. music companies' dominance that year came through loud and clear in RIAA's annual tally of its sales awards. Of the 195 gold records awarded to all the existing record companies in 1974, fifty of them, more than a quarter of the total number, were the products of either Warner, Elektra, or Asylum.

*Circular* wasn't wrong about the miseries waiting to blossom from previous triumphs. The Warner companies' leaps in annual revenue, almost always in the double digits, turned into a mixed blessing when Ross and his financial officers grew to expect similar leaps each year. Ostin and Smith could walk into an annual finance meeting with tens of millions more dollars than they'd boasted the previous year, and they would still get an earful because the year's gains weren't enough to sate Ross's appetite, let alone those of the Wall Street analysts and buyers whose interpretations of a company's prospects for the coming year could send a stock either soaring or tumbling. *Give me the numbers*, Ross would demand, and if he heard a note of caution in the presentation, even one that predicted a larger haul for the coming year, he'd thump the table and roar, *You're lowballing me!* When it was over, Ostin would limp out of the conference room feeling like he'd just been jumped by the Hell's Kitchen Gang over on Ninth Avenue. "They got used to the double-digit increases," he says. But what are ya gonna do? For all that Ross admired the artists who followed their passions and the executives who understood them well enough to fuel the transcendence that led to the production of art beautiful enough to inspire millions of people to buy it, his own pathway to transcendence was making money. And who could say that wasn't an art in and of itself? Ross certainly did it with passion, and even a joyfulness he worked hard to make infectious.

Name an executive incentive program, and Ross had it going on: generous salaries, regular raises, limitless expense accounts, and blizzards of stock options. But the real pièce de résistance at Warner was the profit-sharing program. For every $1 million in profit Warner Bros. Records produced at the end of the year, Ross would keep $500,000 and funnel the other half million back to Ostin to keep and/or distribute among his executives. When Cornyn answered the call to Ostin's office to accept his first profit-sharing check, he was expecting a few car payments at best—five hundred bucks, maybe a thousand, as it had been a good year. Instead, Ostin, with Smith at his side, handed their creative services director a check for $25,000, close to half of his annual salary. What Cornyn intended to be a dignified *thanks* became a yelp: *Holy shit!* Both executives smiled. They knew the feeling. And the feeling would spread as their sales continued to climb through the early seventies, the mid-seventies, the late seventies, and beyond.[2]

People's lives changed. Sitting in his sprawling apartment above Wilshire Boulevard in Beverly Hills, Smith recalls Steve Ross as a boss from beyond your dreams. "He made us all rich," Smith told me. "He'd come to us for advice and give us money. The bonus thing he laid out was criminal." Smith moved his family from their cozy house in Encino to a $250,000 mansion in Beverly Hills, the former residence of Eddie Cantor, complete with expansive lawns, a swimming pool, a detached projection room out back, and an attic converted into a temperature-and humidity-controlled wine storage room for his growing collection of French and Italian varietals.

And Ross's largesse didn't end there. He gave the record company executives access to a company jet they could use at will. Now that he had shifted his entertainment companies into an entity called Warner Communications Inc., or WCI, the delighted Burbank folks dubbed the jet the Wiki Bird (after WCI). Meetings in New York? *Let's take the Wiki Bird!* A James Taylor concert in Chicago? *Take some friends with you, no point in having empty seats.* When Smith caught sight of a beautiful mansion near a hotel he knew in Acapulco, he encouraged Ross to rent it for a couple of weeks. That worked out so well that Smith suggested they simply buy the property and have it ready for whenever the mood struck. Soon the place was theirs, and Smith kept a set of keys in his desk. "I took people there four or five times," he recalled. "I took my mother and father to this spectacular place—the tennis court, the swimming pool. Then we got a number to sign for anything we wanted to buy in the city of Acapulco, and it became part of my identity. We'd get down there, and I'm the guy that signs the big check in the restaurant."[3]

Stan Cornyn's scrapbook from the 1970s tells the story in a series of photos revealing how far the Warner execs would range in their safaris for fun, food, and executive bonding. In the early years, they're perched around numbered tables at industry awards banquets, the cleared-off dinner plates replaced by dozens of empty cocktail and wineglasses. They're posing at company parties with Martin Mull, Randy Newman, and Bonnie Raitt, mustering smiles with drinks in one hand and cigarettes burning inside the cupped palms at their sides. Then it was off to Acapulco, the Ostins and the Cornyns reclining with umbrella drinks at the Princess Hotel, then a postprandial mob at the Cayucas restaurant, faces suntanned and arms thrown convivially over the back of the banquette. Now they're with a couple dozen Warner corporate folks at a meeting in some elegant hotel in Las Hadas, Mexico; in the bar at the Montreux Palace Hotel; a dinner in Mallorca, Spain. There they are inside the Wiki Bird: Ostin, Cornyn, Smith, and Russ Thyret, plus long-haired execs from Chrysalis Records, rocketing off together to another exotic locale. All of it, and so much more, courtesy of Ross, who loved to come along, always ready for maximum fun.

He loved it all, but he might have liked playing the miracle worker even more. When Ross espied Mo and Evelyn Ostin celebrating their thirtieth wedding anniversary at a table across from his in a Paris restaurant, the magnate summoned a portable thirty-piece orchestra to play George and Ira Gershwin's "Our Love Is Here to Stay" to the happy couple. How did he even know they'd be there, let alone the name of the song they'd danced to at their wedding so many years ago? That was Ross's magic: he just *knew*.[4]

Ostin's affection for Ross continues to this day. But appreciating the man's generosity doesn't blind Ostin to the unstated purpose behind his old boss's flights of munificence. Along with everything else, he says, Ross had a genius for understanding human nature and satisfying a person's needs in a way that left him so gratified he'd be willing to do nearly anything. "He felt everybody had a price; that they could be bought," Ostin says. So, while Ross really did love his colleagues, and found delight in giving them the opportunities and rewards they desired, his deeper motivations were a little more purposeful than he let on. "He also had another agenda," Ostin says. "There was a method to the madness."

○

The breakneck rise of Warner Bros. Records in the late 1960s and early '70s triggered a hiring spree that filled the already crowded machine shop at 3701 Warner Boulevard to the brim. By 1970, virtually every office had at least two inhabitants. The dead spaces in the hallways were crowded with desks and temporary plywood-walled offices. The first solution was to install a handful of trailers in the parking lot, the same ones they use for actors' dressing rooms on set, repurposing them into offices for Bob Regehr's Artist Development team. The mail room folks worked out of another trailer. And while trailer offices were better than nothing, they were also stuffy and claustrophobic, and even worse in the summer, when the freon vapors wheezing from the AC window units were too listless to cool and too chemical to breathe.

Clearly, the nation's best-selling record label needed a headquarters that could hold its entire staff, with plenty of space to add the new hires who would surely follow—not just any building, either, but a structure that would animate the spirit of the organization and feel inviting to the artists, managers, and other visitors who came through their offices every day. Ross approved the investment immediately, and after considering a handful of architects, Ostin hired A. Quincy Jones,* a Southern California modernist whose work ranged from austere steel-and-glass university structures to woody private homes that embraced their natural surroundings through expansive windows and natural wall coverings. Ostin deputized art director Ed Thrasher to help the architect understand the spirit of the company. What they needed, Thrasher told Jones, was a building for offices, but not *establishment* offices, a structure that was purposeful but also accessible, open yet cozy. Given a chunk of land at 3300 Warner Boulevard, just down the street from the machine shop, Jones designed

---

* Not to be confused with the famous jazz trumpeter, arranger, producer Quincy Jones.

the entryway as a backward-leaning windowed box rising the full height of the building to give the entryway an open-hearted grandeur. It would be the essence of the Burbank sound made manifest in glass, wood, and cream-colored brick.

But why keep the Warner Bros. Records spirit rooted in one place when they could also take it out on the road and around the world? The idea for a European tour came from Bob Regehr, the oversize whiz at the fore of Artist Development, and it was so old that it was brand-new. They'd send a package tour of Warner acts barnstorming through Europe for a month of concerts, press events, and jinks hi and lo enough to bring European rock 'n' roll fans into the Burbank sound. Sifting through the company's roster, Regehr settled on a half-dozen acts of varying popularity, a genre-spanning array that included consistent hitmakers the Doobie Brothers, the critically acclaimed blues-country-soul surrealists Little Feat, the Led Zeppelin–like rockers Montrose, the funk-soul group Tower of Power, former Sly and the Family Stone bassist Larry Graham's Graham Central Station, and a newly signed Bay Area rock band called Bonaroo. Regehr figured the adventure would lose at least a hundred thousand bucks, but as Ostin had once told Steve Ross and his accountants that was how you built a business.

To make his idea real, Regehr took it to Carl Scott, who partnered with the recently hired Georgia Bergman to work out the specifics. It would be a massive undertaking, a four-nation blitz of theaters, television shows, newspapers, magazines, and record stores, all given the specially produced sampler album featuring two songs from each act, an album that would be available for cheap in record stores and at the shows themselves. Scott and Bergman took on the mammoth task of putting together the weeks-long adventure, booking halls and media appearances, buying airplane, train, bus, and boat tickets. A 125-strong army would be on the road: all the musicians, technicians, roadies, friends, family, and executives, plus Regehr and also label president Joe Smith, who would serve a dual role as cheerleader and adult in the room (Regehr was more likely to be the cause of trouble than its resolution). They dubbed the brigade the Warner Bros. Music Show, and Ed Thrasher's office designed a logo: a vision of Warner Bros.' beloved cartoon rabbit Bugs Bunny in mid-bouncy stride with a guitar in one hand and a furry-fingered peace sign flashed by the other.

The tour's British shows sold out instantly, supported by a special episode of the popular *Old Grey Whistle Test* music TV show, hosted by the rock 'n' roll tastemaker Bob Harris. Ticket sales on the European stops soon soared as well. The touring party coalesced in London for a couple days of interviews and TV performances, and then made for Manchester, where the winter-chilled audience turned to the Burbank sound like sunflowers turning their faces toward sunshine. All the acts earned ovations, but the nights they were on the bill all belonged to Little Feat. Hardly anyone had discovered them but their fans, who included Led Zeppelin's Robert Plant, who talked them up on British TV just as the Music Show tour was about to start. The band was also particularly beloved around the Burbank offices, where the workdays often played out to the tune of "Dixie Chicken," "Fat Man in the Bathtub," and "Oh, Atlanta" grooving away over the building's sound system.

Little Feat was the very model of a Warner Bros. band in the 1970s. Led by Lowell George, a distinctive slide guitarist and singer-songwriter, the six-piece band worked together to craft tunes whose rhythmic and melodic structures wove soul, rock, folk, and jazz influences into a kind of bouillabaisse of sound. The lyrics, meanwhile, made George's polymathic interests into comic book images and breakneck wordplay. "Onamoto-poetry symmetry in motion / They heard about that girl clear across the ocean," went a typical LG couplet. "Two degrees in be-bop, a PhD in swing / He's a master of rhythm, he's a rock 'n' roll king," went another. Many fans considered that one a concise description of its author.

The son of a prosperous Hollywood furrier, Lowell George grew up rebellious and whip smart. When Feat keyboardist and fellow songwriter Bill Payne went to George's rustic house in Silver Lake to have an introductory talk in 1969, he entertained himself while waiting for the notoriously tardy guitarist to show up by examining the contents of his living room, which included a samurai sword, a sitar, a full collection of the Smithsonian Institution's folk and blues recordings, along with works by radical comedian Lenny Bruce, Jack Kerouac, and poet Carl Sandburg, all surrounding the young blond woman sitting in the lotus position at the center of the room. George's brains and wit impressed Ostin, fueling a friendship they continued for the rest of the musician's life. In the meantime, George and Little Feat served as Burbank's hometown heroes. And when they finally took command of the spotlight on the European tour, the folks back home were overjoyed, and not just because the jump in Little Feat album sales added up to much more than the hundred thousand dollars they were losing on the tour.

Little Feat's belated success was also the latest affirmation of Ostin's philosophy of doing business. It was the music that mattered, they chanted to themselves and anyone else who would listen, and if it took some time to find the right audience for it, the company didn't mind waiting.

With the end of the tour approaching in early February, someone got the idea to write a song to celebrate their journey and the company that had invested so much in their music. Larry Graham adapted a Graham Central Station song called "The Jam" into "It Ain't Nothin' but a Warner Bros. Party," an ecstatic groove that name-checked all the acts and left plenty of room for instrumental solos and ensemble vocals. They took to playing it as an encore during the last few shows, with members of all the bands playing and singing along—including Joe Smith, who danced wildly and pitched in background vocals during the song's one-line chorus: "This ain't nothing but a Warner Bros. parrrr-teeee!" Smith took obvious pleasure in the tune's climactic verse, the one that showed exactly how beloved he, Ostin, and the entire record company were among their artists.

> *Warner Brothers*
> *We want to thank you for this opportunity*
> *Warner Brothers*
> *We got love and peace and joy and unity*
> *Warner Brothers*
> *We want to thank the brothers Mo and Joe, yeah.*
> *Warner Brothers*
> *They represent the fights of many mo' . . . YEAH!*

Released as a single to celebrate the end of the tour, "It Ain't Nothin' but a Warner Bros. Party" went on to sell 92,000 copies—another solid hit for the friendly company that couldn't stop making them.

●

Back home, Stan Cornyn and crew celebrated Burbank's tide swell of success by launching a new advertising campaign. To make sure it popped, they took it straight to the billboard-lined stretch of Sunset Boulevard that served as the music industry's showcase for the biggest pop acts and hit albums—except this billboard was filled with the face-splitting grins of Ostin and Smith, posed shoulder to shoulder. WHY ARE THESE MEN SMILING? queried the top left corner. The answer came in equally bold print on the upper right corner. BECAUSE THEY'VE JUST HEARD SOME GREAT NEW ALBUMS. Seals and Crofts, Deep Purple, Van Morrison, the Doobies, Tower of Power . . . all of them riding high on the sales charts.

And then they had a Beatle, too.

Five years since their split in 1970, John, Paul, George, and Ringo still cast long shadows across the pop music business. The members' solo work rarely approached what they had achieved as a group, and in recent years their sales had reflected that distance. But what seemed like a flop record for an ex-Beatle usually meant sales of half a million or more. So, when George Harrison's two-year deal with A&M fell apart, Ostin set up a meeting. As Harrison's widow, Olivia, remembers, her husband felt an immediate kinship with the Warner Bros. chairman. A passionate follower of Ry Cooder's work, Harrison was delighted when Ostin presented him with an advance copy of the other musician's new album. The executive clearly had a deep feeling for music, while the guitarist had a remarkably savvy mind for business. "Everything was cool," Olivia Harrison says. "It was a really inspiring, great musical community. And those were the days when the music business was fun, and people would fly places together. One of the first things we did in 1976, when we were in India, was fly to Acapulco for a big Warner Bros. Records convention. It was all like a big party."

The ex-Beatle's instincts proved to be correct. After so many years of feuds and business hassles, the atmosphere around Burbank felt like a return to Pepperland. But as always with Harrison, the fun could never overshadow his spiritual journey. And if he was hoping to make a spiritual connection with someone at the company, that's where Evelyn Ostin came in.

Evelyn had a way with people; she'd come up to you at a reception or having bumped into you in the offices and ask how you were doing. She'd focus her gaze on your eyes and see more than was immediately visible: the flickers of stress, happiness, lost love, new love, the keening of a wounded spirit. She'd make you feel like Mo's special person, says Russ Thyret. And though Ostin was always concerned with his artists' and staff's well-being, he didn't express it as easily as his wife did, and she did her best to help him open up. "Evelyn made Mo more empathetic and sensitive," he says.

Spiritual by nature, Evelyn had, since the late 1960s, pursued her curiosity with all the energy she could spare. She went to India and spent time in ashrams, taking in every aspect of Eastern culture and spiritualism she could find. She read the tracts and sat for the lectures, learning the power of meditation, chant, and spiritual healing. Once the ex-Beatle recognized how much of his spiritual quest was also Evelyn's, he barely needed to know anything else. He and Evelyn Ostin spoke for hours, meditated together, and recognized one another as fellow travelers among the higher frequencies of existence.

Evelyn was a naturally radiant woman, a warm soul whose presence had a way of calming the people around her. And Mo was well aware of this. When he was worried that he wasn't quite clicking with an artist he hoped to sign, he'd often ask her to drop by. She'd pop in to his office to say hi and then start chatting with his guest, turn her luminescence in their direction, and Mo would just sit back and watch. When she had the visitor's full attention, Mo would step out for a while or suggest that the two of them go to lunch or get a coffee somewhere. Sometimes that would be enough to get the artist on board. And indeed, it worked again, and Warner Bros. Records got themselves a Beatle.

## 12

## FUCK THE BUNNY

The new Warner Bros. Records building opened for business in 1975, all windows, wood, balconies, breezy patios, and plenty of capacious offices. *Non-establishment* offices, just as Ed Thrasher had insisted: a permanent headquarters designed specifically for the needs and spirit of Warner Bros. Records, built to the specifications of its top visionaries. And so, they came happily from the dusty old machine shop, burdened only by boxes of desktop Rolodexes, coffee cup pen holders, windup desk toys, and their favorite posters, postcards, baby snaps, and the like—only to be told to keep it all out of sight. And no, you couldn't put up a bulletin board to stick them into, either. This was Thrasher's doing. He'd been sweating the details on the building for so long, pushing and pulling with Jones to get every touch just exactly right, including the color and texture of the internal walls. So, he imagined every poster-sticking thumbtack like a sword piercing his heart, which meant no pictures, no posters, no *nothing* that was going to scuff one of his perfect surfaces.

The luxurious building came with other new hassles. Back in the machine shop, they had a receptionist named Lynne, and that was the extent of their security operation. But now they had a team of receptionists plus security guards keeping a close eye on visitors and anyone else's furtive movements. Before, all the offices had been the same size and distributed in a random fashion that put junior assistants within arm's reach of senior executives. Now some offices were bigger than others, and other offices positively dwarfed those. The size and extent of office furniture also told a tale: you could measure your place in the company hierarchy by the size of your desk.

It was a lot to get used to, particularly for Ostin, who wandered into David Berson's office one day looking more morose than his top assistant had ever seen him. For all its beauty, the new building had sapped the company's communal spirit. *The artists don't hang out here*, he said. Nobody popped into his office like they used to, sticking their heads in to hand him a demo, tell a joke, or just shoot the shit for a minute or two. They'd done such a good job of ditching the old establishment that they'd become their own kind of establishment, with all their own rules and restrictions to enforce. Woe was Mo.

But, of course, it took only a couple of months for someone to tack the first poster onto one of the immaculate walls. If Thrasher complained, it didn't do any good. Soon, the walls fluttered like they always had, with posters upon publicity pictures upon political and spiritual iconography, a significant percentage of it sporting Bob Regehr's hand-drawn improvements. And as Carl Scott remembers, the office visits picked up again, too. "I mean, there was some decorum, like, *Hey, do you have a minute?* Everybody had a minute."

○

Ostin had first heard about Fleetwood Mac in 1968, when they were a five-man blues outfit recording for the independent Blue Horizon label in England. They were critics' favorites, particularly for lead guitarist Peter Green's guitar playing and imaginative songwriting, supported by drummer Mick Fleetwood and bassist John McVie's spring-loaded rhythm section. And in England they clicked. The group's self-titled debut album hit No. 4 on the British sales charts, and six months later their brooding instrumental "Albatross" topped the singles charts. Not many American music fans had heard of them at the time, but the ones who had were fervent enough to push the imported UK release of *Fleetwood Mac* to No. 198 on the *Billboard* album list. An impressive performance all around.

So, when the group's first 1969 single, "Man of the World," was released by Andrew Loog Oldham's Immediate Records and jumped to the UK charts' No. 2 slot, Ostin looked into buying the entire label from Oldham, a deal that would have netted not just Fleetwood Mac but also the promising young guitarist Peter Frampton and early prog rockers the Nice, led by keyboardist Keith Emerson (soon to form 1970s prog superstars Emerson, Lake and Palmer). When it turned out that the group's deal with Immediate Records was solely for that one single, Ostin went straight to Fleetwood Mac's manager and made a deal. The group's first Reprise album, *Then Play On*, came out in September 1969. It made for a slow start in the United States, peaking at No. 109 on the *Billboard* charts, but it hit No. 4 in the United Kingdom, and the Reprise single that preceded it over there, "Oh, Well," made it to No. 1.

Call it half a promising a start. But from there, Fleetwood Mac fell into slow-motion chaos. Peter Green, whose guitar, songs, and voice anchored the band, quit abruptly in mid-1970 to join a religious commune in Germany and was eventually diagnosed with schizophrenia. Second guitarist Jeremy Spencer took the lead after that, and his songs dominated the group's 1970 album, *Kiln House*. But he left, too, in the spring of 1971, to join a religious sect called the Children of God. Unswayed, the band promoted rhythm guitarist Danny Kirwan to the featured role, then added the keyboardist and singer Christine Perfect to round out the sound. American Bob Welch brought his guitar in next, with Perfect (Christine McVie following her marriage to the group's bassist) elevated to full member status. That version of the band made 1971's *Future Games*, introducing a more laid-back rock sound that flowed through Welch's supernatural-themed jams and Christine McVie's lush ballads and melodic songwriting. The new sound resonated more with Americans, who bought enough copies to earn the group its first American gold album, with more than 350,000 sold. Kirwan, who didn't get along with Welch, was shown the door in 1972, just before the recording of *Bare Trees*, the group's biggest album to date, selling nearly 700,000 copies during its original run. From there the group's next few albums fell back to the earlier albums' sales, moving slowly but steadily enough for the company to break even, more or less, up through 1974's *Heroes Are Hard to Find*, after which Welch struck out on his own.

Setting out again on his familiar quest for a new lead guitarist, Mick Fleetwood happened upon a pair of young Californians who had just made their first album as a duo. Impressed by the male half's guitar playing, the drummer invited him to join his band. The guitarist agreed, but only if his singer-songwriter girlfriend got to join, too. With the addition of Lindsey Buckingham, the guitarist, and Stevie Nicks, his partner in music and romance, Fleetwood Mac was back at it.

After a few months of rehearsing, then playing a series of shows where the new lineup drew so badly that Fleetwood gave the promoters some of their money back, the rejiggered group got to work on an album with a power and clarity none of its earlier efforts had approached. Much of the credit went to the newcomers. Buckingham's California rock sound and Nicks's spectral folk-rock songs, built on Mick Fleetwood and John McVie's rhythmic foundation, made them into a band that could range from the straight-ahead rock of Buckingham's "Monday Morning" and "I'm So Afraid" to the pop balladry of McVie's "Warm Ways" and "Over My Head" and the folk-rock of Nicks's "Landslide" and "Crystal" and the fretful shawl rock of her "Rhiannon."

Knowing that his group's new album marked a significant departure from its previous work, and convinced that it had hit potential, Fleetwood went to Ostin to implore him to put the company's full muscle behind the record. At first, Ostin was skeptical. Fleetwood wanted him to treat Fleetwood Mac like a brand-new band, sinking tens of thousands of dollars into tour support, ads, the works. But they weren't a new band, no matter how many new members they had. Worse, when Russ Thyret sent a few tracks out for market research,* the ensuing report was far from promising. Older teens had next to no interest in Buckingham's cover of the Curtis brothers' "Blue Letter" and "Monday Morning," and Nicks's "Rhiannon" did even worse. No matter. Ostin deferred to Fleetwood and agreed to give the record an extra push. "Artists are usually incredibly smart about themselves," he reflects now. "They know more than we do."[1] The band went back on the road in their customary way, driving them-

---

* Wait a sec. *Market research*? It's hard to imagine that the Warner of that era would have wanted to factor such stultifyingly mainstream analyses into its creative decisions, isn't it? Indeed, it ended up ignoring most of the information, much to its benefit.

selves in two station wagons, one towing the gear in a U-Haul trailer, with their small crew riding in a Winnebago.

Released in July 1975 as the group's second eponymous record, *Fleet-wood Mac* started slowly creeping onto the lower rungs of the sales charts, then perking up a little when McVie's bubbling "Over My Head" hit radio stations in September. Both the album and the single made a few ripples with listeners as the tour wound into the fall, so Fleetwood called the Creative Services department, insisting the company build on the momentum by putting the group on one of those splashy billboards on Sunset Boulevard. Linda York, the advertising executive on the other end of the phone, had a better idea: they should take the five thousand bucks it would cost to lease a billboard and invest it in promoting the record to radio stations. Fleetwood understood this logic, and when he called back a week later to check in, York started shouting. Hadn't he heard the news? The new issue of the *Radio & Records* trade paper had "Over My Head" listed as a pick hit at radio stations all across the nation. The single eventually peaked at No. 20 in January 1976, the highest-charting song Fleetwood Mac had ever released in the United States. Nicks's witchy song "Rhiannon" came out of the box just as "Over My Head" started falling, and with the radio stations already primed for Fleetwood Mac music, it climbed to No. 11 in June 1976. The group's next single, "Say You Love Me," topped out at the same peak in mid-September.

Three solid hit singles in a row would be an achievement for any band, but even this was overshadowed by what happened on September 4, when *Fleetwood Mac*, more than a year after its release, was anointed the No. 1 album in the country. Warner's sales director, Ed Rosenblatt, seemingly still trying to believe that it was true, made a handwritten list of the sales statistics for the seven albums that had preceded their latest, none of which had sold more than 700,000 copies. The group's 1974 album, *Heroes Are Hard to Find*, had attracted only 313,000 buyers. But *Fleetwood Mac*, during its initial run, sold 3,500,000. And they were just getting started.

No longer required to drive their own station wagons on tour, in February 1976 the ascendant musicians jetted north to Sausalito, a sheltered suburban community on the Marin side of San Francisco's Golden Gate Bridge, to work on their next album somewhere beyond the 24/7 pressures of the Los Angeles music business. But while they sequestered themselves in the Record Plant, a windowless wooden structure surrounded by eucalyptus trees, the five members of Fleetwood Mac brought plenty of pressures with them. The year of nonstop touring, an odyssey that began in midsize theaters in the spring and ended in basketball arenas just before Christmas, had transformed their careers and taken a bite out of all their lives. John and Christine McVie broke up in the middle of the tour, just when Lindsey Buckingham and Stevie Nicks's relationship began falling apart. Mick Fleetwood, meanwhile, came home to the news that his wife was leaving him for one of his closest friends. It hardly seemed like a promising atmosphere for a creative collaboration, particularly given the array of new indulgences the gang had taken on, but artistry can ride unlikely currents.

Fueled by their various miseries, the songwriting members of the group produced a catalogue of powerful new tunes that at times seemed like a three-way dialogue about love, heartbreak, and emotional resilience: Buckingham's bitter yet staunch "Second Hand News" leading into Nicks's darkly knowing "Dreams," which gave way to Christine McVie's hopeful "Don't Stop," only to be blown apart by Buckingham's molten rage-pop "Go Your Own Way." Then it was back to McVie's plangent love song "Songbird" and the group's five-way statement of commitment, "The Chain," and its promise, fulfilled or not, to "never break the chain."

Given the puckish title *Rumours* and released just six months after *Fleetwood Mac* crowned the sales charts, the new album became an immediate sensation. With advance orders of nearly a million copies, the largest prerelease order in Warner Bros. Records history, *Rumours* took slightly more than a month to become the top-selling album in the nation, then spent nearly seven months at No. 1 and sold more than ten million copies in its first year. No act had ever sold as many copies of one album so quickly, or stayed on *Billboard*'s album charts for nearly as long as *Rumours* would maintain its residence in the Top 200: just over five years. It was an enormous triumph for Fleetwood Mac, a band that had been struggling for nearly a decade to break through in America and that just three years earlier had been on the verge of nonexistence.

Any other major label chief would have cut Fleetwood Mac loose when the band's sales slipped so drastically after *Bare Trees* in 1972. But the poorer-selling records that came next were every bit as good, and at

Warner that made all the difference. The group's core fans stuck with them, and so did their fans in Burbank, where Fleetwood Mac's latest records were always a popular choice for Warner's in-house sound system. It also made a difference that Mick Fleetwood, who often did double duty as the group's manager, was so smart and easy to deal with. The band worked hard and usually came close to breaking even, so keeping them on the roster was, according to Ostin's measures, a no-brainer. He liked to reward people for doing good work, and by 1977 his faith in Fleetwood Mac had been amply rewarded.

○

At a time when the entire industry was growing by bounds from one year to the next, Warner consistently outstripped its competitors' sales, often by a wide margin. In mid-1976, *Billboard*'s newly computerized sales tracker revealed that the combined Warner/Elektra/Atlantic labels were responsible for 24.3 percent of the songs and albums in the magazine's Hot 100 and 200 singles/albums pop charts. The nearest competitor, *Billboard* reported, counted for only 16.8 percent. By the end of the year, Ostin was thrilled to realize that while the WEA labels had been beating the Columbia/CBS labels for several years, Warner Bros. Records had finally knocked off Columbia in the label-versus-label sweepstakes. The margin was tiny, one tenth of 1 percent, but still, who would have imagined it ten years earlier?

To mark the company's era of dominance, Stan Cornyn launched a new ad campaign that, reversing course from his revolutionary consumer-aimed series in the late 1960s, was directed at the music industry. To emphasize the power of the thriving WEA distribution network, he came up with a central image, the Big Button, and had the art department build a ridiculously oversize model. Then he hired a photographer to go around the record companies snapping photos of the thing with various executives, staffers, and someone in a gorilla suit to illustrate the WEA-powered company's power.

He then published a series of "Big Button" pieces in the industry's leading trade magazines, *Billboard*, the *Hollywood Reporter*, *Record World*, and *Cashbox*. All these shared the basic elements of the "Once You Get Used to It, His Voice Is Really Something" ads: an attention-grabbing headline, a big photograph, playful double entendres. "Is Mo Ostin Ashamed of Having So Big a Button?" asked one Freudian subhead, only to be brushed off with a dash of Parisian cool: *Au contraire.*

But even if they followed the form, Cornyn's new ads didn't have the counterculture sass that had made his furrier, freakier ads so delicious. Oh, you could see traces. The portrait of Ostin in the ad captures him at his desk, richly bearded and joyful, his office stereo on the bookshelf right behind him, a postcard of Richard and Pat Nixon stuck prominently, if sardonically, into the corner of his desktop writing pad. The Button, fifteen times the size of an ordinary triggering device, stands tumescently across from the former First Couple, and he's got his right thumb atop its pusher, poised to mash the thing all the way into next week. And this device, the central headline says, is HOW MO OSTIN CONTROLS AMERICA'S #1 SALES FORCE. What we've got here is an ad for the power of the WEA distribution organization. The size and efficiency of its Los Angeles warehouse and shipping center, which recently shipped fifty *tons'* worth of albums in a single day. And just look at what its sales/promotions staff achieved with Fleetwood Mac, taking them from near obscurity to a multi-platinum band in the course of a few months. "Mo Ostin's thumb is blessed also. It can push the Biggest Button in the record business."

Now here's Ahmet Ertegun in his New York aerie, peering blankly through his glasses. He is neither smiling nor in the company of a jumbo button. Ahmet doesn't *do* props, apparently, but as Cornyn writes, he, too, is perched upon the muscular shoulders of the WEA sales army, including Eleanor Tausch from the Chicago branch office, featured in an ad explaining how she tracks stock and shipments with a futuristic machine that has a keyboard and a TV-like screen that provides instant information from throughout the WEA network. With a glimpse, she can see exactly where the boxes of albums are and where they need to be, and have them on their way within moments.

The ads came week after week—like the old ones, only different. Here's Smilin' Joe, who also has the "Biggest Button in the Business," which means instant access to "seven full-stock branches, 11 sales offices, 92 full-time salesmen, 198 chart records in the past six months, 55 gold records in the last year and great hunger."

*Great hunger.* Everyone needs to eat, and as Cornyn delighted in pointing out in his Loss Leaders series ad copy, Warner/Reprise was a few steps short of being *entirely* benevolent, particularly when it came to its free or cut-price offers. But making not just the profiteering but the entire thrust of the who-we-are-now message visible was jarring to some, and downright off-putting to Lenny Waronker, who thought it unseemly to focus attention on anyone or thing that wasn't one of the company's artists. "And it's like you have the power to push a button and make it a hit? C'mon. That bothered me."[2]

But not nearly as much as it bothered Walter Yetnikoff. The president of Columbia Records was a brainy working-class kid from Brooklyn who had graduated Phi Beta Kappa from Brooklyn College, then attended Columbia Law School on a full scholarship. A brawler by nature, he'd applied his fierceness to his career at Columbia Records, working his way from staff attorney to the company's top chair within just a few years. Once installed, he wielded his power like he'd been taught by the street fighters in his old neighborhood. He'd never liked Ostin or his breezy California record label. The Burbankers seemed like a bunch of unctuous hippies to him, flinging all that holier-than-thou shit about how *groovy* they were, how far above the hustle and hassle of the music biz. Galled by the sight of Ostin's ass ahead of his own in the annual sales race, Yetnikoff declared war. "War is exhilarating," he wrote in his 2004 memoir, *Howling at the Moon.* "War gives us purpose and drive. War was what I wanted. War was who I was."[3] What he didn't know was that lurking behind the beard, smile, and *sotto voce* Ostin style thumped the heart of another working-class kid who knew how to put up a fight.

Yetnikoff struck first. To launch his new campaign at the company's 1976 convention, he had banners printed up: FUCK THE BUNNY. Everyone got a dartboard with a big Bugs Bunny in the bull's-eye. During his speech, Yetnikoff had a staffer dressed as the Warner Bros. Cartoons' trademark rabbit walk onstage, at which point Yetnikoff grabbed a large prop mallet and pretended to beat the creature to death. Three thousand miles away in Burbank, it seemed darkly hilarious, Waronker recalls. "People laughed and said, 'They're scared of us! We win!'"[4]

But it became much less amusing when word came that their bunny-beating rival was already in the act of poaching James Taylor, the perpetual best seller whose contract had expired when he turned in his

1976 album, *In the Pocket*. Yetnikoff came after the artist who had taken Warner/Reprise to the cover of *Time* with a fevered determination to pry him from his rivals' grasp. He came with charm, he came with global ambitions, and he came with jumbo sacks full of money. Once the alarm bells sounded, Ostin leaped into action. He grabbed Waronker and fellow producer Ted Templeman out of their offices for a sprint to the airport, where the Warner jet was raring to fly. He also sent word to Evelyn, who had been close to Taylor and his wife, the singer Carly Simon, for years. Evelyn got on the phone to remind the couple of their place in the family they all had created together. It meant something in the old days, and it still did. Other things mattered, too.

What Ostin and the others didn't know was that Taylor and his manager, Peter Asher, were determined to make the move partly *because* of Warner's cozy family vibe. Because families are essential, especially when it comes to building a foundation for your life, but they can also be limiting. And in recent years, Taylor had felt taken for granted. After his first burst of fame, he had settled into being a reliably good, but not great, seller, consistently moving enough copies to win gold records, but short of the platinum and multi-platinum awards Fleetwood Mac was now minting. Consider Taylor's *In the Pocket*, a Waronker-Titelman co-production that sputtered at No. 16, the lowest-charting album in his Warner Bros. career. True enough, the same team had helped create his far more successful 1975 album, *Gorilla*, which climbed to No. 6 on the strength of hit singles, including his cover of Marvin Gaye's "How Sweet It Is (To Be Loved By You)" (a No. 5 pop hit that topped the adult contemporary charts) and "Mexico" (No. 49 in pop and No. 5 adult contemporary). But even that album, like all of Taylor's previous work, failed to connect overseas, where he now sold fewer records than Little Feat.

There were other factors at work, too. Taylor and Simon lived in New York City, about a half mile from Columbia's offices in Midtown. Knowing how her husband's appetite for liquor and drugs became more acute when he was bored, Simon loved the idea that Taylor would have an office to visit when he wasn't recording or touring. And then there was the money. Determined to take a major artist off Ostin's roster, Yetnikoff was wielding, as Asher says, "an offer we couldn't refuse."[5]

When the Warner crew touched down in New York, they loaded into the waiting limousine and made straight for Taylor and Simon's apartment on Central Park West. There they played the artistic freedom card, the everything we've achieved together card, the brothers-in-arms card, every card in the deck except the of course we'll pay you more than Columbia card. Because as much as Ostin treasured Taylor and his music, he didn't want to get lured into a bidding war. Once that got started, he'd not only end up overpaying, but also set a precedent for every artist looking to cut a richer deal. His loyalties torn, Taylor kept Yetnikoff waiting for hours while the Warner executives made their case. His nerves jangled by cocaine, booze, and guilt, he collapsed into tears, sobbing on the floor of his apartment. No matter what he did, he would hurt someone's feelings, and he couldn't *stand* to hurt people's feelings.

Back on his feet just before midnight, Taylor joined Asher for the short walk to see Yetnikoff in the apartment of Nat Weiss, the former Beatles lawyer whom Asher had known since his days at Apple Records. Once inside the door, they found the agitated Columbia Records president, who responded to the manager's request that his artist be given more time to decide by grabbing Asher by the lapels, calling him a redheaded English traitor, and ordering him to shut the fuck up.[6] "Walter was crazy," Asher says. "But we were all modestly crazy."[7] The night dragged toward dawn, and Taylor vacillated, moving in one direction, then back the other way. He talked about his integrity, about loyalty, about his feelings. Yetnikoff wondered aloud about *his* feelings. Hadn't he given Taylor everything he wanted in this deal? And a million-dollar signing bonus besides? When Taylor stepped out to walk around the block, Yetnikoff, no longer in such a sensitive mood, wheeled on Asher and Weiss and told them that their client had two choices: sign the contract or be physically ripped apart by Yetnikoff's own hands. When Taylor returned, he took Yetnikoff's contract in one hand and a pen in the other and signed "James." Just that much. No "Taylor." That was good enough. Yetnikoff snatched back the contract and handed the musician his million-dollar check. Defeated, the Warner Bros. team slumped to the Wiki Bird and flew back west.

In the end, Yetnikoff delivered on his promise to put Taylor back on top. His 1977 album *JT*, led off by his smash cover of Jimmy Jones's "Handy Man," was (and remains) the biggest-selling album of his career, moving 3.5 million copies in its first year of release. But Yetnikoff failed on his bid to make Taylor an international superstar. "He should have been, but he never was," Asher says. "Columbia said they could do that, but they did not succeed."[8]

While Yetnikoff worked overtime to charm Taylor into switching to Columbia, he put nearly as much effort into alienating Columbia's long-time marquee artist Paul Simon, who had been selling millions of records for the company since the electrified version of Simon and Garfunkel's "Sound of Silence" took them to the top of the *Billboard* charts in late 1965 and early 1966. The duo's innovative yet pop-friendly albums and singles helped define the pop music of the rest of the decade before 1970's *Bridge Over Troubled Water* sold ten million copies, more than any previous album ever released (a record they'd hold until Fleetwood Mac's *Rumours* came seven years later). But at that point, the duo promptly broke up. Columbia's then-president Clive Davis pleaded with Simon to patch it up with Garfunkel, but the musician ignored him, starting a solo career that, while not matching *Bridge*-size sales, continued to produce million-selling records. Simon released his biggest solo album, *Still Crazy After All These Years*, in 1975, less than two years before the time came for the musician to negotiate a new contract. But Yetnikoff, whose professional desire to keep his best-selling artist on the label couldn't match his personal enmity for the man, did the best he could to make the negotiation an ordeal for Simon—or, more accurately, he wanted to get his star re-signed, but without the somersaults and hosannas that usually attended such multimillion-dollar negotiations. Meanwhile, Ostin was already on the case.

Maybe he would have made a play for Simon even if Yetnikoff hadn't just raided his roster. Ostin had been friendly with the artist since Clive Davis took him to a Simon and Garfunkel recording session in the late 1960s. Simon's work, which set new standards for literary and musical sophistication in popular music, fit easily with the rest of the Warner roster. With music, money, and revenge crackling in the air, Ostin went to New York to meet with Ross and his top lieutenants. "I wanted to offer him a really strong deal, an offer he couldn't refuse," Ostin says. "So, before I committed to that, I wanted to make sure the corporation wouldn't have problems with it. And they supported it wholeheartedly." Still in New York, Ostin paid a visit to Simon's lawyer and business partner, Mike Tannen, outlining the offer he was ready to make. Once he was back in California, he sat down with Simon himself. The artist said he admired Ostin and appreciated the offer but, he continued, Columbia had been his professional home for thirteen years. He'd been signed by Columbia's renowned Goddard Lieberson in 1964 and loved being part of the company's gilded tradition. So, thanks, but no.[9]

A few weeks passed. Yetnikoff continued his negotiations with a bottle of scotch in one hand, a cudgel in the other, and a chip the size of Brooklyn on his shoulder. Simon could hold his own and then some, what with the Queens-size chip on his own shoulder, until their negotiations might as well have been taking place on a concrete schoolyard between the Fordham Baldies and the Ditmas Dukes. "For a teeny, tiny little squirt you've got a big mouth," Yetnikoff observed at one point. "I'm tired of your whining," he said later. "I don't want to see you anymore."[10]

And so, he didn't. Manager Tannen called Ostin and suggested that he might take another shot at Paul. Ostin did, and this time the answer was yes. "I never got Walter's firsthand reaction to losing Paul," Ostin told me recently. "But I know he was shocked." He shrugged and smiled.[11]

Yetnikoff tried to steal Bonnie Raitt next, taking her to dinner and passing her a napkin with an astronomical figure written on it. But she wasn't interested in leaving her professional home. They were family, she said, loyal to the end. She would leave the label eventually, it would turn out, but not because she wanted to go.

Even in 2018, Smith remembered it all: the way the air started to crackle, the way the cords in Jerry Wexler's neck drew taut, and how the vein in his forehead started to throb. Ross leaped to his feet and shouted, "No! No!" just as Smith jumped up to wrestle Wexler back, before his balled-up fist made contact with David Geffen's face. The clearest detail of Smith's memory was that Geffen was so obviously enjoying the whole thing. "That was his way," Smith said of Geffen. "If he could say something to make you crazy, he'd do it."[12] Which was just one reason Smith and Ostin never looked forward to the Warner Music executive summits Ross kept scheduling. There were too many of the usual suspects, too many old beefs and unresolvable conflicts. And if Geffen wasn't baiting someone and Wexler wasn't blowing up about something, then Ahmet Ertegun was running his usual game, ignoring everything until he started talking and didn't let anyone else get a word in for the rest of the afternoon. They were all on the same team, all profiting from one another's success with their stock options and profit sharing. But they were also competitors, fierce to the point of relentlessness.

And Smilin' Joe Smith was in the thick of it. As Cornyn recalled, when he couldn't understand why Ostin was so determined to dispense with ten years of tradition and switch the Reprise artists onto Warner Bros. just to rate higher on *Billboard*'s year-end market share ratings, Smith explained the move in just a few words: "It doesn't matter how important the contest is, Stan. It's always better to win than to lose."

It was a philosophy all the Warner music chiefs shared, particularly when it came to besting one another in the pursuit of acts, record sales, profits, and Ross's favor—the last of which wasn't necessarily bestowed upon the man whose company was earning the most money. For example, once Ross got to know Atlantic boss and cofounder Ahmet Ertegun, he was besotted with the executive's wit and refinement.

But as Ertegun and Ostin had revealed during their late-sixties battles for Led Zeppelin and the Rolling Stones, they couldn't help competing, even if Ross had made clear that he didn't want his record companies wasting his money by engaging in bidding wars over some hot new act. But the competition between the Warner labels, particularly between Atlantic and the Burbank-based companies, continued into the mid-1990s, when the rivalry played a role in the most self-destructive moves the corporation's top executives ever made. And maybe it was inevitable. Put that many hotly ambitious, independent-minded chief executives into one operation, and what were the chances they weren't going to fight one another?

The same tension crackled at the heart of the Geffen v. Wexler conflict at that meeting in Smith's projection room. Both men had spent months trying to lift Bob Dylan from his longtime home at Columbia Records, and when it was over the Minnesota bard signed his name on the deal Geffen had offered him at Asylum. Wexler, whose records Dylan had admired for years, had worked hard to convince the world's reigning singer-songwriter that he could do better at Atlantic, an R&B-based company that was smaller and closer to the street than Columbia.* And he was close to getting his man . . . until Geffen swooped in with his talk of solidarity and how he'd fight so much harder for all the artistic freedom, cash, and royalties Dylan deserved. The musician signed the Asylum deal just days before the meeting in Smith's projection room, and Geffen came in to the summit smiling like the cat that had just swallowed the voice of his generation.

Geffen started in on Wexler before the meeting even began, doing his best to get under his skin even as Wexler tried to shrug it off. *Fine. You won,* Wexler said. *Let's just forget it.* But Geffen kept at it, even when they launched the meeting's agenda.

They had a past, those two, going back to 1968, when the young Geffen tried to convince Wexler to release Stephen Stills from the contract he'd signed as a member of Buffalo Springfield so he could join his new partners David Crosby and Graham Nash at Columbia Records. Wexler hadn't met Geffen yet, and the inexperienced agent came on strong, telling Wexler that this was practically a favor, given that Stills didn't have a group anyway. Not the least bit fooled, Wexler levitated out of his chair, grabbed his guest by the arm, and shoved Geffen out of his office, shouting hurtful things along the way. Geffen left with his tail tucked between his legs, but he recovered quickly enough, cultivating Ahmet Ertegun as a mentor. In time, Geffen would follow Ertegun's advice to start his own record company as a joint venture with Warner Bros., a brilliant suggestion that propelled the onetime talent manager into his enormously successful label, Asylum. But Geffen never forgot Wexler's humiliating dismissal, and five years later he was able to exact his revenge on him. Now he wanted to rub it in.

In Smith's projection room, Geffen did just that, telling the Atlantic executive that he had no business working with Dylan because the song-writer was the essence of modern hip while Wexler was just a washed-up relic from the past. Wexler, who had a grudge against talent managers and agents, shot back with more insults, including his famously revolting observation that Geffen, like any agent, would dive headfirst into a bucket of pus if he saw a nickel at the bottom. Then Wexler, whose neck muscles were bulging with rage, leaped up and dove at Geffen, the better

---

* Which Atlantic obviously was, even given its corporate home at Warner Bros. Inc.

to wrap his fingers around his neck and shut him up for good. As Ross jumped to his feet shouting, "No! No!" Smith put everything he had into pulling Wexler off his intended victim before he could lay his hands on him. Ostin, heading for the door, washed his hands of the whole scene. "I'm not staying for *this*," he said. Things calmed down enough for him to stay, but the event left a foul taste in almost every mouth, including that of Stan Cornyn, who had come with Ostin and Smith. It was the first Warner Bros. executive meeting he could remember, he wrote later, where no one had said a word about music.

# THE NAME OF THE GAME
# IS PERFORMANCE

If anyone was built to be a record company president, it was Joe Smith. His years as an AM radio disc jockey and at the fore of the record promotions game had prepared him well. And that experience was built upon a Yale education that had helped hone is mind to see the business from multiple angles. It didn't hurt that he had a set of ears that could recognize hit potential in acts as wild as the Grateful Dead and as mild as Petula Clark. Nor that he could do it all while smiling, laughing, and delivering perfectly timed quips.

Smith had everything it took in such generous helpings that it surprised a lot of observers when he hadn't taken one of the chief executive offers that came his way when Steve Ross elevated Ostin above him in 1970. In 1972, the chairman of EMI offered Smith the keys to Capitol Records. And he was ready to take them, if not for Ross and Ostin. Smith was too valuable to the company, and his contract still had four years to go. Technically, the contract was enough to keep him chained to his desk whether he liked it or not. But Ostin couldn't do that, and Ross wouldn't; it went against the latter's nature as a leader, a businessman, and people pleaser. So, Ross jacked up Smith's salary and—drumroll, please—announced that Smith was now in fact president of Warner Bros. Records, a position he freed up by proclaiming Ostin chairman of the company and all its affiliated labels.

The blizzard of cash Ross unleashed helped keep Smith happy, but it was even more important to him that the work they were doing at the company was so revolutionary. He was an integral part of a record company that was redefining what it meant to be successful in the music industry. He and Ostin also made for excellent teammates, each able to flex his strengths while counting on the other to shore up his weaker spots. Smith had great ears for pop music in every genre, while Ostin leaned more toward the artsy stuff. Smith loved being the face of the company, delivering toasts at the banquets and parties, while Ostin was free to run the show without the high-watt distraction of the spotlight. They also shared the same business ideals, both happy to empower their executives and make sure everyone in the company felt welcome, valued, and as happy as possible.

But when David Geffen decided to get out of the record business in 1975, leaving the recently unified Elektra/Asylum label without a top leader, Smith let Ross know how much he wanted the job. This time, Ross and Ostin agreed the time had come. After all, the Warner Corporation would get the best of both worlds: Ostin running one company and Smith working his magic at another. The winning team would remain in place, controlling even more terrain than before. So, Smith took over Elektra/Asylum in mid-1975. He got a fast start by signing the widely admired Warren Zevon, and set to building on Geffen's work. He expanded into pop-country with Eddie Rabbit, New York punk with the influential band Television, rhythm and blues with the Pointer Sisters, and new wave with the Cars, all of which would help Smith lead the company to an 18 percent market share, the biggest it would ever achieve.

Once Smith moved off to Asylum Records, he left behind a spacious office just next door to Ostin's, where the next president of Warner Bros. Records would sit. Stan Cornyn took particular notice. National sales manager Eddie Rosenblatt did, too. Ostin didn't say anything about when he would fill the job, or how, but the competition for the post, while outwardly subtle, began immediately. You could make a case for either Cornyn or Rosenblatt, and probably three or four other Warner executives, and they'd all have been pretty convincing. But Cornyn and Rosenblatt floated to the top of the gossip line. Both men had been with the company for years. Both had made crucial contributions to the company's success, and you could imagine them doing even bigger, better things once they were installed in a bigger, better office. But only one man, Ostin, would decide who got the job, and he wasn't even talking about it.

◉

In 1976, the Recording Industry Association of America, the organization that tracks record sales throughout the music industry, acknowledged the growth in the marketplace by expanding the terms of its certifications. The gold record, once awarded to singles that sold a million copies and albums that earned a million dollars, now became the prize for selling half a million albums. Now the top prize, the platinum record, was reserved for albums that sold a million copies and singles that moved two million copies. It wouldn't be long before they had to come up with yet another certification, the diamond album, to designate albums that moved more than *ten* million copies. Within the first three years of the diamond album's existence, several artists from other labels would snag the award: Peter Frampton, with his smash live album *Frampton Comes Alive*, on A&M Records; Stevie Wonder's *Songs in the Key of Life*; Billy Joel's *The Stranger*; Pink Floyd's *The Wall*; and the Bee Gees–dominated soundtrack to *Saturday Night Fever*. But within that span, no label would release more diamond records than Warner Bros. Four Warner artists won the new award by the end of 1978, with many more to come.

You could trace it back to the release of Fleetwood Mac's breakthrough in 1975, but the apex of Warner Bros. Records' multi-multi-platinum streak started in early 1976, on sister label Asylum. The Eagles' first greatest hits album, released on February 19, 1976, had sprinted to the top of the *Billboard* album charts, debuting at No. 4 on the March 7 list and then hitting No. 1 the next week. The collection stayed at or near the top of the charts long enough to sell around ten million copies during its first run,* which set up the group's December 1976 album, *Hotel California*. That album jumped to No. 1 in January 1977 and launched two No. 1 singles,

---

* On August 20, 2018, the RIAA certified *Their Greatest Hits, 1971–1975*, for selling thirty-eight million copies in the United States, making it the best-selling album of all time, with Michael Jackson's *Thriller* lagging at a paltry thirty-three million.

the title track and "New Kid in Town," with "Life in the Fast Lane" peaking at No. 11. By mid-1978, the album hit the coveted diamond benchmark: ten million copies sold.* Meanwhile, Fleetwood Mac's *Rumours* was lapping it. That iconic album followed *Hotel California* into the world by six weeks and succeeded in moving ten million copies in its first year.†

At the same time, several longtime Warner acts came through with major records. Gordon Lightfoot released back-to-back smashes in "Carefree Highway" and "The Wreck of the Edmund Fitzgerald." The Beach Boys paid off in 1976 with a Top 10 album, *15 Big Ones*, and its pair of hit singles, a cover of Chuck Berry's "Rock and Roll Music" that hit the Top 5 and "It's OK," which bounced into the Top 30. Even Randy Newman got into platinum territory with his 1977 release *Little Criminals*, which climbed into the Top 10 thanks to his surprise No. 2 single "Short People." The Doobie Brothers, whose initial run of hit songs ended when an illness forced leader Tom Johnston to leave the group, brought in keyboardist/vocalist Michael McDonald, a top-drawer rhythm-and-blues player and singer. His first try at writing for the group yielded "Takin' It to the Streets," which became the title track of the band's 1976 album and the start of a new, even more successful phase in their career.

The company's campaign to strengthen its roster of soul and jazz artists, dating back to 1974, took a significant turn when Bob Krasnow hired on, joining the jazz and pop producer Tommy LiPuma at the fore of a rapidly expanding division. That the artistic leaders of what they called "the Black Music division" were both white would be a scandal today, but both Krasnow and LiPuma had decades of experience and were able to hit the ground running. Krasnow, fresh from the presidency of Blue Thumb Records, moved quickly to sign soul singer Chaka Khan and George Clinton's space-funk orchestra Funkadelic, also known as Parliament. Clinton's bassist Bootsy Collins, renowned for his lunar, thumb-popping style and his supersize *Hey hey, it's Bootsy, baby* vibe, also signed on as a solo artist. On the jazz side, Krasnow brought in the widely admired guitarist George Benson, who had secretly longed to be a singer, only to stop short knowing that edging toward pop vocal music would compro-

---

* The RIAA's August 2018 certification had *Hotel California* passing the twenty-six million mark.
† As of 2013, the RIAA had *Rumours* selling more than twenty million copies in the United States and a total of forty million worldwide.

mise his authority as a jazz player. Tapped to produce Benson's Warner Bros. debut, LiPuma picked up on the guitarist's ambition and brought him Leon Russell's song "This Masquerade," which reached the Top 10 on the pop charts and helped make Benson's *Breezin'* album a chart-topper on the pop, jazz, and soul charts. Jazz singer Al Jarreau started his run to fame at the same time, along with mellow jazz-pop singer-songwriter Michael Franks, whose first album, *The Art of Tea*, featuring the tastefully understated instrumental group the Crusaders, became a kind of classic in modern California jazz-pop.

The company also did good business with Jesse Colin Young, a singer-songwriter/guitarist whose 1973 album, *Song for Juli*, described a rustic world where hippies of means lived in hand-built homes on wooded ridgetops in northern Marin County. "Now my taxes are high, / But I don't believe it's a sin," Young sings, going on to describe the mammoth trees and views in "Ridgetop," one of his most popular songs from the era. Young, once the lead singer of the Youngbloods of "Get Together" fame, captured something of the peace generation's evolution with his sprawling jams about sunlight, songbirds, and the beauty of hilltop mornings. His voice is both airy and strong, and his band, including a woodwind player on saxophone and flute, give his folkish songs a jazzy lilt and come across on his 1976 live album, *Jesse Colin Young on the Road*, as the ur-band of the post-Woodstock 1970s. "We gotta stop killing one another," he sings in "Peace Song," but it all comes home in the end to that remote ridgetop where the ruts in the twisting hillside road keep the tourists at bay.

A half dozen years or more after joining the company, a lot of the hippie artists who had once made up pop music's underground or even avant-garde began to slip quite easily into mainstream stardom. The diamond-selling likes of Fleetwood Mac and Asylum's Eagles, along with regular top sellers Neil Young, Joni Mitchell, and Rod Stewart, now radiated the vaporous glam of private jets, hand-buffed limousines, sterling champagne buckets, and gilded mirrors lined with rails of white powder whose provenance you didn't have to consider as long as you kept snorting.

The back-to-back-to-back years of hits and mega-profits made it seem as if the Big Button really did exist, and not just on the big desks in the corner offices. The numbers kept insisting that the Warner Bros. team really did have the best ears and the best taste in the business. And as long as they kept on doing what they were already doing, it seemed like they could keep on going forever. And that's what always happens in pop culture. The rebels had ousted the old guard, and after a few years of glory, they were becoming the new old guard. And the only thing less surprising than that was how surprising it seems each time it happens. *How could it be?*

Well, the clock keeps ticking. The younger brothers and sisters come of age in a different time, with a different cultural landscape: kids for whom political assassinations and protest marches were not the backdrop to their adolescence. And then there's the constant morphing of the popular unconscious, whose fancies, phobias, appetites, and preferred illusions shift according to some unknown combination of shared experience, the flapping of distant butterfly wings, and, perhaps, the whims of gods on high. The culture keeps changing, is the thing. And no one's cultural radar can keep up with it forever.

In early 1975, Ostin met with a pair of publicists named Bob Gibson and Gary Stromberg who were trying to pitch him a movie they'd dreamed up with a concept so slight it struck Ostin as nothing short of outrageous. And yet they practically leaped out of their chairs with excitement when they told him about it.

*It's called "Car Wash,"* Ostin heard. *'Cause it's all going down in the car wash, right?*

Ostin blinked. *And . . . ?*

*And "Car Wash"!*

The picture would be a day in the life at a Los Angeles car wash, and all the characters would be there: the owner, the workers, the customers. Some would be rich, some would be poor, everyone would have his own story, and it'd all come together at the car wash! *See?*

Perplexed, Ostin asked to see a screenplay or at least a treatment. They had to have something to show him, right? Nope. Just the idea and the title: "Car Wash." Because that's where it's all going down! And if that weren't enough, they had the storied former Motown producer Norman Whitfield on board to produce a soundtrack album! So, if Ostin agreed to fund the project, he stood to make *two* fortunes, one on the movie itself and the other on the soundtrack. What else did he need to know?

*A lot more than that,* he told them.

That was the end of the meeting, but Ostin was so flabbergasted by the guile of Gibson and Stromberg that he went on a building-wide orbit to tell everyone he could see about this ridiculous meeting he'd just had with these *lunatics* who'd tried to pitch him the stupidest movie idea he'd ever heard. Eighteen months later, after Universal bought the idea and made it into a smash hit starring Richard Pryor, George Carlin, Garrett Morris, and others, and after after its Norman Whitfield–produced, double-disc album sold more than two million copies, Ostin's former assistant-turned-executive David Berson came into his office to make some good-natured sport of his boss.

"I want you to produce my movie," he said. It would be called "Commissary" and would take place at the cafeteria that Warner Bros. Pictures used to feed its workers during the day. "It's all going down in the commissary," Berson proclaimed. Glamorous movie stars, scheming executives, teenage prop assistants, comically starstruck visitors—all coming together every day to eat! *So, how about that?*

Ostin nodded ruefully. "If you can get Norman Whitfield to produce the soundtrack, I'm in."

The *Car Wash* incident might have been too silly to be a real indicator, but there's no denying that by the mid-seventies some people were having a hard time seeing beyond the Burbank borders. The Warner A&R team missed out on the punk rock rebellion and the rise of disco, in all its outsider, gay, Latino, and African American jubilation. Eager to catch up, Ostin started paying attention to the punk scene, and when he saw that England's leading punk group the Sex Pistols had lost their deal with A&M Records after the band members concluded a visit to the company's Los Angeles headquarters by smashing desks and chairs and then peeing on things that weren't toilets, he took an immediate interest. Long accustomed to dealing with eccentrics, Ostin sent Artist Development czar Bob Regehr and Bob Krasnow to London to check out the engagingly egregious band and see if they might fit into the Warner family.

Once in England, the executives found the Pistols and their manager, Malcolm McLaren, in the grotty underground warren they used as a rehearsal space. The room was unventilated and brimming with trash and half-destroyed bits of furniture someone had rescued from a nearby tip, plus the remnants of spitting battles, nausea attacks, and worse. Krasnow and Regehr's appearance incited a hail of verbal abuse from Johnny Rotten, Sid Vicious, and their bandmates, much of it directed at Regehr, who for some reason showed up smoking a cigar. When they started playing, the Pistols thrashed their instruments while lead singer Johnny Rotten snarled and sneered. When it was over, the executives returned to their hotel and took turns wiring their impressions back to Burbank. Krasnow compared the experience to sinking a foot into dog shit. Regehr, on the other hand, felt the group's anarchic charge lift the hair from his forearms and urged Ostin to sign them as quickly as possible. Thoroughly puzzled, Ostin sent the same response to both men: *Did you go together?*

Even Krasnow couldn't deny the star power flashing from Rotten's ice-blue eyes, so Ostin worked out terms with McLaren to welcome the Sex Pistols to their new home in Burbank. Though accustomed to the hi- and lo-jinks of professionally unhinged young musicians, the Warner staffers were still a little terrified of the British punk rockers. If they had peed on the desks at A&M, what mementos would they try to leave in the Warner Bros. offices? When advertising executive Shelley Cooper was given an invitation to join the band at a Moroccan restaurant that encouraged diners to eat with their hands as actual Moroccans did, she made plans to be as far away as possible. Imagine the food fight the Pistols would start in a place where they were *allowed* to touch their food! But Regehr was having none of it. Just don't wear your good clothes, he suggested. Cooper appeared as requested, only to be surprised at how well-mannered the punks turned out to be. And not just once. Invited to a lunch for the group not long after that, she was surprised when Rotten arrived with his aged mum in tow. And as finance executive David Berman recalls, there was nothing rotten about the lad born John Lydon when his mother was about. "She was a sweet old lady, and he was very nice," he says.*

The Pistols were about to set off on their first American tour to promote their debut record, *Never Mind the Bollocks . . . Here's the Sex Pistols*, but the performances in mostly small, rural cities turned into a disaster that set bassist Sid Vicious and his girlfriend Nancy Spungen on a heroin-

---

* The only member of their party who misbehaved turned out to be Cooper's aunt's mother-in-law, who had a few too many drinks and decided that splashing through the fountain outside the restaurant would be a most excellent goof.

addicted spiral that would lead to both their deaths. The only Sex Pistols record Warner Bros. Records ever released was the soundtrack to the group's quasi-documentary, *The Great Rock 'n' Roll Swindle*, made up almost entirely of leftovers, live recordings, and tracks recorded after Rotten had quit the group.

○

If they'd been late on the Sex Pistols, the A&R crew in Burbank had, save for Joe Smith's landing Television for Elektra, entirely missed the new wave acts coming together at CBGB in New York and the dance music booming out of the clubs farther uptown. That was Seymour Stein's world, the focus of his Sire Records, an old-style NYC indie he'd packed with the likes of punk godfathers the Ramones, Cleveland's the Dead Boys, and the art school visionaries Talking Heads, who were already on their way to defining the new wave music of the late 1970s and early '80s. Stein and his partner, Richard Gottehrer, an accomplished songwriter and producer, had everything going for them, but they faced a familiar conundrum: they had the music but no reliable way to get it out into the world. Stein struck a distribution deal with Ostin in 1977 and liked the corporate money enough to sell his company outright to Warner a year later. At which point, Warner Bros. Records, by the grace of Stein, stepped into the fore of the latest revolution in sound.

It was the same move that Seven Arts executives had performed with Atlantic Records in 1967, expanding Warner's grasp of the music market by buying another company lock, stock, and artist roster. Given the vast machinery of the WEA distribution network, arguably the most powerful marketing system in the world, Warner became a hub for a growing galaxy of smaller labels, each expanding the company's reach to cities and scenes no individual company could ever have hoped to cover. And so, they came to Burbank from all over: the Georgia-based Capricorn Records, home to the Allman Brothers Band, the Marshall Tucker Band, and a handful of other Southern rock acts; England's Chrysalis Records, the UK home of Jethro Tull and guitarist/vocalist Robin Trower; the Bearsville label founded by Bob Dylan/Peter, Paul and Mary manager Albert Grossman, which offered up Todd Rundgren, Foghat, and the NRBQ; and Chris Blackwell's Island Records, known primarily as the home of Bob Marley,

Toots and the Maytals, and other reggae acts from Jamaica. Those and more came, each covering a genre, subgenre, and geographic region not within range of the ears in Burbank. Casablanca Records, founded in 1973 by Neil Bogart, brought a newer wave of artists onto the Warner books. Bogart had worked the New York City nightclubs for Casablanca to find acts that came to include the cartoon rockers KISS, disco superstar Donna Summer, and the gay icons the Village People, who would break into the mainstream with smash singles "Macho Man" and "YMCA."

The distribution and buyout deals proved spectacularly profitable for Warner, and provided more evidence of how the global WEA network, with all its many arms, branches, and tentacles, could keep the money gushing in from dozens of directions at once. But they could also lead to some strange relationships, as when Ostin did a deal with the young A&R executive/producer/record company owner Mike Curb, who was in many ways the opposite of everything Ostin and Warner Bros. Records had ever wanted to be.

Clean-cut and politically conservative, Curb made his breakthrough as a college freshman by writing a jingle the Honda motorcycle company used in a splashy ad campaign. Dropping out of school, he busied himself writing scores for B movies (e.g., *The Born Losers*) and then started a small record company he merged in 1969 with MGM Records, becoming the merged labels' president. One of his first moves was to cleanse the company of artists that appeared to him to be drug takers, including the Velvet Underground and Frank Zappa's Mothers of Invention, though the latter group was led by a staunch opponent of drugs who routinely fired musicians he saw puffing on a joint.* The stunt brought Curb to the attention of Richard Nixon, and Curb wrote "Nixon Now (More Than Ever)" for the president's 1972 reelection campaign.

Eventually, Curb started a self-titled label he stocked with what Stan Cornyn described in his memoir as "Mormon hitmakers, singers without facial hair [and] thin kids who caused shivers on teen-magazine covers sold in towns with feed-and-seed stores." Curb had the Osmond family, a tableau of mustaches called Exile, the pop-country Bellamy Brothers,

---

* Fun fact: MGM artist Eric Burdon, late of the Animals, was a very public advocate of psychedelic drugs, but he also sold a lot of records, so Curb made an exception for the leaping, overfed, pinwheel-eyed gnome.

blond heartthrob Shaun Cassidy (younger half brother of dark-haired heartthrob David Cassidy, late of the *Partridge Family* sitcom), and Debby Boone, a young woman with a pop music pedigree like no one else.

All cultural differences aside, Ostin knew about Curb's abilities as an A&R man and hitmaker, and in 1975 he struck a deal to distribute Curb Records through Warner Bros. The deal paid off almost immediately, with No. 1 singles from the country-rock act the Bellamy Brothers and the reinvigorated early 1960s hitmakers the Four Seasons, whose chart-topping "December 1963 (Oh What a Night)" turned out to be one of the biggest hits of the group's long career. None of it was particularly on-brand for a company that many still considered the hippest and most artistically progressive of the major record companies. But everyone knew the benefit of keeping the cash flowing, if only because it helped subsidize the acts that made the great albums that didn't stand much of a chance with mainstream record buyers. Then came "You Light Up My Life."

The tune was direct and plaintive, a declaration of love from a once-lonely woman for a man who gives her hope and helps her carry on and a lot of other familiar love song tropes that seemed especially obvious and annoying, particularly given the singer's background. Previewed at one of the regular new-release meetings in early 1977, "You Light Up My Life" caused a resounding uproar. *Holy shit*, the executives in the room cried. *Are you fucking kidding me?* When it turned out that the singer, Debby Boone, was the daughter of Pat Boone, the baby-faced vision of country club society who had built a following in the late 1950s by recording watered-down versions of songs by Little Richard, Fats Domino, and other rhythm-and-blues artists, the room nearly choked on its indignation. Pop was pop, and it had its place. But "You Light Up My Life" was *bad* pop with a politically retrograde heritage. They'd released a lot of mediocre and even bad records before, but for fuck's sake, this was an *embarrassment*.

All heads swiveled to Ostin, who sat silent and unflappable through the whole kerfuffle, tapping the end of his pen against the table. *Tap-tap-tap.* This was his usual, if unconscious, signal that the time had come for everyone to stop talking, please. Silence achieved, he shrugged. "I don't know what's so wrong with this song," he said. "It's catchy, it's nice. I think this could sell." *WHAT!?* Now they were all yelling at Ostin, asking if he'd cleaned his ears lately because the song *sucked*—all the things you could never tell *your* boss but definitely could shout at Mo Ostin because he never wanted anyone to tell him what they thought he wanted to hear. Finally, one promotions guy threw up his hands and said, *Okay, fine. I'll service a couple radio stations on it, but no more. I've got a reputation to protect. Let's just get this over with.* Then the strangest thing happened. "You Light Up My Life" not only caught on, but became the biggest hit single in the history of the *Billboard* Hot 100, sticking at No. 1 for ten weeks and selling more than a million copies.

You had to give Ostin credit. For a guy who'd come up through the business side of the company, he could spot a record whose potential evaded every other set of ears. Whether "You Light Up My Life" also represented the ultimate contradiction of his edict to make good records rather than just hit records is another question. But then, he'd said that in 1967, when dreams were so much dreamier and the financial stakes not nearly as high. Times had changed, and would soon change even more, in an increasingly unhip way.

○

One morning in the fall of 1979, Adam Somers, lately elevated to Warner Bros. Records' director of merchandising and national director of operations,* came into work and found a note on his desk: report to Stan Cornyn's office immediately. Finding his boss looking hassled at his desk, Somers took Cornyn's invitation to sit down and steeled himself for what came next. "Fire ten percent of your people. Then cut five percent of your budget and get the memo on my desk by the end of the day." That was the end of the meeting. Somers went back to his office, pulled out his list of the staffers who reported to him, and commenced with the dreadful task. "It'd be guys in warehouses who'd been there for fifteen years," he says. "And you'd have to fire executives and not just secretaries, because you needed someone to do the work. So, it would get ugly, and you'd end up with blood up to your elbows. But the numbers boys in New York just wanted the number."[1]

---

* A sweeping administrative post that put him in charge of the company's payroll, administration, and warehouses and gave him responsibility for the care and management of the company's buildings around the country—all duties Cornyn had earned when he was named a vice president in 1970. While thrilled to be a VP, Cornyn had zero interest in such prosaic tasks and handed them immediately to Somers.

For more than a decade, the numbers on the Warner Bros. Records ledgers had done nothing but get larger and larger, leaving Ross's financial officers without much to complain about. Yes, they always asked whether Ostin and his compadres might save a few shekels here or there, and yes, they demanded the richest possible projections for the next year in order to escalate Warner Communications Inc.'s stock price. Ertegun, with his aristocratic sangfroid set on stun, had always given a variation on the same forecast every year. *We're going to put out a bunch of records, and some of them will be hits and some of them won't, and we'll see how it goes.* The numbers guys didn't like this answer, but for a long time they lived with it—until 1979.

The surprising thing was that the year prior had been breathtaking. The company celebrated its twentieth anniversary in 1978; it also mourned the death of its founder, Jack Warner. Yet, at the time of his death, Warner's fantastical charge to founding president Jim Conkling—that he eclipse the industry's twin towers, Columbia and Capitol—had come true and then some. In 1978, every day seemed to bring a new platinum-selling album, except for the days that produced multi-platinum sellers. Established acts, including the Rolling Stones, solo Eagle Joe Walsh, Linda Ronstadt, Neil Young, and Rod Stewart, among many other WBR-related artists, moved more than a million copies of their latest records, as did new discoveries Van Halen, Dire Straits, the Cars, Blondie, and the Dostoyevskian singer-songwriter Warren Zevon. Blockbusters released in previous years, including Fleetwood Mac's *Rumours*, the Eagles' hits compilation, and *Hotel California,* added a few million more to their sales tallies. The other record companies were doing just as well, A&M raking in mountains with Peter Frampton's mega-platinum breakthrough concert album, *Frampton Comes Alive*, while RSO Records' Bee Gees–dominated soundtrack to the hit movie *Saturday Night Fever* passed the ten-million mark and kept right on going, powered by four No. 1 singles and a handful of other Top 20 hits.

Riches don't come much more embarrassing than that, and with the clatter of the cash registers and the zoom of the private jets and the popping of champagne corks, it was difficult to imagine the money train ever slowing down, let alone flying off the rails. But that was before the global economy slipped into a ditch in 1979, caused in part by the Islamic Revolution in Iran, which choked off the oil supply. From there, the dominos tumbled: inflation sped up, and spending slowed everywhere, including in the record business.

Nothing goes on forever, particularly the kind of market growth the record industry, and particularly Warner Bros. Records, had been riding for more than a decade. The company's expenses had grown at nearly the same pace as its profits, and what had once been a two-hundred-person staff now numbered two thousand. The top executives had been riding the Wiki Bird to and fro, while budgets for every department had grown on an annual basis because, what with all the cash flooding into the building day in and out, it didn't make any sense *not* to spend more. It had never been a problem, not as long as business kept thundering along.

But now business was sputtering. New releases, even from the super-star likes of George Harrison and Fleetwood Mac,* didn't sell nearly as well as anticipated. Unsold vinyl avalanched back into the warehouses, most for contractually guaranteed full refunds. The fall 1979 meeting where Ostin and his top lieutenants sat down with Ross and his finance people didn't include nearly as much backslapping and calls for champagne as in the previous year, or any year over the last decade. Ostin insisted they stay the course, investing in the artists and promoting their work with all the oomph they could muster. *And did you notice how many Grammys we won this year?* The Doobie Brothers got Song of the Year for "What a Fool Believes" and the Best Pop Vocal Performance by a Duo, Group, or Chorus for the *Minute by Minute* album; Donna Summer won for Best Pop Vocal Performance by a Female; Rickie Lee Jones got Best New Artist, and . . .

Ross nodded at first. Yes, very impressive. Then he tapped the big book of numbers in front of him on the conference table. It wouldn't be long before the story within regained its cheerful narrative, but as Ross explained so succinctly, there could be no happy ending until the numbers said so.

"The name of the game, Mo, is performance."

---

* Whose *Rumours* follow-up, *Tusk*, was a largely experimental double-album set that, while sell-ing three million copies, fell short of expectations.

## JUST GO DO

R egehr looks a little hazy at first, his eyes dull, hair rumpled, an unlit cigarette shifting from one hand to the other. He's sitting on the sofa in his office in Burbank, but he has just flown back from a stay in New York City, where he'd been moving full tilt from his first morning meeting to the final encore of the concert he caught at the Palladium. God only knows what happened after that. Regehr's brain spins too fast to let him sleep more than a few hours a night, and when everyone else drowses, he keeps right on going, sometimes playing, sometimes working, sometimes ploughing through novels or whatever else catches his attention. By 1981, when the Canadian music channel MuchMusic corralled him for an on-camera interview, Regehr had transcended his role as the director of publicity in so many ways that it was hard to say what part of Warner Bros. Records his expertise *hadn't* touched.

The interviewer lets Regehr sleepwalk through the background stuff, how he came to the company, what he'd done so far. But when the questions turn to the current state of the business, and where it might be headed in the 1980s, the executive's eyes come into focus. And as he continues talking, the modern viewer comes to understand that by the spring of 1981, Regehr had already identified some of the most significant technical and artistic forces of the coming decade. Music videos were going to be huge, he promised, and you could already see them on the growing number of video shows being broadcast on local channels. He also had a recommendation to offer: the "nice little band" he'd seen at the Palladium just the other day. "They're called U2. The oldest kid is like nineteen years old." But they had great songs and a passion for the stage he hadn't seen in years. "They were totally unknown in New York, playing to two thousand people, a tough audience. But they got two encores. And one of them was a song they'd played earlier that they said they could play better." Which they did, to the thunderous cheers of the now thoroughly convinced audience. Soon, U2, whose label, Island Records, was distributed by Warner Bros. Records, would be among the most successful video artists, too.

Three years earlier, promotions director Russ Thyret came to Lenny Waronker with a three-song demo from a teenage musician he'd met through a friend of a friend in Minneapolis. The kid, a petite singer-songwriter/multi-instrumentalist, who played and sang every note of the songs he also produced, impressed Waronker and everyone else who heard the tape—so much so that Warner's campaign to sign him resulted in a contract that included more concessions than they'd ever given an untested artist, let alone a teenage one. It was just as unprecedented as Prince turned out to be, and though he would always be a challenging personality—in the early 1990s he would respond to a contract disagreement by changing his name to an unpronounceable symbol and writing "Slave" on his face—it was one of the most profitable deals they ever signed.

Prince was one of several artists who joined Warner Bros. just before the 1979 downturn who would help rocket the company back to stratospheric success in the early 1980s. Another was Christopher Cross, whom Ostin's son Michael had discovered in 1978. Hired on as a junior A&R scout after graduating college a year earlier, Michael Ostin was digging through boxes of unsolicited demos and came up with a tape by the Texas singer-songwriter with an appealingly feathery voice and an album's worth of songs that would feature some of the biggest pop hits of the early 1980s.

Business was booming again, and the vision Ostin had described in 1967, of a major league record company that could both support the work of great artists and make great profits in a creative, collegial atmosphere, had come true. Warner Bros. Records had outlived the sixties and the Age of Aquarius, gained strength into the mid-seventies, led the way through the mega-platinum years, and despite the horrors of the 1979 recession had managed to turn the corner into the eighties with the purring grace of an Italian roadster.

The core of executives Ostin had gathered around him remained almost entirely in place, working together easily even as they fought the predictable battles over competing ideas, strategies, and turf. They'd made their concessions to the changes around them, not just in popular taste but also in their own ways and means, paying more attention to artists' sales and potential for future revenue and, in the wake of 1979, being more, shall we say, *realistic* about expenses and promotional budgets. "I think it's inevitable that the label got more sleek and corporate,"[1] Russ Thyret says. Indeed, the company's gleefully subversive "weekly promotional device," *Circular*, had issued its final act of corporate wisecrackery in 1974, its place taken by the glossier monthly *Wax Paper*, whose wit hewed a more traditional promotional line. Stan Cornyn, meanwhile, took his leave of Creative Services for a post higher up the corporate chain, overseeing product launches, packaging, new formats, and anti-piracy efforts for the entire Warner Music Group. And yet, as Thyret adds, some things never changed much at all. "I can't even count the number of times when I walked into Mo's office and found him listening to new albums, track by track, making notes about everything that was released."[2]

It took nearly seven years for Mo Ostin to fill the presidential post Joe Smith left in 1975, but he'd had one candidate in his sights the entire time. When Ostin first brought up the idea back in the late 1970s, Lenny Waronker wondered if his boss had lost his mind. Waronker had built his life around making records. And all of it—the time he'd done exploring the other departments in his dad's record company, the summer he spent at the publishing company offices in New York plugging songs to other producers and A&R men, the executive meetings he'd observed—had fascinated him. But none of it rivaled the feeling he got working with musicians in the recording studio. And he was one of the best at it, too, creating a signature sound that stripped away everything that didn't spring directly from the emotion at the heart of the piece. Waronker didn't, and doesn't, know anything about the technical aspects of music and musicianship. "I'm not one of those guys who can walk into the studio and start calling out chords and notes or anything like that," he says.[3] He relied on Van Dyke Parks and then Russ Titelman to keep track of that stuff while he sat in the control room, often shutting his eyes and resting his head on the control board while he listened. When he raised his head, he'd be tuned in to the piece's spiritual core and homing in on how slowing it down a hair and adding a single oboe, or a banjo, or simply stripping away everything but the twelve-string strum, could draw the essential feeling to the surface.

Mo Ostin sensed that gift in Waronker the day he first talked to him in 1965. But Ostin was just as impressed by the clarity of the young man's gaze. Waronker said what he thought, with no apologies or attempt to spin it into something he thought you'd prefer to hear. "He was incredibly honorable," Ostin says. "He could recognize artists, and he could recognize quality." And more important: "He *believed* in quality."[4] As they both ascended in the company, the two drew even closer. Ostin depended on Waronker to find the artists who expressed the artistic and cultural ideals he wanted Warner/Reprise to animate. And he made a point of bumping the producer up the company ladder, first by appointing him chief of the A&R department, then making him a vice president, then elevating him to executive vice president, the top tier of his executives. For Ostin, the thing that made Waronker such a crucial executive was that, along with all his strengths as a thinker and leader, he had the spirit of an artist. But if Waronker was a romantic at heart, he also had the brain of a realist. He wouldn't sell out an artist's creativity to squeeze more profit out of her. But he had the rare ability to put the opposing forces of music and commerce into equilibrium. And though he never required an artist to adopt any of his suggestions, he understood artists well enough to know that virtually all of them were eager to connect with an audience. So, if Waronker, one of the most successful producers in the industry, had an idea for them, they paid attention.

Ostin had left the Warner Bros. Records president's office vacant since 1975 for a reason. Stan Cornyn and Eddie Rosenblatt, worthy candidates both, couldn't have known what was on his mind, and he let them down as easily as he could. He wasn't rejecting them, he told them, as much as trying to figure out what the job should be. Ostin could handle all the administrative duties himself; it didn't make sense to bring in someone to duplicate what he could already do. What he needed, Ostin figured, was a partner who knew the creative side of the business, someone who understood good music and knew how it was, and wasn't, made.

Ostin had always known it would be Waronker. But he didn't tell him that for a while and when he did Waronker couldn't imagine how it could work. As far as he could see, he had no qualifications, or even interest, in business. Ostin disagreed. "Lenny's always underestimating his ability," he says. "He's one of those guys who thinks less of himself than he should."[5] Still, Ostin didn't push. A year went by. Then another. And then, one day at lunch, Waronker started musing. *What if there were a place for a creative executive?* he asked. *Someone in the top ranks who could represent the artists' side of the company?*

Ostin nodded. "That," he said, "would be a great job for you."

Waronker didn't disagree. Plus, he'd started to burn out on making records; working with Russ Titelman on a new album for Paul Simon, one of Waronker's favorite artists on Warner's or anyone's roster, he kept catching himself glancing at the clock, wishing it was time to go home. It was really time, he realized, for him to find something else to do.

A day or two later, he poked his head through Ostin's door. *I think I'd like to try that creative executive job*, he said. Ostin's eyes sparkled. *Terrific!* Waronker nodded, took a few steps down the hall, then did a quick one-eighty back to Ostin's doorway. Did the job have a title?

Ostin, without looking up from the papers on his desk, nodded. "President."

Now Waronker stepped into Ostin's office. *We'd better have a meeting tomorrow*, he said.

Ostin shrugged. *Sure.*

After a restless night of wondering how he could possibly pull off the impossible job he'd foolishly agreed to take, Waronker got into the office the next morning and went straight to the supply room to gather what he'd need to track all the crucial information Ostin was about to give him. He left loaded down with multiple yellow legal pads, a couple of ballpoint pens, a rainbow of colored felt pens, manila folders and hanging files, nearly enough gear to open his own OfficeMax. But, my God, the *immensity* of what he needed to learn: the intricacies of cash flow and budgeting; of supply chains, product distribution; all that shit they put into the contracts that Waronker never bothered to read. And now he had to learn it all, quickly, and do his best to master it before anyone had a chance to figure out how incompetent he was. *Fuck!*

When the time arrived Waronker padded into Ostin's office with his armload, taking a moment to organize it all on his side of the chairman's desk, and then looked up expectantly, waiting for what he knew would be a lengthy disquisition, one that would certainly take up the morning and probably run through lunch and deep into the afternoon. Instead, he got those three encouraging but maddeningly indistinct words.

*Just go do.*

Waronker could only take Ostin at his word, that he should just continue doing what he'd been doing as an executive president, focusing on the artists and the music. So, that's what he'd do, with one significant difference from his predecessor: he wanted a grand piano installed at the center of the room. Not for him, of course; Waronker didn't play. But a lot of his visitors would. And everyone else who entered his presidential lair would immediately understand one thing for sure: Warner Bros. Records, above everything else, was in the business of making music.

Art and commerce, hand in hand—it was the keystone of both Ostin's business philosophy and his company's years of success. And if you needed a visual metaphor to see what that looked like, all you had to do was glimpse the two of them together, Warner Bros. Records' chairman and his chief A&R man. As the years passed, they were all but inseparable, Mo and Lenny, Lenny and Mo. Can't find one? Look for the other, and chances are you'll find your quarry. And if you found them together anytime over the next dozen years, you'd be looking at the most admired and successful pair of record company chiefs in the music industry.

The friendly integration of music and business at Warner had always paid steep dividends for the company. Rather than sequester the non-music executives from their counterparts on the creative team, Ostin regularly encouraged them to get to know one another. He wanted each side to understand what the other did, how they did it, and why it was so important to the company. He expected all the executives to go to concerts, including acts that had nothing to do with Warner Bros., to keep current on their artists and the pop music scene in general.

Ostin's philosophy on the role of his executives set Warner Bros. apart from other record companies, and set the company up for success decade after decade. You could see the difference in Regehr's easy expertise as a pop music prognosticator in that 1980 interview. And one of the most crucial signings in WBR's history came through the company's promotions chief, Russ Thyret, after a chance meeting with a Minnesota advertising executive.

Thyret had been visiting a branch office in Minneapolis when regional exec Cliff Siegel introduced him to Owen Husney, a musician turned adman who did a little artist managing on the side. Not long afterward, Husney met Prince Nelson, a recent high school graduate so overflowing with talent and desire that he taught himself to play every instrument in a funk or rock band with something like virtuosic skill. Nelson could also compose and arrange pop songs and then produce recordings of himself playing and singing every part. Husney took Nelson on as a client, and when he was ready to make a play in Los Angeles, he took the youngster to Thyret in Burbank.

Thyret, who'd been listening to Warner's bands and their demos for years, could hear how special Nelson's three-song tape was, and quickly handed it off to Waronker. The A&R chief could hear the magic, too. The songs weren't just funky but also pop-friendly and cleanly produced. The instrumentation was just as striking: the guy used keyboards like horns and could do things with his guitar that Waronker hadn't heard since Jimi Hendrix died. Every other set of ears in the A&R offices heard it, too, so from that point, signing Nelson became the company's top priority. So, when Nelson and Husney demanded that Nelson be allowed to produce his own records, and that the company be required to release at least three of his albums regardless of how well their predecessors sold, Waronker took the offer to David Berman, who had already heard the intensity of the A&R team's excitement in their most recent weekly meeting and accepted the terms with few questions.

The only holdup came from Waronker, who wanted to make sure the teenager was as capable of producing sessions in a professional studio as he was in the smaller setup he'd used to record his demo tape. He booked some time at a nearby studio, told Husney and Nelson what he wanted to see, and corralled a few other A&R executives to listen in. Russ Titelman consulted briefly on the drum sound, then joined the others in the control room to see what would happen next—which was that the leonine young musician laid down a perfect drum part in one take. Leaving his sticks on the floor, he picked up the bass, called for the tape to roll, and once it did, he locked in with his drum track to form a tight one-man rhythm section. When he got to the end, he picked up a guitar to play *that* part, but Waronker hit the Talk button in the control room and called him off. "Okay, okay, I've seen enough," he said. "You're the producer." The entire session had taken less than fifteen minutes.

The first album, *For You*, credited simply to Prince, came out in the spring of 1978 and sold about 175,000 copies during its initial run, establishing the newcomer with its lead single, "Soft and Wet," which climbed to No. 12 on the R&B charts. The 1979 follow-up, *Prince*, did even better, hitting No. 3 on the R&B album charts and No. 22 on the pop list while launching the single "I Wanna Be Your Lover" to No. 11 on the pop charts and No. 1 on the R&B chart. The album sold more than five hundred thousand copies, enough to earn gold status during its initial run, making Prince one of the hotter rising acts in soul music. But Prince wasn't satisfied being just a soul star. His third album, the last of the three he had insisted he be guaranteed to make, abandoned the gloss of mainstream R&B for the wilder world of his own imagination. It was called *Dirty Mind*, and every part of it lived up to its title. The cover featured the artist in full androgynous regalia, clad only in bikini briefs, a bandana knotted loosely around his neck, and a studded trench coat. Recorded in a comparatively stripped-down, rocked-up style, the album boasted suggestive titles, including "Head," "Sister," and the title track, which only hinted at the transgressive notions the songs contained.

*Dirty Mind* didn't sell as well as its predecessor, but it did establish Prince as a revolutionary artist whose extraordinary musical chops were matched by his creative daring. *Rolling Stone* published a full-throated rave by critic Ken Tucker, who described the album as "a pop record of Rabelaisian achievement . . . *Dirty Mind* jolts with the unsettling tension that arises from rubbing complex erotic wordplay against clean, simple melodies." A few months after its release, Mick Jagger invited Prince to open the Rolling Stones' two stadium shows in Los Angeles. Ever since they booked Ike and Tina Turner for their 1969 tour, the Stones had made a practice of using the opening slots at their shows to showcase musicians they admired, but this time their mainstream rock crowd threw a fit at Prince's sexily avant-garde act, chasing him from the stage with a hail of bottles and roars of racist, homophobic displeasure. Still, Jagger urged Prince to shake off his impulse to not play the second show, recalling how many times his band had suffered just as much resistance during its early years. Prince followed Jagger's advice, and it would take only a year for his 1982 single, "Little Red Corvette," to hit No. 6 on the *Billboard* pop charts, lifting its creator on his way to bigger things.

◉

Regehr's confidence in the future of music videos, long before MTV would air its first video in August 1981, was based on something more than a lucky guess. The nascent cable network was owned in part by corporate parent Warner Communications. Regehr had also approved the launch of an in-house video production unit that, like Van Dyke Parks's audio and visual services department in late 1970, set out to develop new ways to spread and promote the work of WBR artists. This time the energy center for Warner's video projects was Georgia "Jo" Bergman, a young but deeply experienced staffer who had started her career as a teenager in 1963 when she stumbled into a job with Brian Epstein's NEMS Enterprises, just as the Beatles were becoming something more than a regional pop band. From there, the California-born Bergman moved to jobs with Marianne Faithfull and Faithfull's boyfriend Mick Jagger, who put Bergman in charge of the Rolling Stones' London offices, where she remained through the band's 1972 tour of America.

Along with everything else she did for the band, Bergman helped the Stones make promotional films for their songs, and it didn't take long for her to get Regehr fired up about making videos for Warner's bands. Some of the films she'd produced for Jagger and company were straightforward performance pieces, but the psychedelic era brought forth a wave of more artful, often surrealist films that gave other visual form to the songs. Some videos were as striking and beautiful as the music itself. As with so many things in the sixties, the catalyst came from the Beatles, whose 1964 film *A Hard Day's Night* was built around staged performances and tightly shot narrative sequences that would soon be followed by promotional films full of surrealistic washes of color, backward action, and other psychedelic touches. The Stones were half a step behind, but when the Beatles split in 1970, the other band continued creating the mini-films. Few were memorable, but they were cheap to make and brought their music to fans and TV watchers all around the world.

Bergman spent most of the seventies at Warner working with Carl Scott on Artist Development projects, setting up concert tours and other career-building projects for the company's acts. But as the new decade approached, she focused more attention on the music video producers and broadcast outlets sprouting up around the nation and the world. Rod Stewart was the sole WBR artist who consistently made videos for his records. And though they were flimsily made and often downright silly, they were broadcast across the world at nearly no expense to the company. But they sure kept the records moving, driving sales in distant corners of the planet that Stewart hadn't visited in years, or maybe ever.

The potential for music videos had, like so many good ideas, occurred to more than a few people. Monkee guitarist/actor turned country-rock singer-songwriter and media innovator Mike Nesmith experimented with the form in *PopClips*, a music video program co-produced by Elektra Records founder Jac Holzman, who had been exploring media opportunities for Warner since the early seventies. *PopClips* debuted on the Nickelodeon cable network in early 1980 and made such a splash that Warner Cable offered to buy the show outright, then set to adapting the concept into a twenty-four-hour-a-day cable network they would eventually call MTV, with former Movie Channel president Bob Pittman taking the lead. Nesmith, meanwhile, developed an hour-long special he called *Elephant Parts*, which combined music performances with skits, fake advertisements, and other amusing bits and bobs. Holzman co-produced the program, which came to market as a VHS tape and video disc in 1981, sold well, and was eventually awarded the first-ever Video of the Year Grammy in 1982.*

Bergman expanded her video work with Fleetwood Mac's 1979 release, *Tusk*, the follow-up to the mega-million-selling *Rumours*, starting with a video for the new album's title track, a mini-epic featuring the group and the fully garbed USC marching band playing the song in Dodger Stadium. A stage performance of Stevie Nicks's ballad "Sara" followed, taken from a long-form concert video that Bergman released to the market in 1980. Successful artistically and commercially, the Fleetwood Mac projects led to more videos for Warner's acts. When MTV, co-owned by Warner Communications and American Express, premiered on August 1, 1981, the very first video aired was by a British duo called the Buggles, a Warner Bros. Records act whose "Video Killed the Radio Star" became something like a theme song for the next epoch of popular music.

Oh, but that song title. It sounded so sinister, particularly once MTV began its rapid ascent into the definitive pop music platform of the 1980s. Maybe this really was the end of popular music as we knew it. Maybe now the musicians would be shunted aside for a new wave of pretty pop-bots who looked good jumping around and shaking their hair to and fro, but who had no idea how to form a G chord, let alone where to put the bomp-ah-bomp-ah-bomp. And some of that did come true. You could moss out in front of MTV for hours at a time and be assaulted with an endless procession of haircuts, eyeliner, dancers, and spandex. A lot of the new stars were every bit as tuneless and dull-eyed as anyone feared. But when *isn't* that the case in pop music?†

As it turned out, some of the definitive musicians of the next two decades turned out to be brilliant video artists, too. One of them was U2, that thrilling baby band that had fired Bob Regehr's faith at the New York Palladium in spring 1981. Another was Prince, whose musicianship rivaled that of any popular artist of the twentieth century. And another

* Which makes him exactly 50 percent of all the award's recipients, given that in 1984 the Academy of Music Arts replaced the category with one designated for "Best Music Video."

† Consider WBR's first signee, Tab Hunter, the spectacularly handsome actor who, even by his own admission, had approximately none of what it took to be a good or competent or even passable singer. His fans sure did buy his records, though, at least for a little while.

was a willful young woman from Detroit who had already taken the New York dance clubs by storm and had no intention of stopping there.

Unfortunately, Regehr wouldn't be alive to see either of their greatest successes. After having moved to the New York office in 1983, he was diagnosed with a gruesome form of cancer on one side of his jaw. The doctors removed part of his jaw to treat it, but when the disease struck the other half of his jaw a few months later, and he realized that further surgery would end his ability to speak, he decided to end treatment. He died in the spring of 1984. "We miss him now," the company's official obituary said; "we will always miss him."

●

As it had in the first half of the 1970s, the Warner Bros. Records' artist roster of the early to mid-1980s included a significant percentage of the moment's most popular and influential musical artists. True to form, the list spanned the pop horizon to include Van Halen, Rod Stewart, pop-jazz guitarist George Benson, and soul singer Chaka Khan; artier acts like Rickie Lee Jones, Bonnie Raitt, Ry Cooder, and King Crimson; and popular yet substantive ones like Fleetwood Mac, Devo, Paul Simon, and Prince. The company's ongoing success, along with its reputation for supporting its artists, made it a popular destination for veteran bands, with the top-rank likes of the Who and Simon and Garfunkel and others moving their operations to Burbank. The company's affiliated labels, including wholly owned subsidiaries such as Elektra, Asylum, and David Geffen's self-named label, added to the riches with definitive acts that included John Lennon, Elton John, Queen, Jackson Browne, and the Eagles.

But when it came to the cutting-edge acts, the ones that would define the next decade or two or three, most of those were now joining the company through Sire Records and its mercurial president, Seymour Stein. A longtime record man who learned the business in the rough-and-tumble world of New York's indie labels, Stein had a knack for finding the next big thing, and not just because he could party his way through so many of New York's bars and showrooms in the course of a night. He also had an ear for the edgier, more explosive stuff that echoed his own full-volume pursuit of life. After finding the punk rock prototypes the Ramones in

1975, Stein had become a regular at CBGB, the Lower East Side bar that was the cradle of New York's progressive rock 'n' roll scene. All bug eyes and high-speed raps, he could barely articulate the difference between a great artist and a decent-but-unmemorable one, but it didn't matter. He did even better after joining the Warner Bros. organization in 1977, signing the art college band Talking Heads, the London-based rock band the Pretenders, and more. Soon Stein snapped up British rockers the Smiths, the Minnesota neopunks the Replacements, Depeche Mode, and others.

Then there was a signing of a different sort: that wildly ambitious woman from Detroit whose dance tracks were shaking up the clubs in New York. Her name was Madonna Ciccone, and in 1982 Stein got her name on a contract, too.

All Stein's artists became part of the Warner Bros. Records empire, which had been designed in large part to help offbeat artists of their caliber become something like superstars. The Warner system was churning away, so prepared to transform talent and inspiration into sales that Madonna's self-titled debut album, released in mid-1983, jumped into the Top 10, selling nearly three million copies during its first year.

But the company's fast recovery from the 1979 sales slump didn't make it immune to the next economic plague. And despite Madonna's success in 1983, Warner Bros. Records suffered its first truly bad year. It couldn't have come at a worse time for Warner Communications. Steve Ross had invested in the Atari video game company in 1976, back when the rudimentary video ping-pong game *Pong* reigned over the entire toy and game sector. Ross bought the company just as its designers were developing smash games that included *Pac-Man*, *Asteroids*, and *Atari Football*, all of which were enormously popular in arcades and then found even greater success as cartridges for home gaming systems, which sold in fantastic quantities, too. Starting in 1977, Warner's gaming division earned about 40 percent of what the Warner Record Group, including Atlantic, Elektra, and all the related music companies, brought into the company. Both divisions' numbers ticked up in 1978 and 1979, but Atari outpaced them each year, and by 1980 it was outearning the record companies by half a billion dollars. Ross and everyone else in top management couldn't believe their luck. By the end of 1982, the game company's skyrocketing sales jacked up Warner Communications' stock price by *300* percent compared to five years earlier, and its prospects seemed limitless.

But by the Christmas season of 1982, the Atari games seemed to lose their tang. Then, in 1983, the bottom fell out of the video game market—or, more specifically, out of Atari's piece of the market—and just when the dire effects of the 1981–82 recession, including more than 8 percent unemployment, leveled consumer spending. Warner Communications Inc. earnings tanked, and took WCI's stock price down the chute with them, triggering a financial crisis that sent the corporation reeling. There could not have been a worse time for the company's cash cow to go dry, but that's exactly what happened. And though the same slump hit every record company in 1983, Warner Bros. once again led the way, having its first money-losing year since before Bob Newhart came strolling into that Chicago warehouse. Only a tiny scattering of Warner's releases in 1983 cracked the *Billboard* charts' Top 10. Paul Simon's *Hearts and Bones*, no longer the long-awaited Simon and Garfunkel reunion it had been teased as, stalled at No. 35. The Doobie Brothers' *Farewell Tour* live album was the group's first in a dozen years not to earn gold or platinum status, barely cracking the Top 80 at No. 79. Even Rod Stewart, an evergreen pop artist if ever there was one, couldn't crack the Top 30 with his *Body Wishes* album. And that was just the top rank of the artists who released records that year; it only got worse from there.

With the Warner Communications Inc. stock price burrowing toward China, Rupert Murdoch, the media baron from Australia, plotted a hostile takeover, which forced Ross to hustle up additional financing to hang on to his company. Ross did his best to keep his record company presidents from panicking and, perhaps, stampeding for other companies. "Let me worry about the stock market," he said. "Just keep doing what you do."[6] But budget cuts came quickly, and deeply. There were steep layoffs across all departments, and they had to do the one thing they hated most: drop artists from the roster. After so many years of standing by artists whose sales didn't match their musical achievements, the time had come for the company to grit its teeth and let the Grim Reaper do his business.

It was gruesome. Thirty acts were shot down, including some who had been at the company more than long enough to be family. Bonnie Raitt, the beloved blues singer and guitarist, tasted the knife after twelve years of richly celebrated, if not mass-selling, work for the company. To add insult to injury, she got the news the day after finishing her new album, with an extensive tour booked and ready to start. Next was Van Morrison. He had been on the team for nearly fifteen years and sold many millions of records before his pace slowed. Then came Arlo Guthrie. The catalytic modern folkie behind "Alice's Restaurant" and the 1972 hit single "The City of New Orleans" went, too, despite Waronker's attachment to the musician and his many years of excellent work. Also cut were the promising multi-instrumentalist T Bone Burnett, the former Modern Lovers leader Jonathan Richman, and too many others. They were dark days, but they wouldn't last for long.

○

Prince wanted to make a movie. He had come up with a loosely autobiographical story and more than enough songs to make up a soundtrack. And, of course, he'd play the lead, not just because he figured he had all the looks, charisma, and talent to make it work, but also because he would essentially be playing himself in the guise of "The Kid," a talented young Minneapolis man fighting his way to his spotlit destiny. As movie pitches go, it was better than the one for *Car Wash*, but it still required a bailetic leap of faith. To that point, Prince's commercial high point had come with "Little Red Corvette." Who knew if he would even be able to hit No. 6 again? Nevertheless, Ostin supported the project, and though the executives at Warner Bros. Pictures at first shot it down as ridiculous—why would they want to bet millions of their dollars on a vanity project for some less-than-famous musician from out of frigid Minnesota?—Ostin dug in and eventually found a compromise. Prince's new manager, Bob Cavallo, would put up $1 million for production costs, and if the movie ran over budget, Ostin would use record company money to cover the difference. They shot the film for about $7 million, a drop in the bucket compared to most movie budgets, and its July 27, 1984, premiere came with only muted studio promotion.

But the movie didn't need studio promotion. The first single released from the soundtrack, "When Doves Cry," leaped to the top of the *Billboard* chart almost immediately in June, and its accompanying video, rich in sequences from the movie, played constantly on MTV through the first half of the summer. It was then joined by "Let's Go Crazy," another chart-topper with a video that also played as a trailer for the *Purple Rain* movie. Released on the heels of two No. 1 singles, the movie *Purple Rain* earned surprisingly good reviews en route to becoming one of the biggest hits of the summer, grossing $80 million at the box office. The soundtrack album did even better, dominating the top slot in the *Billboard* album chart for a full six months and selling nearly ten million copies in its first year. It also transformed Prince into a superstar, one of the three or four pop giants straddling the planet in the mid-eighties, alongside Michael Jackson, Bruce Springsteen, and Seymour Stein's New York dance music auteur Madonna.

If Prince had made a steady climb to superstardom, Madonna arrived there at a sprint. And she knew exactly where she was going from the moment she got started. When the aspiring performer had visited the Burbank offices for the first time in 1982, she made the rounds of executive offices, shaking hands, giving hugs, and doing everything in her considerable power to sparkle and charm every person she found into fully uniformed soldiers in the Madonna campaign for stardom. And she was great: full of bluster, smiles, and laughs. When she got to Bob Regehr's office and found him missing, she grabbed a piece of paper lying around and left a note pinned to the center of the bulletin board behind his desk. "Dear Bob," it read. "I'm sorry you missed me . . . I'm going to be a STAR." She was on to something. It took nearly six months for *Madonna*, her debut, to climb to No. 8 on the *Billboard* charts, dragged out of the doldrums by her first across-the-board hit single, "Lucky Star," which reached No. 4 on the Hot 100. From there the stage was set for 1985's *Like a Virgin*, which soared into diamond record status with sales of ten million. With that, she was right alongside Prince, Springsteen, and Jackson, and together they formed the Arthurian court of the 1980s. Just one year past the disaster of 1983, Warner Bros. Records was back on course for what would become the most successful decade in its history.

The watery numbers of 1983 were followed by a 51 percent jump in revenue for 1984. The next year was just as gilded, headlined by the former Creedence Clearwater Revival front man John Fogerty's celebrated No. 1 comeback album, *Centerfield*, which sold two million copies and reestablished the blue-collar rocker for the 1980s and beyond. Multi-platinum albums also came from veteran acts Dire Straits, ZZ Top, Van Halen, and Peter Gabriel, and 1986 was no letdown thanks to Madonna, whose *True Blue* fell just short of diamond status with nine million sold, and an array of hot-selling newer acts.

But the standout album of 1986 came from Paul Simon, the high-priced superstar whose first two albums for Warner had fallen well short of sales expectations. Feeling creatively adrift, Simon fell under the spell of South African pop music and decided to center his new album on the exotic rattletrap sounds that had lit up his imagination. Advanced tapes of the sessions struck some Warner executives as portents of another failure for the company's best-paid artist. On top of that, a number of the sessions were recorded in South Africa, a politically controversial move in the apartheid era. Yet even as doubts rose within the company, both Waronker and Ostin heard brilliance in the unique sound of the album, and backed Simon all the way. When *Graceland*, as Simon titled the album, was finished, Ostin called for an all-staff listening party, which he concluded with a rare speech to say how strongly he believed in the album, not just as art, but also as commercial pop music that would bend mainstream culture in its direction. And, again, Mo was right. *Graceland* sold five million copies and won Album of the Year honors at the 1987 Grammy Awards.

The hot streak wouldn't quit. Along with everything else, the increased popularity of compact discs, the latest technology in music formats, spurred a stampede of fans eager to retrofit their favorite albums to the shiny new format. Given Warner's twenty-year emphasis on artists with staying power, the rush of archival sales grew into another gusher of new profits. And it wasn't just the original albums, either. Thanks to the ongoing popularity of the company's landmark artists, the backlist of hit records could be sold in expanded versions with bonus tracks and enhanced packaging and as expansive multi-disc box sets, often at premium prices.

Even as their catalogues sold in record numbers, many of the legacy artists continued making new and often wonderful records. In 1987, George Harrison produced his biggest hit for Warners with *Cloud Nine*, an acclaimed million-seller that led to even more hit music when he gathered a few friends to help record a bonus track for the B-side of a European single. The song, a group-written tune called "Handle with Care," turned out so well that Harrison and his pals Bob Dylan, Tom Petty, early rock 'n' roll singer-songwriter Roy Orbison, and Electric Light Orchestra's Jeff Lynne, decided to keep going, writing and recording an album's worth of songs they released in 1988 as the Traveling Wilburys. The unbelievable lineup, a real-world variation on 1969's mythical Masked Marauders, created all the buzz you'd expect from such a conglomeration, with the group's debut album selling more than three million copies.

As Petty got to know Ostin and Waronker, he began to consider dumping MCA Records, the label he'd been with for a decade, and switching his allegiance to the Burbank company. When he mentioned the prospect at a dinner at Ostin's house one night in 1988, Ostin's antennae sparked. *You're serious?* Petty said that he was *very* serious, and Ostin and Waronker gave each other a long look. It wouldn't be immediate: as Petty pointed out, his current deal wouldn't expire for another five years. Both Warner executives shrugged. So what? They could work out a deal right then and there. Petty was game, and the outlines of a deal sketched quickly. Petty's manager, Tony Dimitriades, came in to work out the specifics a day or two later, and once that was done they printed two copies of what had to be a secret deal, signed them, and tucked them into their respective safes until Petty had delivered his final record to MCA.

Of course, when the time came in 1993, there would be a hitch in the plan. The numbers they had agreed upon in 1988, which had been generous for that time, had since been eclipsed by richer deals awarded not just to Petty's peers, but also to artists whose sales didn't approach his. Feeling belatedly shortchanged, Petty would send Dimitriades back to Ostin, who sat mutely while the manager sheepishly delivered his artist's request to renegotiate. It was, they both knew, a ridiculous ask, and Ostin only needed to hear a few sentences before he held up his hand. *Stop*, he said. For a moment Dimitriades thought he was about to get tossed out of the office. Instead, Ostin cut to the chase: *Just tell me what you want.* Dimitriades came up with a list of what other best-selling artists had signed for in the previous year or two, Ostin bumped Petty's number accordingly, and that was that. Released in 1994, Petty's first Warner Bros. album, *Wildflowers*, climbed into the Top 10 and sold three million copies during its initial run. Petty, already one of the most popular rock 'n' roll artists of the age, would continue making acclaimed albums for Warner Bros. for more than twenty years.

○

By 1988, nineteen years had passed since Peter Buck first filled his teen-age room with the strange sounds of Van Dyke Parks, Captain Beefheart, and a choice sampling of Warner/Reprise's first wave of outsider artists. Leaving home for Atlanta's Emory University in the fall of 1975 Buck dropped out after a year and eventually moved to Athens, the home of the University of Georgia, where he worked for a record store and met the three music-besotted friends with whom he would form the art rock band R.E.M. Driven by equal parts ambition and creative exploration, the group blazed a unique path to pop success, rising from campus favor-ites to alternative demi-stars to the highest tiers of the album charts in the space of half a dozen years. The group's million-selling 1987 album, *Document*, was the last record on their contract to the independent IRS Records, and though fourteen major labels made a run at signing them, Buck and his bandmates had a strong sense of which company would best serve their vision.

When the band and its representatives got to Burbank for their first meeting in the Chalet, it was near the end of the day. They found Ostin and Waronker in the chairman's office, where they all settled into the sofas and chairs for what turned out to be two hours of convivial banter, a long getting-to-know-you session. Warner Bros. was the top-selling label in the nation at the time, but neither executive brought this up. Instead, they talked about music and musicians, about the work the group had done and the kind of music they wanted to make next. It was a relaxed visit, and for Buck it confirmed the impression he'd formed so many years earlier, not just in the eccentric grooves of the albums but also in the wry liner notes and ads Stan Cornyn wrapped around them. That any label stocked with artists and staffers as diverse and strange as Warner/Reprise had to be different from the other major labels.

Two decades later, Buck and his bandmates were intent on making sure that the outsider–friendly philosophy he'd intuited from the Loss Leaders series of albums still existed. Because, along with the money and promotional support they knew they'd earned, the members of R.E.M. needed to make certain they would always have complete authority over their songs, their records, and how they were presented. That had been their top priority since the day they first came together to make music, and no amount of corporate money was going to change it. Not that they wanted to shut down all avenues of collaboration. If Waronker or whoever their A&R rep turned out to be had any thoughts or advice for the group, they'd be happy to hear them. But that didn't mean they were necessarily going to *change* anything, and that needed to be clear from the get-go. As far as Waronker was concerned, they didn't even have to ask. It had been part of the company's core philosophy for more than two decades, and neither Ostin nor Waronker would have considered giving them anything less.

So, while the chief executives at other companies might have made richer offers, the combination of artistic freedom, Ostin and Waronker's good faith, and the stability of the company's management made the decision clear. R.E.M. took Ostin and Waronker's ten-million-dollar, five-album deal. The mutual trust paid off almost immediately. The group's first WBR album, *Green*, released near the end of 1988, earned even greater acclaim than its predecessor while also selling twice as many copies. *Out of Time*, which followed in 1991, dwarfed *Green*'s sales, selling more than ten million copies around the world during its initial run, including two spells at No. 1 on the *Billboard* charts in the United States. By the time its 1992 follow-up, *Automatic for the People*, repeated the diamond-plus sales achievement, R.E.M. had joined U2 as one of the two most admired and beloved rock bands in existence. Their albums were so consistently strong, and their group identity so perfectly in tune with the times, that you could watch their progress and hear echoes of the Beatles' path through the 1960s. As their music continued to evolve into the mid-nineties, R.E.M. only got hotter, in both commercial and critical terms. All told, the foursome became the very model of a perfect Warner Bros. band: a group of committed artists who, though their collective muse might veer off in any direction, could still appeal to an audience big enough to hoist them to the top of the sales charts.

Ostin had always put his bets on the long game, the artists who needed a year or three (or even five or eight) to find their voices; the ones who might not wow the followers of the Top 10, but who would build a fan base dedicated enough to follow them from one album to the next, fans who would haul their friends to the shows until the band was filling bigger halls and selling ever more records. Van Dyke Parks, the Fugs, Captain Beefheart, and the rest of the outsider artists from the late 1960s may have sold fewer records among them than Debby Boone's "You Light Up My Life" sold in Wichita in a month, but their presence at the company drew R.E.M. into the fold just as the band was about to start selling records in the multiple millions. At the same time, influential modern alternative groups such as the Replacements and Husker Dü were already working with the company, all of them trusting in the Warner executives' well-documented willingness not to meddle in anyone's creativity.

From 1986 to 1989, Warner Bros. Records' annual revenue jumped from $270 million to $350 million, a 77 percent increase over three years. It's hard to find a problem in those numbers, especially during a period of overall stagnant-to-fading revenue in the record industry as a whole. But at least one executive in the Warner corporation's New York headquarters thought it wasn't enough. What's more, he already had some ideas on how he'd fix things to make Warners' record companies even more profitable. He wasn't in a position to do anything about it just yet. But he would, in time. And decades later, they'd still be wondering what he could possibly have been thinking.

15

## COMING FOR THE COWBOYS

In the early months of 1992, Lenny Waronker was in his office having a chat with Howie Klein, then the general manager of the Sire label, when the telephone rang. The call was from Mo Ostin, who was in his office just beyond the bathroom that separated the chairman's office from the Warner Bros. Records president's lair. Ostin was on a phone call with a Warner executive from New York and he wanted Waronker and Klein to come in and observe. When they settled into the chairs across from Ostin's desk, the fellow on the other end was grousing about the superstar guitarist, songwriter, and bluesman Eric Clapton. Why did they still have him on the label? Clapton had sold a lot of records when they signed him in the early eighties, but he had an inordinately expensive contract that guaranteed huge advances for each of his records. And though he usually sold enough to earn gold and sometimes platinum status, he had faded beneath the point that would justify what they were paying him. *He's not a modern artist*, the guy on the line said. *I want you to drop Clapton and bring in some artists who appeal to today's record buyers.* He didn't phrase it as a suggestion. It was a declarative sentence: *Drop Eric Clapton.*

Waronker and Klein could hear only Ostin's half of the conversation, a litany of neutral conversational space holders. *Mmm-hmm. I see. Modern artists. Got it. That's it?* It was like the ticking of a detonator. Something was about to happen. "The ice storm that dropped on that telephone call," Klein says, "is something I've never forgotten."[1]

There was no screaming. Ostin was not engineered for tantrums. His anger, to the extent he ever expressed it, could be found in what he *didn't* say: the black holes between the words.

*Let me explain something to you,* Ostin said to the man on the other end of the phone. He didn't mention Clapton. He wasn't talking music with this guy; he didn't have to. Ever since Steve Ross took over Warner Bros. more than twenty years earlier, Ostin had reported to only one person: Steve Ross. It was in his *contract*. Of course, he might entertain ideas from lower-ranking executives, and he was open to anyone's thoughts, including the folks working in the mail room. But the only person at Warner Communications Inc. who could actually *tell* him what to do was Steve Ross. So, now that we've got that straight, *never call me here again.* Ostin cut off the connection, glanced up at his visitors, and thanked them for coming in.

When Clapton's latest album, the one the executive had told Ostin not to bother releasing, hit the record shops, everything he had said about the artist turned out to be not just wrong but spectacularly so. *Unplugged,* the album Clapton recorded while taping an episode of MTV's stripped-down performance series, shot to the top of the *Billboard* album charts. It became the most successful album of the storied guitarist's career, selling ten million copies in the United States and more than fifteen million overseas, adding up to global sales of twenty-six million copies. At the same time, Clapton's catalogue, including a few albums that had been overlooked by record buyers the first time around, roared back onto the charts as his new and revived fans dug deeper into his more recent work, spurring even more millions of sales and a shower of new platinum and multi-platinum certifications.

It was a spectacular display, not just of Clapton's lasting appeal to mainstream record buyers, but also of the core strategies Ostin and Joe Smith set in motion when they took control of their conjoined record labels in 1967. And what of that executive in Steve Ross's New York headquarters? You would think he might have learned something from the experience, but you would be surprised. So many years later, Ostin, Waronker, and

Klein aren't entirely sure which executive called Ostin's office that day. But they all have the same theory: "I can't say for certain," Ostin admits. "But I *suspect* it was Robert Morgado"[2]—a name that was soon to become dismayingly familiar to anyone who worked in the Chalet or released their music through a label housed in or distributed through its offices.

●

For the most part, Warner Bros. Records purred through the first half of the 1990s with the same tuneful ease it had brought to the previous two decades. R.E.M.'s string of multi-platinum records put the group alongside their Warner Music Group fellows U2 as the dual kings of rock 'n' roll, while Prince's work continued to sell in the millions, hitting a latter-day peak with his 1991 release, *Diamonds and Pearls*, which earned multi-platinum status in countries around the world. The B-52s, signed to WBR in 1979, hit their commercial apex with 1989's *Cosmic Thing*, which boasted a string of hit singles that pushed the album into the Top 10 of 1990's best-selling albums. Neil Young, who had jumped to David Geffen's self-named new label in 1982, celebrated his return to Burbank with 1992's *Harvest Moon*, his first platinum album since *Rust Never Sleeps* in 1979. Veteran acts, including Rod Stewart, Paul Simon, and Van Halen, continued to sell at platinum or multi-platinum levels. And the array of successful subsidiary and distributed labels continued to grow, building the gold mine that was Seymour Stein's Sire Records with the addition of Los Angeles punk company Slash, the hip-hop focused Tommy Boy, Irving Azoff's Giant Records, hip-hop impresario turned record producer Rick Rubin's Def American, Quincy Jones's Qwest, and Madonna's Maverick Records. They cranked out hits by a genre-spanning universe of artists, ranging from Depeche Mode, David Byrne, k.d. lang, and Lou Reed to the aggro comedian Andrew Dice Clay and former Smiths singer Morrissey.

But Ostin's signature success of the new decade came in 1991, with the release of the Red Hot Chili Peppers' *Blood Sugar Sex Magik*. The Chili Peppers, a four-man punk-funk-rock group from Los Angeles, had been building a moderate-size cult of fans since the early 1980s, and as their album sales climbed into the low hundred thousands, they seemed on the verge of big things. Several companies chased after the band when their contract with EMI expired in 1989, and Ostin put together what struck him as the best contract he could offer. But when Sony/Epic ponied up a richer deal, the group decided to take it. Disappointed to lose but still charmed by the Chili Peppers themselves, Ostin called each of the four band members at home to say he was sorry to have come up short but was still happy that they had made such a great deal for themselves. "It's a small world," he told them. "Maybe we'll meet again down the line."

When the group started working out the specifics of their contract with Sony/Epic, problems emerged. Stipulations the Peppers had counted on, particularly the company's promise to provide the $1.5 million it would cost to free the band from their final EMI obligations, started to evaporate. Feeling as if they'd been taken in by a bait-and-switch operation, the group ducked out of their Sony deal and made a beeline for Burbank and the one record executive they felt they could trust. Ostin agreed to bump up his offer, and they sealed the deal with a round of handshakes. The Chili Peppers, now Warner Bros. artists, got to work on their next album, and when *Blood Sugar Sex Magik* was released in September 1991 lightning struck. While the band's previous albums had sold in the low to mid-hundreds of thousands, just enough not to crack the Top 50 on *Billboard*'s album charts, *BSSM* shot into the Top 3, producing a No. 2 single in "Under the Bridge" and selling long and strong enough to move seven million copies in the United States alone, plus several more million across Europe and Asia. Elevated to the top echelons of rock 'n' roll stardom, the Chili Peppers have produced nothing but million-plus sellers ever since.

●

No one competed with the ferocity and joy that Steve Ross brought to his job. After twenty years of consistent expansion, in 1990 the CEO pulled off what many considered the greatest corporate merger of the era by joining forces with Time Inc. to create a mammoth media company he dubbed Time Warner. It was a tough deal to pull off, one that attracted a hostile competing bid from Paramount Inc., accusations of monopoly building, and more. But it was tougher than anyone knew for Ross, who had been quietly battling prostate cancer for most of the negotiations. The hard-living executive had reined in his diet and quit cigarettes after being stricken with a heart attack in 1980, but cancer was another story. He was able to stave off the tumor that troubled him during the Time

Warner talks, but it recurred in 1991 with even more force. The struggle continued into 1992, when Ross was also besieged with criticism for his mammoth salary, which topped $78 million in 1990, just after the new company laid off 605 employees in its media division due to a short-term economic recession.

With the accusations of greed and irresponsibility gaining steam, all while Ross continued to fight prostate cancer, an even bigger controversy erupted out of Warner Bros. Records. The rap artist Ice-T, who was signed to Sire Records as a member of a rap-metal group called Body Count, released a song called "Cop Killer," a thrash rocker sung in the voice of an African American man pushed too far by the brutality of the racist cops in the Los Angeles Police Department. Citing the notoriously savage 1991 police beating of unarmed African American construction worker Rodney King, the song lays out a revenge fantasy involving a sawed-off shotgun, a long knife, and a lot of murderous ambition. "Cop killer, it's better you than me," Ice-T snarls. "Cop killer, fuck police brutality."

In the midst of a presidential election year, the song became a front in that year's culture war between supporters of free expression and a conservative sensibility that found Ice-T's antiauthoritarian vision horrifying. As usual, Ostin drew a hard line against censoring his artists' lyrics, but as the political heat sparked threats of a Time Warner boycott, the already beset Ross all but ordered Ostin to take "Cop Killer" off the Body Count album.* Ostin resisted the move until Ice-T made the call himself, asking the company to reissue the album without the song. Ostin approved the move, but also had the song distributed to record stores as a free single. The move ended the controversy but did nothing to ease the stressors Ross was facing. His cancer continued to progress, and by the end of the year it had spread too far. He passed away just before Christmas 1992.

As the company mourned Ross's death, it also became clear that the chief executives throughout the Warner Music Group were facing a crisis. One of Ross's greatest strengths as a leader had been knowing how much he didn't know. It had long been clear to him that running a record company was nothing like leading a more traditional business. It required a very different set of skills, some of them seeming to verge on shamanism.

---

* Ross also forbid the Warner record companies from signing rap acts, though Body Count was a racially mixed heavy metal band whose vocalist also happened to be a rapper.

No ordinary middle-aged executive would have been able to walk into the Avalon Ballroom in 1966, take in the wild psychedelia of the Grateful Dead without making head or tail of the music, and still be able to peg them for an entertainment attraction. But Joe Smith could, and he could also weather three years of expensive failures before seeing them produce the first trickles of profit. More than fifty years later, the band's catalogue is a bottomless annuity, yet it has earned on an investment that no sensible corporate accountant would ever have allowed.

It took an extraordinary businessman to recognize the importance of keeping his nose out of business he didn't understand. But not everyone Ross hired could live up to his example. And as he fought against his cancer and for his merger with Time Inc., he came to lean on an ambitious young executive he had brought into the company a decade earlier from the office of New York governor Hugh Carey.

A native of Hawaii, Robert J. Morgado had moved to New York State to attend graduate school and then joined Governor Carey's staff, rising quickly to become chief of staff. His hot-wired ambition was one of the things that endeared Morgado to Ross. He'd spent most of his early years at the company with the amorphous title of "special assistant to the CEO," taking on whatever assignments the boss threw his way. Ross, who thrived on being loved, delegated the cost-cutting and layoff decisions to Morgado, who had no problem wielding the axe. Smart, aggressive, and a little ruthless, he proved a valuable asset for Ross, though the CEO was also careful to keep him away from his thriving record companies. But as cancer robbed the chief executive of his energy, his attention wavered. And that's when Ostin began to field calls from corporate executives with opinions on Eric Clapton.

Morgado first turned his attention to Warner's record companies in the mid-1980s, and he took a dim view of the independence Ross had granted Ostin, Ahmet Ertegun, and the chairman of Elektra/Asylum/Nonesuch, who at that point was ex–Warner Bros. Records executive Bob Krasnow. Morgado was suspicious of what struck him as the imperial powers allowed the three chief executives, and his first impulse was to gain control over Atlantic Records, but he reversed course when he realized how much influence Ertegun had over Ross. Fixing instead on the WEA International division founded and run by Ahmet's brother,

Nesuhi Ertegun, he identified a few of the organization's weaknesses and got Ross's approval to hire a new executive to co-chair the division. Nesuhi was relieved of his remaining duties in 1987. Two years later, Morgado elevated an Atlantic executive named Doug Morris to serve as the record company's chief executive, leaving Ahmet as the company's chairman, but with significantly reduced control over its day-to-day operations.

Morris had the tools, at least, to be a top music executive. He had launched a successful label, Big Tree Records, and sold the operation to Atlantic Records in 1974. Four years later, he became president of Atlantic subsidiary Atco, and in 1980 he graduated to president of Atlantic. Successful from the start, Morris grew close to Ertegun, who gave him a first-year bonus that equaled three times his annual salary of $250,000, taking him under his wing in order to share his wisdom while also keeping the golden boy as close as possible. The company thrived through the 1980s, but lost enough momentum by 1989 that Morgado elevated Morris to Ertegun's coequal as Atlantic's CEO.

When Ross died in 1992, Time Inc. boss Gerald Levin became the merged corporation's sole chief executive. Coming from the world of publishing, Levin had only a limited perspective on how the empire's music companies worked. At the time, Morgado was the most highly placed corporate executive with any record company purview, so Levin elevated him to the job Morgado had coveted for a decade: CEO of the entire Music Group.

From that point forward, Morgado decreed, all the once-untouchable record company chairmen would report to him—or so it seemed, until Ostin reminded him of his contractual guarantee to report only to the chairman of the Warner Corporation, now Gerald Levin. This was true, but so was another fact: Ostin's contract would expire at the end of 1994, less than two years away. And Morgado was a patient man.

Over the next few years, Morgado tightened his grip on the Warner Music Group, largely through Doug Morris at Atlantic. Morris continued to rise and was given control of Atlantic's day-to-day operations. When hiring the next president of Atlantic, he reached outside the company to hire Danny Goldberg, an artist manager whose clients had included Bonnie Raitt, Sonic Youth, Rickie Lee Jones, and the reigning grunge rockers Nirvana. Goldberg had never worked for a major record company, and he worked closely with Morris to succeed, winning the support of not just Morris and Ertegun but also uber-boss Jerry Levin. More important for Morgado's plans, Goldberg and Morris represented an influx of new executives into the Music Group who didn't have the same expectation of independence or comradeship that figures like Ostin and Ertegun had.

As 1994 began, Ostin was already negotiating the terms of the contract that would extend his tenure as chairman of WBR for another five years. Most of it was basic stuff, slight revisions of numbers, dates, and so on. But Morgado threw a few curveballs, too. He insisted that Ostin anoint an official successor, as if he hadn't spent the last twenty years preparing Lenny Waronker to be exactly that. But Morgado wanted it in writing, so he could add another catch. Ostin would serve as chairman for only the first half of the term, after which Waronker would take control of the company, ascending to chairman while Ostin focused his energies on smoothing the transition to the new administration. And there was one more thing. From the moment the new contract took effect, Ostin would no longer answer only to the chief executive of the Warner Corporation. Instead, he would report to the chief executive of the Music Group, Robert J. Morgado.

Ostin resisted. Morgado said that he couldn't have it any other way. Ostin took his case to Levin, who shook his head. No matter how things had always been, Ostin would have to get used to having Morgado as a boss. And who said that had to be bad? Levin was sure it would all work out. Hoping to ease the conflict, he set up a dinner at Primavera, an Italian spot on Manhattan's Upper East Side that Ostin had long favored. Far less talented at brokering relationships than he was at putting together business deals, Levin made reassuring overtures about how Morgado and Ostin should just relax, work it out between themselves, and let things slip into gear. Ostin, shaking his head, turned to face Levin while gesturing at Morgado. "I don't trust this man," he said.[3] But Levin didn't care, and what was Ostin supposed to do? Warner Bros. Records was his life's work, the animation of who he was and what he'd spent his life achieving. Was he really going to sacrifice it all because of one supercilious *pisher* from Hawaii?

"I couldn't do anything about it, and I didn't want to leave," Ostin says. "So, I agreed I would sign the contract. I accepted that provision [to report to Morgado], but it really gnawed at me."[4] The finished contract arrived in Ostin's office a few days later. He tucked it into a desk drawer, figuring he'd give it a look and sign it within a few days. But then he kept finding other things to do. For a while, one of those things was to pick up his telephone and hear Morgado or Levin urging him to open the contract to the last page, pick up his pen, and finish the job. He'd say he would, if not today then definitely tomorrow, but then something wouldn't let him do it, and eventually he stopped taking the calls. "There was something inside me that kept telling me not to sign that contract."[5]

Meanwhile, Morgado kept finding ways to reinforce Ostin's distrust. When the Warner Music Group record companies traveled to Montreux, Switzerland, to present their release schedule for the year, Ostin and Waronker showed off WBR's slate as a team, taking turns introducing the records and hyping their hit potential. The presentation went well, but afterward Morgado declared himself furious. Ostin, he said, had hogged the spotlight, shoving Waronker aside in order to draw attention to himself. Waronker, who thought Ostin had been perfectly collegial at the event, had no idea what Morgado was talking about. But that didn't matter. Going directly from the convention to a few days of rest in Italy, Ostin was interrupted by a call from Elektra chairman Bob Krasnow. Had he heard the latest? Now that Morgado had gained control of the corporation's music operation across the globe, he was going to create a new umbrella organization, Warner Music–U.S., to oversee the domestic operations of Warner, Atlantic, and Elektra. And, Krasnow continued, Morgado had already decided to make Doug Morris its president—which meant that Ostin would report to Morris, who would report to Morgado, who would then check in with Levin.

Cutting his Italian trip short, Ostin flew to New York to meet with Morgado. At first the executive filibustered, talking about everything else under the sun until Ostin forced the point: "Is there anything else you want to tell me?" Morgado nodded. *Oh yeah*, he said, as if he'd just remembered something. He'd been thinking of making Doug Morris the chief of American music operations. What did Ostin think of that? Ostin, who didn't like the idea one bit, said he'd think about it. Morgado asked him to keep what he'd just heard close, because he hadn't told anyone yet and didn't want it to slip out. Ostin agreed, made for the Warner corporate jet, and flew to Aspen, where his family had gathered for a ski break. When the plane landed, he found his son Michael waiting at the airport with news: Morgado had appointed Morris the CEO of American music operations. Ostin, with Morgado's plea for confidentiality still clattering in his ears, was astonished to discover that Michael hadn't heard the news from Time Warner's corporate HQ but from Irving Azoff, the Eagles manager, who was then launching his own Warner subsidiary label. Azoff, meanwhile, had heard it from David Geffen, who had gotten the news from the president of Capitol Records—which meant that Morgado had deliberately kept Ostin in the dark even while the news was fast spreading through every other record company in America.

Of course, diminishing Ostin's power had been a central part of Morgado's plan for years. Not long after Ross's death in late 1992, Joe Smith, nearing the end of a six-year run as president of Capitol Records, had bumped into Morgado at an industry party in New York. The Time Warner executive introduced himself and told the former president of Warner Bros. Records and Elektra/Asylum Records all about what was going on at the company and how things were changing. One thing they were definitely going to do, Morgado said, was rein in all those record company bosses who had gotten so used to doing whatever they wanted, with no corporate control.

Morgado smiled as he said it: "We're coming after all the cowboys."

Smith's face hardened. "If it weren't for the cowboys," he said, "you'd have nothing."[6]

Morgado shrugged and walked away.

David Geffen, whose long, competitive relationship with Ostin had included fruitful partnerships, bitter conflicts, grand displays of friendship, and hard-eyed brinksmanship, saw Ostin's slow-motion defenestration as an insult to the entire music industry. Spying Levin at an exclusive get-together for top media executives in Sun Valley, Geffen waved him over to his table and let him have it. "You're making a terrible mistake," he said. "Mo Ostin is the single most important music executive in the world." Geffen, not known for his self-deprecation, explained to Levin how long he had been competing with Ostin, who persisted in beating the crap out of him far more often than not. "Jerry," he concluded urgently, "this is NOT a good idea for you."[7] Levin listened, nodded, and paid no attention. More than twenty years later, the subject still gets Geffen irate. "Morgado was a complete and total asshole who didn't have a clue as to what he was doing," he says. "What he was doing there in the first place is beyond me. Morgado caused the demise of that company as the most important one in the music business."[8]

Ultimately, it was too much for Ostin. On August 15, 1994, he released a statement saying that he would be leaving Warner Bros. Records when his contract expired at the end of the year. His decision took Levin and Morgado by surprise; they urged him to stay on as chairman emeritus, but he wasn't interested. Waronker, who hated the thought of abandoning all his artists and colleagues, at first agreed to stay on and succeed Ostin, though he would do so only with the reduced title of CEO—nobody other than Mo Ostin, he insisted, could be the company's chairman. But Waronker couldn't stick with it. Realizing that his greatest loyalty was to Ostin, he reversed himself and resigned his job, too.

When it was time to go home at the end of his final day as chairman of Warner Bros. Records, Ostin stepped out the front door to discover the entire staff of the company, hundreds strong, all wearing red Warner Bros. Records hats, their faces covered by masks of Ostin's own smiling mug. They cheered their toppled leader with the kind of emotional abandon that bordered on the religious. Their feelings were compounded by the fact that no one was quite certain why Ostin was being pushed out. Clean-shaven, pink-faced, and bright-eyed at sixty-seven years old, he was obviously in excellent health. The company he was leaving was in excellent financial condition. Nothing was wrong—except for the fact that Ostin had been sent away.

The cheering and applause went on for some time. Ostin, never entirely at ease in front of even the friendliest mobs, applauded for them and finally climbed into the front seat of his gold Mercedes sedan. He gave a last wave through the windshield and then shifted into gear and was gone. To many WBR people, and to a legion of observers, too, he took the spirit of Warner Bros. Records with him.

## LOSING MY RELIGION

At 10 a.m. on Saturday, March 9, 2019, the current owners of Warner Bros. Records opened the Chalet doors to let the old crew come in and take one last look. The invitations had gone out less than a week before the reunion/farewell party, and no one knew what to expect. A lot of the WBR veterans hadn't been in the building for years. Maybe they weren't always welcome, but once the invitations went out, the RSVPs blizzarded back, nearly all of them saying yes. By 9:45 a.m., the Warner Boulevard sidewalk was so crowded you would have thought Prince had come back from the Purple Beyond to play another surprise show on the building's patio. But it was just the folks whose voices used to ring in the conference rooms and hallways, who had hired on as bony hippie kids and left as well-fed middle-agers with real estate, mortgages, and, in more than a few cases, stock options that were even more mature than their kids (who now had kids of their own).

It was a chilly spring morning, and when the security guards pulled open the glass doors, the folks came flooding in. Soon the reception area was mobbed, cacophonous with recognition, laughter, and tears, those tears that come when you rediscover a feeling you forgot you missed—like the way it felt when the idea of changing the world, even one small piece of it, seemed realistic. Take it from Stan Cornyn, back in his old faux-wood-paneled office in 1972, a fortyish businessman gone shaggy with beard and belief, telling *Record World* that his mission at Warner/Reprise was to turn the usual dynamic of art and commerce on its head. "I'm trying to stop record companies from using artists, and start artists using record companies," he said.[1]

One persistent rumor had a lot of heads swiveling to and fro throughout the WBR reunion. I'd heard it myself a day or two before, that Lenny Waronker, as per the habit they'd developed during the good old days, would arrive at the party with Ostin at his side. I couldn't figure out how likely that was. Waronker had returned to the company in 2009 and had been a regular presence ever since. Ostin had also reentered the scene, awarded the title of chairman emeritus, meeting with the company's leaders from time to time either to consult on some specific issue or to serve as a spiritual guide, a living conduit to the company's most glorious era. It'd be special for them to turn up, the old generals addressing the troops, thanking them for their service, invoking the names of the fallen, and giving everyone a chance to feel a part of it one more time.

Robert Morgado's luck ran out soon after he had pushed Ostin out of Warner Bros. Records. Waronker's unexpected departure created another crucial vacancy that Morgado tried to fill with a loyalist, but that put him afoul of Doug Morris, his handpicked chief of the American record companies, who preferred to have one of *his* allies running the Burbank shop. Morris handed the WBR chairmanship to Danny Goldberg, the former talent manager who had jumped into the record business and rose quickly to be the president of Atlantic Records, where he worked closely with Morris. The forty-four-year-old Goldberg, however, got to Burbank tainted by his association with both Morgado and Morris, which made his bid to stabilize the company difficult. Goldberg dropped mountains of cash to hold on to company pillars, including promotions boss Russ Thyret, product management vice president Steven Baker, Reprise Records president Howie Klein, and business manager David Altschul, along with signature artist Neil Young. And while some executives at WBR say they'd heard him dismiss Ostin as an elitist, Goldberg reached out to his predecessor, who not only agreed to meet his successor for lunch, but also proved surprisingly friendly. "He associated me with the forces that had fucked up his professional life," Goldberg says. "I would have understood if he didn't want to meet with me. But he was professional and thoughtful."[2]

With chaos breaking out in the corporate offices and major WBR acts lining up to leave the staggered company, Levin finally realized he'd put his trust in the wrong executive. Six months after he climbed into his car and left the Chalet for the last time, Ostin received an invitation from Time Warner's CEO to spend a few days with him at the company's vacation house in Acapulco. Levin described it as a fun getaway. Ostin and his wife were both invited, and Quincy Jones, one of Ostin's closest friends, would be there with his wife. But within a day of Ostin's arrival, Levin pulled him aside to say he'd made a terrible mistake and wanted the former Warner Bros. Records chairman back in his old job. When Ostin said he'd never work for Bob Morgado, Levin assured him that wouldn't be a problem. He was already going to fire him. Now Ostin was interested.

Levin replaced Morgado with former HBO chief executive Michael Fuchs, who promptly fired Doug Morris. Levin flew to Los Angeles to pitch Ostin again, with Fuchs alongside, but Ostin ended up turning them down. The sticking point was that Fuchs wanted to keep authority over the WBR chairman even while allowing him to do whatever he wanted; this would have re-created the old Mo-and-Joe setup, but with Mo in Joe's role and without the time-tested trust that had held the original duo together.[3] Ostin had an array of other offers, including one from David Geffen and his new partners Steven Spielberg and Jeffrey Katzenberg to team with Waronker and his son Michael in launching a record company for their DreamWorks enterprise. The terms were as good as the job was exciting, and they launched DreamWorks Records in 1996 with a logo designed by the influential modern artist Roy Lichtenstein.

Back at Warner, Fuchs asked for Goldberg's resignation in August 1995 and hired Russ Thyret to replace him as WBR's chairman. At first Thyret refused to move into Ostin's old office; he couldn't bear the thought of trying to replace the man who had changed his life in so many ways. When Ostin heard this, he told Thyret to stop being ridiculous. No one was more qualified to be the chairman than he was, and he owed it to his employees to be firmly in charge.

Everywhere else in the company, chaos reigned. Corporate executives on multiple levels came and went, sometimes within months of one another. Thyret stayed as WBR chairman until resigning in 2001, when he was replaced by Tom Whalley, who had started his career in the Chalet's mail room many years earlier. Time Warner's disastrous 2000 merger with the AOL internet company led to the sale of the Warner Music Group to one new owner, then another and another. Hoping to telegraph a reformation of the old days, Whalley asked Ostin to rejoin the company as its chairman emeritus, then took his predecessor's advice to invite Waronker back, happily accepting the former company president's condition that he go back to the staff A&R job he'd started with in 1965, working with artists, making records, and nothing else.

Their run had never been perfect. There were territorial squabbles between executives, retrograde attitudes about women, and pitched battles on which artists to sign, how to divide the promotions budget, and whose most beloved artist had to be dropped so they could sign someone else's hot new prospect. They couldn't always put the art above the profits. Some artists never really did get the shot they deserved. Some staffers felt the same way about their careers. As the years passed, the communal vibe ebbed, too. And the relatively gentle pot and LSD that had fueled the bonding rituals in the 1960s mutated into toxic powders that ruined careers and short-circuited lives. But it was so hard to say no. "The excesses were like a football player on steroids," says longtime executive Steven Baker. "You had to do it just to be a part of it. Getting high was part of the business at any record company." If you were lucky you could find your way through without paying too much for your indulgences. Not everyone was that lucky.

But the work went on, the music continued to play, and along with everything else Warner Bros. Records boasted the most content and loyal workforce of any major entertainment company in Los Angeles. Job turnover was nearly nonexistent during the Ostin era, with many employees staying with the company for a decade, for two decades, for even longer than that. "People didn't want to go," says Russ Thyret. "There are so many people I know, men and women who came up the ladder, spent years [at WBR], who still swear it was the greatest job they've ever had. And it didn't make them complacent. They had to compete to stay on top of what was going on. They wanted to maintain their jobs and their own growth."[4]

○

Back at the Chalet reunion, the current WBR staffers were doing their best to be as welcoming and relaxed as possible. *Of course you can go upstairs*, they said. *Go see anything you want to see, and help yourself to any CDs or posters or T-shirts or anything you can find lying around. That's all for you guys.* They had all kinds of security guards drifting here and there, but they were instructed to dress casually and remember that this was a family gathering, that these were honored guests who'd earned respect and admiration. But there was tension in the air there, too, and it felt a little more freighted than the usual disconnect between generations you find at college reunions or old-timers' games.

Today's WBR has all kinds of cool acts: the Flaming Lips, Tegan and Sara, the Black Keys, NLE Choppa, Gary Clark Jr., and dozens of others. Nothing to be ashamed of in that lineup, but compared to the likes of Jimi Hendrix, Fleetwood Mac, Prince, the Grateful Dead, R.E.M., Joni Mitchell . . . well, it doesn't have quite the same *oomph*.

Except maybe these modern folks at Warner Bros. Records, which in mid-2019 ditched the "Bros." to be known simply as Warner Records, don't see it like that. Because pop music is always a forward-looking game, and because they're just as young and disruptive as their hippie-era predecessors, who also didn't care much about the music of bygone decades. I've spent enough time talking with current Warner staffers to know that a lot of them are smart, cool people who live, breathe, and dream music with as much passion as anyone else who has devoted their lives to helping artists make records that matter. Only, it's so much more difficult now. In this age of digital copying, online streaming, collapsed record sales, and the primacy of megacorporations that make the old Time Warner seem like a mom-and-pop outfit, it's all but impossible for any record company to achieve what Warner Bros. Records did during the Mo Ostin era. Or maybe that's just how it seems to a middle-aged white guy whose tastes started forming when Lyndon Johnson was president of the United States, the Beatles were still clean-shaven, and Lil Pump's *parents* had yet to be born.

I visited the Chalet half a dozen times during its last few years and it was always a thrill. The long, brown leather sofas in the reception area, original pieces from when the doors first opened in 1975, seemed like artifacts from a sacred time. The framed photos and memorabilia lining the walls recalled artists and albums whose songs had filled my ears since I was running across playgrounds, dancing at high school parties, getting married, holding newborn babies, doing my work, succeeding, failing, driving kids to college, getting divorced, and then starting over. There are dozens of Warner Bros. (including Reprise, Sire, Elektra/Asylum) albums that on certain days feel like religion to me. Sometimes it's an entire album, other times a song, and sometimes it all comes down to a single moment in a song, as when the Replacements distilled everything I'm struggling to say now into the two-line chorus of "Alex Chilton": "I'm in love—what's that song? / I'm in love—with that song." That was the feeling Ostin urged his A&R staff to chase back in 1967, and it was at the heart of his vision of a commercial record company that ran like a for-profit art commune. It shouldn't have worked. Art is supposed to exist in the shadow of commerce, not the other way around. But it did work, and on every level. It continued working for nearly three decades and might still be working had it not been for the death of Steve Ross and the rise of corporate executives who figured that producing high-quality popular art came down to another formula with a solvable $x$. And as they would soon learn, it didn't.

The invitations made clear that the party would end at noon, and when the digital clock flicked toward twelve, the casually dressed security folks fanned out across the building's three floors to suggest that guests start finding their way back to the reception area. Not everyone was ready. A pair of women stood outside Ostin's old office and cupped their hands against the glass, hoping to catch a glimpse of . . . something. They walked away frustrated, but there was nothing to see in there anyway. All of Warner's Los Angeles record companies were moving to a converted Ford auto factory in the growing arts district downtown. A few totems from the old building would be joining them, including those rich leather sofas and armchairs in the lobby. But once the doors closed this afternoon, the Chalet would be just another memory about Warner Bros. Records.

# POSTLUDE
## On Vine Street

Mo Ostin lives alone in a modern house at the top of a large hill overlooking the Pacific Palisades section of West Los Angeles. When I drove my rental car up to see him, I navigated long, curling streets past houses that each defined *luxuriant* in their own special way. There were pink-stone châteaux seemingly plucked from a waterfront cliff in Saint-Jean-Cap-Ferrat, stone balconies and red ceramic tiled roofs included; a lavish Italianate mansion that could have been six hundred years old, except it was built in 1927. If you drive a long way up the hill, you'll find the house where former California governor Ronald Reagan lived when he was elected president in 1980. Keep climbing another few hundred feet, and Ostin's house is on the right.

There is a big wooden gate, immaculate gravel in the driveway, and half a dozen parking spots separated by small trees. You approach from the high side of the house, entering a cool, dark chamber that leads to an airy kitchen opening onto the dining area and an informal living room, all of it fronted by floor-to-ceiling windows. The view spans the shipping lanes of the Pacific Ocean to the San Fernando Valley in the east, with San Diego off in the southern distance and Marina del Rey, Venice, Santa Monica, and Brentwood in the foreground. Panning from the windows to the walls reveals Ostin's taste in modern art. Priceless works by Jean-Michel Basquiat, Cy Twombly, René Magritte, and contemporary abstractionists Joe Bradley and Jeff Elrod, among many others, can be found nearly everywhere you turn.

Ostin famously loathes interviews, particularly ones that focus on him. When I started talking to former WBR executives in early 2017, all of them said the same thing: *You can't tell this story without talking to Mo, but Mo will never talk to you.* Then word of my project got to Michael Ostin, who helped convince his dad to have an off-the-record lunch with me in early 2018. Michael brought Mo to the restaurant and sat by proudly as his father proved to be everything I'd heard he would be: charming, focused, sharp as a razor, and surprisingly happy to talk about the old days. He gave me his blessing to do my work and, six months later, agreed to speak with me on the record. It took nearly nine months to set up the meeting, but it was worth the wait. Michael, who has partnered with his father on everything he's done since leaving Warner Bros. Records in 1994, hired a video crew to capture our talks, which stretched to more than twenty hours over three days.

We set up in the sitting area near the kitchen, and when Ostin appeared he didn't make an entrance as much as slip in from some unseen portal, giving a small hello on his way to the cold buffet arrayed across the kitchen counter. Salads, small cut-up sandwiches, half a salmon chilled with lemon, dill, and a creamy sauce. Ostin fixed himself a plate and forked up some salmon. "Hey, that's really *good*," he exclaimed, as if he were surprised by his luck. And he has been lucky, as he repeats several times over the next few days.

Ostin is ninety-three now, his hair completely gone, and his head mottled with those dark age spots you see on older folks in sunny climes. He's quite thin these days, and concerned about his posture, mostly because his yoga teacher won't stop yelling at him about it. For all the convincing it took to get him to talk, he dives into the task enthusiastically, and the clarity of his recall is astounding. He remembers not just the specifics of contracts he negotiated fifty years ago, but also how particular clauses evolved in subsequent renegotiations, right down to the specifics of the royalty rates.

Ostin has his regrets, particularly regarding his treatment of Sire Records president Seymour Stein, who complained for years that he was never paid adequately for his contributions to the company, which included signing Madonna, Talking Heads, the Pretenders, and dozens of other platinum-selling artists. Stein was a brilliant record man, but he also spent mad amounts of money and came across to Ostin like a tornado, equal parts kinetic, frenetic, and out of his fucking mind. As Stein grew more obstreperous, Ostin became more determined not to renegotiate the terms of his original deal, whether he deserved it or not. Eventually, Steve Ross interceded in Stein's favor, but the bad blood between Ostin and the Sire chief turned so sour that Stein used his 2018 memoir, *Siren Song*, to lash out at his former boss, making several legitimate points but also launching wild allegations that made Stein seem bitter and unmoored. Ostin felt less angry than sad about how he'd helped create the mess. "I was just too hard on those things. You need to compromise, and I wouldn't."

He has other regrets, some almost too devastating to acknowledge. "It was tough for the boys to grow up as my sons," Ostin says in his unflinching way. "I think I wasn't a great father. I was so immersed in the music business. I was away most of the time, either traveling or in the office late." Michael cuts in to demur, pointing out what a great dad Mo was when he *was* home, always on the sidelines of their Little League games, always interested in their lives and concerned for their happiness and well-being. Ostin shrugs.

What's happened to his family in the last fifteen years has been almost too devastating to bear. Mo and Evelyn's youngest son, Kenny, had troubled the family for years. The most handsome and charismatic of the boys, Kenny excelled at baseball and other sports, and his charm was as effortless as it was irresistible. But drugs held a similar power over him, and when cocaine first took hold of him in his twenties he was gone for good. Kenny worked closely with Ahmet Ertegun at Atlantic Records for a time and did well when he was focused. He checked himself into rehab programs, but the cure never stuck, and the years of anxiety and frustration took a toll on Ostin and the whole family. "We had an argument about drugs once, and I actually punched him in the nose, I got so furious," Ostin says. "And he was a fabulous kid. I loved being with him. We played golf together a lot. But then he'd get to the country club stoned, and it was embarrassing." Kenny died of an OxyContin overdose in 2004, at forty-eight.

The tragedy devastated Mo and Evelyn, just as she was battling a melanoma that spread into her brain. This time the disease would not be beaten, and she died in October 2005, less than a year after Kenny. Evelyn's memorial packed UCLA's Royce Hall with friends ranging from beauticians to the apex of show business's A-list. *Saturday Night Live* impresario Lorne Michaels produced the service, which included Evelyn's close friend Barbra Streisand singing two songs.

Ostin was staggered by Evelyn's death, but tragedy wasn't done with him yet. His eldest son, Randy, who had built a career as a promotions man at Asylum Records and went on to work for the Eagles before becoming an investor focusing on nightclubs and restaurants, developed liver cancer in his mid-fifties and died from the disease in 2014, when he was sixty, leaving behind a twenty-four-year-old son. So much loss in such a short period of time—how could any father and husband stand it?

Ostin shrugs again. "You have to go on."

○

Books about music shouldn't have sad endings, not if the music is still playing somewhere in the world. And maybe no music ever dies. It takes to the air and stays aloft, a vibration on the breeze, a dream adrift, always ready to float into another set of ears and implant itself into another living spirit. That's the great miracle of music, this invisible presence that can travel through walls, air, and time. And for everything they achieved at Warner Bros. Records during the Ostin era, for all the money they made, the awards they won, the parties they threw, and the ecstasies they traversed, they always kept their focus on the empty air. Always ready for magic to strike. And it did.

Maybe this is why Van Dyke Parks opened *Song Cycle*, the album Ostin still considers one of his company's most significant achievements, with "Vine Street." Parks played the song one last time at his farewell performance at Los Angeles' Largo at the Coronet in 2015. And with Ostin, Waronker, Newman, and a cadre of his old Warner Bros. Records compatriots looking on, Parks took them all into another lost time, when ears were open, hearts were full, and music filled the air.

*Swingin' along on the wings of a song . . .*
*We've things to say that the people would pay to hear us play, on Vine Street.*

# NOTES

## 1: Song Cycle

1 Author interview with Lenny Waronker, February 2018.
2 Joe Smith memo to promotion staffers, November 1, 1967 (author's scan from Rock and Roll Hall of Fame archives).

## 2: Welcome to the Chalet

1 Author interviews with Mo Ostin, March 2019.
2 Author interview with Lenny Waronker, May 2013.
3 Ibid.
4 Ibid.

## 3: Warner Bros. Records: Terribly Sophisticated Songs

1 Stan Cornyn and Paul Scanlon, *Exploding: The Highs, Hits, Hypes, Heroes, and Hustlers of the Warner Music Group* (New York: HarperCollins, 2002), p. 17.
2 "The Ira Ironstrings Hoax: How to Sell 25,000 Easy," *Billboard*, September 8, 1958, p. 4.
3 Avakian memo to Jim Conkling, October 9, 1958, quoted in Stan Cornyn and Ellen Pelissero, "What a Long, Strange Trip It's Been: An Authorized History of Warner Bros. Records," vol. 1, pp. 154–55 (unpublished manuscript, c. 1981, volume and page numbers refer to author's privately scanned version).
4 Cornyn and Pelissero, "What a Long, Strange Trip," vol. 1, p. 162.
5 For chart/sales numbers, see ibid., vol. 1, pp. 167–71.
6 For a description of the meeting with quotes, see ibid., vol. 1, pp. 205–6.
7 Ibid., vol. 1, pp. 206–7.
8 Details via author interview with Bob Newhart, October 9, 2018.
9 Ibid.
10 Cornyn and Pelissero, "What a Long, Strange Trip," vol. 1, p. 252.
11 Author interview with Newhart.
12 Ibid.; and Cornyn and Pelissero, "What a Long, Strange Trip," vol. 1, pp. 266–68.
13 Cornyn and Pelissero, "What a Long, Strange Trip," vol. 1, pp. 266–68.
14 Author interview with Newhart.
15 Stan Cornyn, "Starting Over in 1961," Stay Tuned, *Rhino*, February 21, 2013.
16 Cornyn and Pelissero, "What a Long, Strange Trip," vol. 1, pp. 307–9.

17  Ibid.

18  Lyrics, etc., from ibid., vol. 1, pp. 391–95.

19  Cornyn and Pelissero, "What a Long, Strange Trip," vol. 1, pp. 395–400.

20  Ibid., vol. 1, p. 401.

21  Ibid., vol. 1, pp. 401–5.

22  Wikipedia entries for "Hello Muddah, Hello Fadduh" and *My Son, the Nut.*

23  For financial specs and background on Peter, Paul and Mary history/deal, see Cornyn and Pelissero, "What a Long, Strange Trip," vol. 1, pp. 368–72.

24  Cornyn and Pelissero, "What a Long, Strange Trip," vol. 1, pp. 609–11.

**4: Reprise Records: Newer, Happier, Emancipated**

1  Foregoing paragraphs from author interviews with Ostin, March 2019.

2  Ostin family information from ibid.

3  All background information from ibid.

4  Background info on Granz, Clef, and Verve from ibid.

5  Ibid.

6  Ibid.

7  Gay Talese, "Frank Sinatra Has a Cold," *Esquire*, April 1966.

8  Stan Cornyn, "Mike and Mo Go Toe to Toe," Stay Tuned, *Rhino*, February 28, 2013.

9  Author interviews with Ostin, March 2019.

10  Stan Cornyn and Paul Scanlon, *Exploding* (New York: HarperCollins, 2002), p. 48.

11  Ad in author's collection.

12  Author interviews with Ostin, March 2019.

13  Ibid.

14  Author interviews with Jimmy Bowen, April 2018.

15  Ibid.

16  Ibid.

17  Author interviews with Ostin, March 2019.

18  For the financial details of the Warner Bros.–Reprise deal, see Cornyn and Pelissero, "What a Long, Strange Trip," vol. 1, pp. 557–71.

**5: Warner/Reprise: A Quite Unlosable Game**

1  Author interviews with Joe Smith, November 2017 and February 2018.

2  Author interviews with Ostin, March 2019.

3  Author interviews with Smith.

4  Author interviews with Ostin, March 2019.

5  Cornyn and Pelissero, "What a Long, Strange Trip," vol. 1, pp. 609–12.

6  Ibid., vol. 1, p. 608; and author interviews with Ostin, March 2019.

7  Author interviews with Ostin, March 2019.

8  Scene from *What's Happening!*, dir. Albert and David Maysles (Maysles Films, 1964).

9  Philip Larkin, "Annus Mirablis," collected in *High Windows* (New York: Faber and Faber, 1974).

10  Letter from Mo Ostin to Louis Benjamin, August 22, 1964 (author's scan from Rock and Roll Hall of Fame archives).

11  Cornyn and Pelissero, "What a Long, Strange Trip," vol. 2, p. 16.

12  Telegram from Mo Ostin to Desi, Dino, and Billy, April 13, 1965.

13  Cornyn and Scanlon, *Exploding*, p. 69.

14  Ibid.

15  Author interviews with Ostin, March 2019.

16  Cornyn and Pelissero, "What a Long, Strange Trip," vol. 1, pp. 38–42.

17  Author interviews with Smith.

18  Scene from author interviews with Smith and from accounts in Cornyn and Scanlon, *Exploding*, p. 111; and Dennis McNally, *A Long Strange Trip: The Inside History of the Grateful Dead* (New York: Broadway Books, 2002), p. 171.

19  Author interviews with Smith.

20  Stan Cornyn, "'Greatful' Dead," Stay Tuned, *Rhino*, April 2, 2013.

**6: Christmas and New Year's and Your Birthday All Together**

1  From *Monterey Pop*, dir. D. A. Pennebaker (American Broadcasting Company, 1968).

2  Ibid.

3  Michael Lydon, "Monterey Pop: An Int'l Pop Festival," in *Monterey Pop*, dir. D. A. Pennebaker (Criterion Collection, 50th anniversary DVD, 2017).

4  From *Monterey Pop*, dir. D. A. Pennebaker.

5   Cornyn and Pelissero, "What a Long, Strange Trip," vol. 2, p. 12.

6   Author interviews with Ostin, March 2019.

7   Cornyn and Scanlon, *Exploding*, p. 73.

8   Author interviews with Lenny Waronker, 2017–19; and author interview with Randy Newman, July 2, 2018.

9   Author interview with Newman.

10  Author interviews with Waronker, 2017–19.

11  Author interview with Newman.

12  Ibid.

13  Author interviews with Waronker, 2017–19.

14  Ibid.

15  Author interview with Newman.

16  Ibid.

17  Author interview with Arlo Guthrie, November 2018.

18  Author interview with Ry Cooder, September 2018.

19  *Billboard*, November 25, 1967.

20  *Variety*, July 20, 1968.

**7: Once You Get Used to It, His Voice Is Really Something**

1   Quotes from broadcast air check audio, KRLA, September 17, 1967.

2   Cornyn and Pelissero, "What a Long, Strange Trip," vol. 2, pp. 171–72.

3   Ibid., vol. 1, p. 176.

4   Ibid.

5   *Newsweek*, November 28, 1966, p. 66.

6   Cornyn and Pelissero, "What a Long, Strange Trip," vol .2, p. 94.

7   Ibid., vol. 2, p. 111.

8   Ibid., vol. 3, pp. 106–7.

9   Ibid., vol. 3, pp. 104–5.

10  Author interviews with Mo Ostin, August 2019.

11  Author interviews with David Berson, March 2018.

12  Jerry Hopkins, "Inside the L.A. Scene," *Rolling Stone*, June 22, 1968.

13  Stan Cornyn, liner notes for Frank Sinatra, *September of My Years* (LP, Reprise FS 1014, 1965).

14  Author interview with Newman.

15  Author interview with Peter Asher, May 2018.

16  Cornyn and Scanlon, *Exploding*, p. 117.

**8: How Can We Break the Rules Today?**

1   Cornyn and Pelissero, "What a Long, Strange Trip," vol. 2, p. 203.

2   Ibid.

3   Author interviews with Smith.

4   Author interviews with Carl Scott, 2017–19.

5   Liner notes for the Lyman Family with Lisa Kindred, *American Avatar* (LP, Reprise RS 6353, 1969).

6   Cornyn and Scanlon, *Exploding*, pp. 124–25.

7   Cornyn and Pelissero "What a Long, Strange Trip," vol. 3, pp. 46–50.

8   Author interview with Greil Marcus, July 2018.

9   Cornyn and Pelissero, "What a Long, Strange Trip," vol. 3, pp. 46–50.

10  Ibid., vol. 3, p. 49.

11  Author interview with Langdon Winner, July 2018.

12  "Rock Album Was a Rumor Spin-Off," *Los Angeles Times*, December 1, 1969.

13  *Circus*, December 1969.

**9: The Gold Dust Twins**

1   Author interviews with Smith.

2   Cornyn and Pelissero go into exhaustive detail in "What a Long, Strange Trip," vol. 2, pp. 304–40.

3   Cornyn and Scanlon, *Exploding*, pp. 131–32; and Connie Bruck, *Master of the Game* (New York: Simon and Schuster, 1994), pp. 48–49.

4   Bruck, *Master of the Game*, pp. 19–20.

5   Author interviews with Ostin, March 2019.

6   Author interview with Charlie Springer, May 2018.

7   Author interview with Marcus.

8   *Vogue*, March 1, 1970, described in Cornyn and Pelissero, "What a Long, Strange Trip," vol. 3, p. 58.

9   Cornyn and Pelissero, "What a Long, Strange Trip," vol. 3, p. 58.

10  *New York Times* obituary, September 19, 1984.

11  From email interview with "Pete Johnson," who prefers to not be identified.

12  Cornyn and Pelissero, "What a Long, Strange Trip," vol. 3, pp. 262–73.

13  Author interview with Tom Johnston, October 2018.
14  Author interviews with Smith.
15  Ibid.
16  Author interview with Peter Buck, August 2017.

**10: The Rock Morality**

1  "The New Rock: Bittersweet and Low," *Time* cover, March 1, 1971, interior article: "James Taylor, One Man's Family of Rock," pp. 45–53.
2  Author interviews with Carl Scott, 2017–19.
3  Author interview with Ted Templeman, May 17, 2018.
4  Van Dyke Parks memo to Mo Ostin, "Steel Band Album Musicians Payments," March 1, 1971.
5  Van Dyke Parks memo to Joan Taylor, "Steel Band Recording Payment," March 1, 1971.

**11: It Ain't Nothin' but a Warner Bros. Party**

1  Cornyn and Scanlon, *Exploding*, p. 112.
2  Ibid., p. 199.
3  Author interviews with Smith.
4  Bruck, *Master of the Game*, p. 362.

**12: Fuck the Bunny**

1  Author interviews with Ostin, March 2019.
2  Author interviews with Waronker, 2017–19.
3  Walter Yetnikoff, *Howling at the Moon* (New York: Broadway Books, 2004), p. 94.
4  Author interviews with Waronker, 2017–19.
5  Author interview with Asher.
6  Yetnikoff, *Howling at the Moon*, p. 95.
7  Author interview with Asher.
8  Ibid.
9  Author interviews with Ostin, March 2019.
10  Yetnikoff, *Howling at the Moon*, p. 97.

11  Author interviews with Ostin, March 2019.
12  Author interviews with Smith.

**13: The Name of the Game Is Performance**

1  Author interview with Adam Somers, November 2018.

**14: Just Go Do**

1  Author interviews with Russ Thyret, July–September 2018.
2  Ibid.
3  Author interviews with Waronker, 2017–19.
4  Author interviews with Ostin, March 2019.
5  Ibid.
6  Author interview with Eddie Rosenblatt, February 2018.

**15: Coming for the Cowboys**

1  Author interview with Howie Klein, July 2018.
2  Author interviews with Ostin, March 2019.
3  Dinner details via ibid.; and Cornyn and Scanlon, *Exploding*, p. 379.
4  Author interviews with Ostin, March 2019.
5  Ibid.
6  Author interviews with Smith.
7  Cornyn and Scanlon, *Exploding*, p. 396.
8  Author interview with David Geffen, September 2018.

**16: Losing My Religion**

1  John Gibson, "Stan Cornyn: Free Wheeling with a Purpose," *Record World*, November 25, 1972.
2  Author interview with Danny Goldberg, March 2018.
3  Author interviews with Ostin, August 2019.
4  Author interviews with Thyret.

# BIBLIOGRAPHY

Bergman, Jo. *The Book of the Road*. Burbank, CA: Warner Bros. Records Inc., 1975.

Bowen, Jimmy, and Jim Jerome. *Rough Mix*. New York: Simon and Schuster, 1997.

Browne, David. *Fire and Rain*. Cambridge, MA: Da Capo Press, 2011.

Bruck, Connie. *Master of the Game*. New York: Simon and Schuster, 1994.

Cale, John, and Victor Bockris. *What's Welsh for Zen?* New York: Bloomsbury USA, 2000.

Cornyn, Stan, and Ellen Pelissero. "What a Long, Strange Trip It's Been: An Authorized History of Warner Bros. Records." Unpublished manuscript, 1981.

Cornyn, Stan, and Paul Scanlon. *Exploding*. New York: Harper Entertainment Publishing, 2002.

Cross, Charles R. *Room Full of Mirrors: A Biography of Jimi Hendrix*. New York: Hyperion, 2005.

Dannen, Frederic. *Hit Men: Power Brokers and Fast Money Inside the Music Business*. New York: Crown, 1990.

Fletcher, Tony. *Perfect Circle: The Story of R.E.M.* London: Omnibus Press, 2018.

Goodman, Fred. *Mansion on the Hill*. New York: Crown, 1997.

Greenfield, Robert. *The Last Sultan*. New York: Simon and Schuster, 2011.

Jackson, Blair. *Garcia: An American Life*. New York: Penguin Books, 2000.

King, Tom. *The Operator: David Geffen Builds, Buys, and Sells the New Hollywood*. New York: Random House, 2000.

McDonough, Jimmy. *Shakey: Neil Young's Biography*. New York: Random House, 2002.

McNally, Dennis. *A Long, Strange Trip: The Inside History of the Grateful Dead*. New York: Broadway Books, 2002.

Yetnikoff, Walter, with David Ritz. *Howling at the Moon*. New York: Broadway Books, 2004.

Zanes, Warren. *Petty: The Biography*. New York: Henry Holt and Company, 2015.

———. *Revolutions in Sound: Warner Bros. Records, the First Fifty Years*. San Francisco, CA: Chronicle Books, 2009.

# ACKNOWLEDGMENTS

Writing is supposed to be a lonely profession, but what they don't tell you is that if you're doing it on the nonfiction side of the aisle, you're actually working with dozens, sometimes hundreds, of other people: editors, agents, subjects, sources, publicists, personal assistants (not yours, generally), librarians, archivists, computer repair folks, baristas, bartenders, and many more. Then come the family, friends, and colleagues, and then your *therapist*, and the gang's all here.

So a great ringing chorus of thanks to all these folks, and to a hundred others, too.

At Writers House: my great friend and agent Dan Conaway, Simon Lipskar, and Lauren Carsley.

At Henry Holt and Company: as crazy as it sounds, this book has had no fewer than *four* editors. Crazier still, the transitions all went smoothly, and all four contributed something valuable to the project. Gillian Blake acquired the book and encouraged me during the early going; Libby Burton gave excellent assistance during the writing process and helped me sharpen my thinking; Jonathan Cox did a masterful line edit; and Kerry Cullen came in to help push the thing over the goal line.

I spoke to a legion of Warner Bros. Records people, but I owe my greatest thanks to Carl Scott, who volunteered to be my WBR rabbi and then did everything but perform my bris, much to the relief of both of us. Georgia Bergman was also an invaluable source and supporter throughout.

Mo Ostin gave me an extraordinary amount of his time and access to his long and astonishingly precise memory. Lenny Waronker was also essential to the creation of this book going back to our first meeting in 2013, when neither of us knew I'd be working on it. I also owe enormous thanks to Michael Ostin, Jeff Smith, Chris Cornyn, David Berson, and Bob Merlis, all of whom sat for multiple interviews, connected me to other crucial sources, and/or provided invaluable archival materials. Also key: Russ Thyret, Ted Templeman, Russ Titelman, Pete Johnson, Eddie Rosenblatt, Bill Bentley, Adam Somers, Steven Baker, Gene Sculatti, Larry Butler, Jimmy Bowen, Barry "Dr. Demento" Hansen, Jac Holzman, Mark Maitland, Oscar Fields, Joe Boyd, Richard and Linda Perry, Tom Whalley, Lou Dennis, Howie Klein, Michael Linehan, Jeff Gold, Charlie Springer, Danny Goldberg, Lee Herschberg, Sig Sigworth, Jeff Ayeroff, David Altschul, David Berman, Shelley Cooper, Jim Ed Norman, Eugene Sculatti, Ted Cohen, Nina Berson, Paul Almond, Seymour Stein, and Rebecca Thyret. Also at WBR: Liz Morentin, Peter Standish, Laura Swanson, Bob Kaus, and Michelle Finn.

Thanks also to Arlo Guthrie, Geoff Muldaur, Maria Muldaur, Bob Newhart, Bill Payne, Tom Johnston, Patrick Simmons, Peter Buck, Ry Cooder, Randy Newman, Jim Yester, Andy Paley, Olivia Harrison, Clive Davis, Bertis Downs, Irving Azoff, Shep Gordon, Lorne Michaels, David Geffen, Peter Asher, Greil Marcus, Langdon Winner, John Rockwell, Mike Bone, Owen Husney, Al Teller, Jon Landau, Rick Rubin, Tony Dimitriades, and Larry Solters.

At the Rock and Roll Hall of Fame archives: Andy Leach and Jennie Thomas. Mike Wilson and Andy Fischer in the WBR archives, and Matthew Bass at RIAA.

To friends and colleagues for their encouragement and advice: Brian Hiatt, David Browne, Brad Rosenberg, Tim Riley, David Leaf, Patterson Hood, Scott Gould, Ryan White, Warren Zanes, and, once again, the excellent transcriber and volunteer research consultant Craig Williams.

Warren and Sheryl Rosenberg gave me a place to write and a spectacular view of Haystack Rock.

Thank you to the founders and staff of the PLAYA artists' residency in Summer Lake, Oregon.

To my family: Sarah, Abie, Teddy, and Max.

And to the memory of Elizabeth Shippen Ames.

# INDEX

A&M Records, 78–79, 149, 177, 197, 201–2, 207

Abrams, Benny, 41

Abramson, Herb, 88

Abramson, Miriam, 88

Academy Awards, 131

Academy of Music Arts, 219n

Acapulco property, 171–72, 177

Adler, Lou, 83, 86

"Albatross," 180

Alden, Ronald, 104

"Alex Chilton," 246

Alice Cooper, 109, 135–39

*Alice's Restaurant*, 131

"Alice's Restaurant Massacree," 79–80, 95, 223

"All Day and All of the Night," 58

Allen, David, 26

Allen, Steve, 31

"All Golden, The," 4

Allman Brother Band, 203

Altschul, David, 242

Alvin and the Chipmunks, 75

*Amahl and the Night Visitors* (Menotti), 5

America, 109, 157, 169

*America*, 157

*American Beauty*, 132, 151–52, 155

*America's Favorite Organ Hits*, 47

Andersen, Eric, 105

Animals, 70, 82, 204n

Ann-Margret, 134

"Annus Mirablis" (Larkin), 57

*Anthem of the Sun*, 150

Antonioni, Michelangelo, 118

"Anything Goes," 78

*Aoxomoxoa*, 150

"Aphrodite Mass," 79

Apple Records, 105, 110, 189

*Aqualung*, 153

*Are You Experienced*, 71–72

Armstrong, Edwin, 97

Arnaz, Desi, Jr., 59

*Art of Tea, The*, 199

Asher, Peter, 105, 110–11, 188–90

Ashley, Ted, 116, 129

Association, 2, 9, 81, 97

Asylum Records, 169–70, 192–93, 196–97, 199, 246, 250

Atari company, 221–22

Atco, 236

Atlantic Records, 70, 77, 79, 88–92, 127–29, 154, 157, 192–93, 203, 235–36, 242, 249

*Auntie Mame*, 26
*Autobiography of a World Savior* (Lyman), 117
*Automatic for the People*, 228
Autumn Records, 61–62, 74, 98, 140
Avakian, George, 25–26, 29–30
Avalon Ballroom, 63–65, 111, 149
Azoff, Irving, 232, 239

B-52s, 232
"Baby It's You," 49
Backus, Jim, 33
Baez, Joan, 115
Baker, Ginger, 119–20
Baker, Steven, 242, 244
Ball, Lucille, 59
Band of Joy, 120
Bardavid, Evelyn, 42
*Bare Trees*, 181, 184
Basie, Count, 47
Basquiat, Jean-Michel, 248
Battin, Skip, 6
Beach Boys, 2, 5, 7, 9, 61, 84, 118n, 153–54,
    156, 164, 198
Bearsville label, 203
Beatles, 2, 5, 7, 56–59, 69–70, 84, 86, 101, 105,
    110, 120–21, 177, 217–18, 245
Beau Brummels, 61, 74, 140
Beefheart, Captain, 81, 100, 113, 140, 143–45,
    149, 227, 229
Bee Gees, 197, 207
Beethoven, Ludwig van, 6
Belafonte, Harry, 48
Bellamy Brothers, 204–5
Benjamin, Louis, 58
Benson, George, 198–99, 220
Bergman, Georgia "Jo," 174, 217–19
Berio, Luciano, 62
Berman, David, 202, 215
Berry, Chuck, 25, 198
Berson, David, 94–95, 116–17, 119, 180, 201
"Big Bad Jim," 32
"Big Bad John," 32
Big Brother and the Holding Company, 71–72
Big Button ad campaign, 185–86, 199
Big Tree Records, 236
Bikel, Theo, 17, 81
*Billboard*, 15, 24–27, 30, 34, 37, 47, 44, 51, 58,
    61, 69, 74, 81, 99, 110–11, 123–24, 131–33,
    136, 139, 150–51, 157–58, 169–70, 180–81,
    184–85, 190, 197, 206, 217, 222, 224, 228, 231

Bizarre/Straight label, 135–36
"Black Jack Davy," 2–3
Black Keys, 245
Black Sabbath, 12, 53, 109, 153
Blackwell, Chris, 203
Blind Faith, 120
Blondie, 207
*Blood Sugar Sex Magik*, 232–33
Bloomfield, Mike, 120
"Blowin' in the Wind," 36, 60
Blue Horizon label, 180
"Blue Letter," 182
Blue Thumb Records, 198
Body Count, 234
*Body Wishes*, 222
Bogart, Neil, 204
Bonaroo, 174
Bonham, John, 120
*Bonino* (TV show), 5
*Bonnie and Clyde* (film), 81
Boone, Debby, 205, 229
Boone, Pat, 26, 205
*Born Losers, The* (film), 204
Bowen, Jimmy, 50–51, 57–58
Box Tops, 2
Boyd, Joe, 110, 163
Bradley, Joe, 248
Bread, 154
"Break on Through (To the Other Side)," 98
*Breezin'*, 199
*Bridge Over Troubled Water*, 190
Brown, Bruce, 94
Brown, James, 120
Brown, Ruth, 88
Browne, Jackson, 110, 169, 220
Bruce, Jack, 119
Bruce, Lenny, 175
Bruck, Connie, 127
Brunswick Records, 23
Buck, Peter, 145, 227–28
Buckingham, Lindsey, 109, 182, 184
Buckley, Tim, 154
Buckley, William F., 36
Bucks County Kennel Club, 139
Buffalo Springfield, 5, 71, 76–77, 87, 119, 193
Buggles, 219
Bugs Bunny, 174, 187
Burdon, Eric, 82, 204n
Burke, Joe, 131
Burke, Solomon, 119

Burke, Sonny, 132
Burnett, T Bone, 223
*Button-Down Mind of Bob Newhart, The*, 30–31
*But You've Never Heard Gershwin with Bongos*, 21
Byrds, 5, 68, 84, 87, 119
Byrne, David, 232
Byrnes, Edd "Kookie," 27
"By the People," 4

Cale, John, 163–65
"California Dreamin'," 68–69
*Callboard* (newsletter), 106
*Can-Can* (soundtrack), 45–46
Canned Heat, 115
Cano, Eddie, 49
"Can't Get No Nookie," 120–21
Cantor, Eddie, 171
Capitol Records, 20, 22, 24–25, 31, 33, 35, 45–47, 63, 72, 108, 123–24, 147, 195, 239
Capricorn Records, 203
"Carefree HIghway," 198
Carlin, George, 201
"Carolina on My Mind," 110
Carr, Joe "Fingers" (Lou Busch), 33
Cars, 196, 207
*Car Wash* (soundtrack), 129n, 200–201, 223
*Casablanca* (film), 87, 126
Casablanca Records, 204
Casady, Bill, 123
"Casey Jones," 150
*Cashbox*, 99, 123, 185
Cassidy, David, 205
Cassidy, Shaun, 205
Castaneda, Carlos, 96
"Cathy's Clown," 28–29
Cavallo, Bob, 223
CBGB, 203, 221
*Centerfield*, 224
"Chain, The," 184
Chalet (WBR headquarters), 13–14, 18, 173–74, 179–80, 227, 232, 241, 243–46
Chamberlain, Richard, 137
Chandler, Chas, 70
Charles, Ray, 58, 70, 88, 101
Checker, Chubby, 47, 49
*Cheetah* (magazine), 98
Children of God, 181
"Chipmunk Song, The," 75
Chrysalis Records, 172, 203

"Cigarettes, Whiskey and Wild, Wild Women," 26
Cipolla, Barbara, 103
*Circular* (newsletter), 107–8, 122–23, 130, 152–53, 157–58, 170, 211
*Circus* (magazine), 124
"City of New Orleans, The," 165, 223
Clapton, Eric, 119–20, 230–32, 235
Clark, Gary, Jr., 245
Clark, Petula, 9, 58, 81–82, 195
Clay, Andrew Dice, 232
Cleanliness and Godliness Skiffle Band, 121
Clinton, George, 198
*Cloud Nine*, 225
"C'mon and Swim," 61
Coasters, 88
"Coca-Cola Douche," 79
Cochran, Eddie, 75
Cockettes, 136, 137, 138
Cole, Buddy, Trio, 56
Cole, Nat King, 42
Coleman, Ornette, 5
Collins, Bootsy, 198
Collins, Judy, 102, 154
Columbia Records, 24, 72, 106, 147, 155–56, 163, 185, 187–93
"Come to the Sunshine," 78
Conkling, Jim, 19–32, 63, 207
Cooder, Ry, 80, 109, 140–45, 149, 177, 220
Cook, Hal, 27
*Cool Scene, The*, 21
Cooper, Shelley, 136, 166, 202
"Cop Killer," 234
Cornyn, Stan, 10–14, 20–21, 24, 26, 58, 62–64, 70, 86, 96, 99–106, 110–15, 122–24, 133–34, 146–48, 151–53, 162–65, 168, 171–72, 177, 185–87, 192–97, 204, 206, 211–13, 227, 242
Cosby, Bill, 56, 97
*Cosmic Thing*, 232
Country Joe and the Fish, 115
*Court and Spark*, 169
Covay, Don, 119
"Cow Pie," 120, 122–23
*Crawdaddy* (magazine), 98
Cream, 90, 119, 120
Creedence Clearwater Revival, 115, 224
Crimson, King, 220
Crosby, Bing, 48, 56
Crosby, David, 5, 68, 87, 119, 193

Crosby, Stills, and Nash, 119–20, 193
Crosby, Stills, Nash, and Young, 90, 116, 119
Cross, Christopher, 210
Crusaders, 199
"Crystal," 182
Curb, Mike, 204–5
Curb Records, 205
Curtis, Tony, 91
Cushing, Richard, 36

"Dance of the Hours," 34
Darin, Bobby, 88
Davies, Ray, 107
Davis, Clive, 72, 190
Davis, Sammy, Jr., 7, 47–48, 112
Day, Dennis, 47
Dead Boys, 203
Dean, Jimmy, 32
Decca Records, 91, 147
"December 1963 (Oh What a Night)," 205
Deep Purple, 109, 153, 177
Def American Records, 232
Deity Records, 123
de Mello, Jack, 49
Denver, John, 110
Depeche Mode, 221, 232
Devil at Four O'Clock, The (film), 39–40
Devo, 13, 220
"Diamond Girl," 169
Diamonds and Pearls, 232
Diken, Howard, 30
Dimitriades, Tony, 226
Dino, Desi, and Billy, 59
Dion, 49
Dire Straits, 13, 207, 225
Dirty Mind, 216
Discover America, 142, 162–63
"Dixie Chicken," 175
Dixieland Sound, The, 25
Document, 227
Domino, Fats, 17, 25, 44, 205
Donahue, Tom, 60–65, 98, 121n, 139–40
Donovan, 120, 137
Don Quixote (animated film), 45
Don't Leave Your Empties on the Piano, 21
Don't Look Back (documentary), 94
"Don't Stop," 184
Doobie Brothers, 13, 135, 140–42, 149, 174, 177, 198, 208, 222

Doobie Brothers, 141
Doors, 8, 98, 110, 154
Dorsey, Tommy, 48
Dot Records, 24–25
"Downtown," 58
"Do You Want to Dance," 61, 74
Drake, Bill, 107
"Dreams," 184
Dream Works Records, 243
Drifters, 88
Dubin, Al, 131
Dunn, Lloyd, 25
Durante, Jimmy, 56
Durgom, George "Bullets," 32–33
Dylan, Bob, 34, 36, 60, 94, 120–23, 192–93, 203, 225

Eagles, 87, 169, 197, 199, 207, 220, 239, 250
Eddie Cano at P.J.'s, 49
Ed Sullivan Show, 56, 58
Edward Gould Orchestra, 137
Einstein, Albert, 6
Electric Light Orchestra, 226
Electric Prunes, 69, 81, 114
Elektra-Asylum, 196, 203, 220
Elektra-Asylum-Nonesuch, 235
Elektra Records, 8, 125, 154–55, 157, 170, 218, 238, 246
Elephant Parts (video), 218–19
Ellington, Duke, 47, 81
Elliott, Cass, 68–69, 87
Elrod, Jeff, 248
Emerson, Keith, 181
Emerson, Lake and Palmer, 181
EMI, 195, 232–33
Endless Summer, The (documentary), 94
Epstein, Brian, 217
Errico, Jan, 77
Ertegun, Ahmet, 77, 88–92, 127–29, 138, 154, 157, 186, 192–93, 207, 235, 237, 249
Ertegun, Nesuhi, 89, 90, 154, 235–36
Esquire, 10
Esquivel, Juan, 56
Esso Trinidad Steel Band, 161–63
Esso Trinidad Steel Band, 162
Everly, Don, 29
Everly, Phil, 29
Everly Brothers, 13, 28–29, 47, 56, 114, 149
"Everybody Loves Our Jim," 32
"Everybody Loves Somebody," 21n, 51

*Exciting Sounds of the South Seas, The*, 47
Exile, 204
*Exploding* (Cornyn), 63

Faithfull, Marianne, 217
Family, The, 120
Family Dog company, 64
*Farewell Tour* (Doobie Brothers), 222
Farkle, 3–4
Fass, Bob, 80
"Fat Man in the Bathtub," 175
Faulous Farquahr, 109
Fellini, Federico, 65
Ferragnio, Della, 107
*15 Big Ones*, 198
"59th Street Bridge Song (Feelin' Groovy),"
    15, 77–78
"Fire and Rain," 110
*Fireball*, 153
First Edition, 74
Fischer, Wild Man, 81, 114
Fitzgerald, Ella, 17, 81, 149
Flaming Lips, 245
Flatt and Scruggs, 81
Fleetwood, Mick, 149, 180, 182–85
Fleetwood Mac, 12, 95, 109, 149, 180–90,
    197–99, 207–8, 219–20, 245
*Fleetwood Mac* (1968), 180–81
*Fleetwood Mac* (1975), 183–84
Fogerty, John, 224
"Foggy Mountain Breakdown," 81
Foghat, 203
Fonda, Peter, 5
*For You*, 216
Four Seasons, 205
"Foxy Lady," 70
Frampton, Peter, 181, 197, 207
*Frampton Comes Alive*, 197, 207
Franklin, Aretha, 70, 88, 90
Franks, Michael, 199
Frechette, Mark, 118
Freeman, Bobby, 61, 74
Friedman, Joel, 24–25, 74, 99
Friends of Ed Labunski, 109
Fuchs, Michael, 243
Fuck the Bunny campaign, 187–88
*Fuck You: A Magazine of the Arts*, 79
Fugs, 17, 74, 79, 81, 93, 97, 100, 103–9, 113,
    129, 229
*Fugs Eat It, The*, 79

Funkadelic (Parliament), 198
Furay, Richie, 76
*Future Games*, 181

Gabriel, Peter, 225
Garcia, Jerry, 150, 152
Garfunkel, Art, 190
Garrett, Snuff, 76
Gaye, Marvin, 188
Geffen, David, 116, 160, 169, 191–94, 196,
    220, 232, 239–40, 243
Geffen Records, 220, 232
Gentry, Bobbie, 2
George, Lowell, 148, 175–76
Gershwin, George and Ira, 172
"Get Together," 199
Giancana, Sam, 48, 51
Giant Records, 232
Gibson, Bob, 200, 201
Gilligan, Matt, 22
Gitlin, Murray, 70, 72
Gleason, Jackie, 5
Gleason, Ralph J., 5
"Glory, Glory, Harry Lewis," 33
*Go, Go Radio Moscow*, 109
*God Bless Tiny Tim*, 131
Goldberg, Danny, 236–37, 242–43
"Golden Road (to Unlimited Devotion), The,"
    111
Goldstein, Richard, 132
*Gone with the Wind* (film), 126
Gordon, Shep, 135–36
*Gorilla*, 188
Gossage, Howard Luck, 100–101
Gottehrer, Richard, 203
Gottfried, Martin, 131–32
Gould, Edward, 137
"Go Your Own Way," 184
*Graceland*, 13, 225
Graham, Bill, 64
Graham, Larry, 174, 176
Graham Bond Organisation, 119
Graham Central Station, 174, 176
Grammy Awards, 24, 26, 99, 162, 208, 219, 225
Grant, Peter, 90–91
Granz, Irving, 41–42
Granz, Norman, 42–46, 73
Grateful Dead, 5, 9, 12, 13, 17, 53, 62–66,
    69–74, 97, 103, 111–16, 129, 132, 149–52,
    195, 235, 245

*Grateful Dead* (1967), 81, 111
*Grateful Dead* (*Skull Fuck*, 1971), 152
*Great Italian-American Hits*, 47
*Great Rock 'n' Roll Swindle, The* (soundtrack),
   203
Great Society, 61
Grech, Ric, 120
*Green*, 228
Green, Peter, 149, 180–81
Green Day, 13
Greenspan, Seymour, 29
Grey Advertising, 86
Grossman, Albert, 34–36, 123, 203
GTOs (Girls Together Outrageously), 81, 138
Guinness, Alec, 6
Guthrie, Arlo, 9, 12, 79–80, 93, 95, 113–16,
   131, 142, 149, 165, 223
Guthrie, Woody, 79

Haley, Bill, and the Comets, 28
Halprin, Daria, 118
Halverstadt, Hal, 122, 144–45
"Handle with Care," 225
"Handy Man," 189
*Hard Day's Night, A* (film), 218
Harpers Bizarre (*formerly* Tikis), 15, 78, 140,
   149
Harris, Bob, 175
Harris, Emmylou, 148
Harrison, George, 120, 123, 177–78, 208,
   225
Harrison, Olivia, 177
*Harvest*, 157
*Harvest Moon*, 232
"Head," 216
Hear Here Records, 132
"Heart of Gold," 157
*Hearts and Bones*, 222
"Hello Muddah, Hello Fadduh," 34
Helms, Chet, 64
Hendrix, Jimi, 12–13, 53, 69–72, 81–82, 93,
   97, 113–16, 129, 215, 245
Herman's Hermits, 103
*Heroes Are Hard to Find*, 181, 183
Herschberg, Lee, 7
"Hey Joe," 69–70
"High Coin," 6
Hilburn, Robert, 124
Hinsche, Billy, 59
Hollies, 120

*Hollywood Reporter*, 85
Holzman, Jac, 8, 125, 154–57, 218
*Honeymooners, The* (TV sitcom), 5
Hopkins, Jerry, 97
"Horse with No Name," 157
*Hotel California*, 197–98, 207
*Howling at the Moon* (Yetnikoff), 187
Howlin' Wolf, 5
"How Sweet It Is (To Be Loved By You)," 188
Huebner, Louise, 109
*Hullabaloo* (magazine), 101
Hunter, Tab, 23–25, 219n
Husker Dü, 229
Husney, Owen, 215, 216
Hyman, Eliot, 87–90, 92, 125–27, 154

Ice-T, 234
"If You Could Read My Mind," 132
Iggy and the Stooges, 154
"I Had Too Much to Dream Last Night," 69
Ileindorf, Ray, 26
"I'm a Believer," 2
"I'm a Fool," 59
"I'm Eighteen," 136
Immediate Records, 181
"I'm So Afraid," 182
"I'm Walkin'," 44
Ink Spots, 26
*In the Pocket*, 188
Invincibles, 109
*I Remember Tommy*, 48
Iron Butterfly, 90, 110
Ironstrings, Ira, 20–21, 24–25, 99, 122
IRS Records, 227
Island Records, 203, 210
"It Ain't Nothin' but a Warner Bros. Party,"
   176
*It Crawled into My Hand, Honest*, 81, 103
"It's OK," 198
Ivy League Trio, 50
"I Wanna Be Your Lover," 216

Jackson, Calvin, 47
Jackson, Michael, 197n, 224
Jacobs, George, 50, 51
Jagger, Mick, 91–92, 120, 123, 217
"Jailhouse Rock," 49
"Jam, The," 176
*James Taylor*, 110
*Jammin' the Blues* (short film), 45

Jan and Dean, 61
Jarreau, Al, 199
*Jazz & Pop* (magazine), 10, 144
Jazz at the Philharmonic, 42–43
*Jazz Variations on Movie Themes*, 47
*Jazz Singer, The* (film), 23, 87
"Jealous Heart," 25
Jefferson Airplane, 61, 64, 72, 115
Jeffries, Mike, 70
Jeremy and the Satyrs, 74
*Jesse Colin Young on the Road*, 199
"Jesus Is Just Alright," 141
Jethro Tull, 95, 101, 109, 153, 203
Joel, Billy, 197
John, Elton, 129n, 220
Johnnys, The, 109
Johnson, J. J., 42
Johnson, Lyndon, 85, 245
Johnson, Pete (Solomon Penthaus), 107,
   122–24
Johnston, Tom, 141, 198
Jolson, Al, 23, 120
Jones, A. Quincy (architect), 173–74, 179
Jones, Brian, 71
Jones, Davy, 103
Jones, Jimmy, 189
Jones, John Paul, 120
Jones, Quincy (musician), 93, 232, 243
Jones, Rickie Lee, 208, 220, 236
Joplin, Janis, 71–72, 115
Jourdan, Louis, 6
*JT*, 189
"Just a Little," 61, 74

Kalmenson, Ben, 27, 28, 31
Katzenberg, Jeffrey, 243
Kay, John, 137
Kaye, Danny, 47
Kelly, Grace, 6
Kennedy, John F., 48–49
Kennedy, Joseph, 48
Kennedy, Robert F., 48
Kerouac, Jack, 63, 96, 175
Kessel, Barney, 42, 44
Khan, Chaka, 198, 220
Kienholz, Ed, 134
*Killer*, 139
*Kiln House*, 181
King, BB, 70
King, Ben E., 47

King, Rodney, 234
Kingston Trio, 34
Kinks, 13, 53, 57–58, 81, 93, 107, 114, 132
Kinney National Service, 127, 154
Kirwan, Danny, 181
KISS, 204
Klein, Howie, 230–32, 242
KMPX-FM, 98, 121n, 123
Knotts, Don, 31
Kooper, Al, 115, 120, 123
Kornfeld, Artie, 116
KPPC-FM, 98
Krasnow, Bob, 198, 201–2, 235, 238
Kristofferson, Kris, 110
KRLA-AM, 84–85, 108
KSAN-FM, 121–22
KTTV-TV, 144
Kupferberg, Tuli, 79, 103–4
Kweskin, Jim, 117–18
KYA-AM radio, 60–61

Lambert, Kit, 70
"Landslide," 182
lang, k.d., 232
Lang, Michael, 116
Larkin, Philip, 57, 68
"Laugh Laugh," 61, 74
Led Zeppelin, 90–91, 115, 120, 175, 192
"Lend Me Your Comb," 21n, 27
Lennon, John, 120, 123, 177, 220
LeRoy, Mervyn, 40
Lesh, Phil, 65, 111, 150
"Let's Go Crazy," 224
"Letter, The," 2
Levin, Gerald "Jerry," 236–40, 243
Levy, Morris, 50
Lewis, Jerry Lee, 25
Liberty Records, 15, 75–76
Lichtenstein, Roy, 243
*Lick My Decals Off, Baby*, 143–44
Lieberson, Goddard, 191
"Life in the Fast Lane," 198
*Life* (magazine), 45
Lightfoot, Gordon, 109, 132, 137, 198
"Like a Rolling Stone," 59
*Like a Virgin*, 224
"Like I Love You," 27
Lil Pump, 245
Linkletter, Art, 50
LiPuma, Tommy, 198, 199

"Listen to the Music," 141
*Little Criminals*, 198
Little Feat, 143, 148, 174–76, 188
"Little Red Corvette," 217, 223
Little Richard, 205
*Live at Fillmore East* (Frank Zappa), 153
*Live/Dead*, 132, 150
Livingston, Alan, 72
Loma Records, 82n
London, Julie, 75
Lopez, Trini, 54, 58
*Los Angeles Times*, 106, 124, 138, 162–63
Loss Leaders (sampler albums), 113–15, 187,
     227
"Louie, Louie," 59
*Love It to Death*, 136, 138–39
"Lucky Star," 224
Luke Warm, 109
Lulu, 2
Lydon, Michael, 68
Lyman, Mel, 117–19
Lynne, Jeff, 226
Lynyrd Skynyrd, 129n

"Macho Man," 204
*Mad* (magazine), 63
Madonna, 12, 13, 221–25, 232, 249
*Madonna*, 221, 224
*Magic Christian, The* (Southern), 121
Magritte, René, 248
Mailer, Norman, 79
Maitland, John K. "Mike," 31–37, 55–59,
     72–73, 88–90, 99, 126, 128–29
Makeba, Miriam, 81, 114
Mamas and the Papas, 68–69, 77
"Mammy," 120
Mancini, Henry, 21
"Manic Depression," 70–71
"Man of the World," 181
Manson, Charles, 118n, 119
Marcus, Greil, 120–23, 132
Marinello, Frank, 68
Marley, Bob, 203
Martin, Dean, 47, 51, 59, 81–82, 112
Martin, Dewey, 76
Martin, Dino, 59
Martin, Steve, 13
Marvelows, 109
Masked Marauders, 120–24, 226
*Masked Marauders, The*, 124

*Mass in F Minor*, 81
*Master of Reality*, 153
*Master of the Game* (Bruck), 127
"Masters of War," 120–21
Maverick Records, 232
Maxim, Arnold, 46
May, Elaine, 31
Maysles, Albert and David, 56
MC5, 154
MCA Records, 44, 129n, 226
McCartney, Paul, 56, 68, 101–2, 120, 123,
     177
McDonald, Michael, 198
McGuinn, Roger, 5
McGuire Sisters, 50
McKenzie, Scott, 68
McKuen, Rod, 137–38
McLaren, Malcolm, 201–2
McVie, Christine, 109, 181, 184
McVie, John, 149, 180, 182, 184
Melcher, Terry, 118n
Menotti, Gian Carlo, 5
Mercer, Johnny, 32
Mercy, Miss, 138
Merman, Ethel, 47, 48
"Mexico," 188
Meynard, Raoul, 26
MGM, 6, 127
MGM Records, 46, 204
Michaels, Lorne, 250
Midwest Rock Festival, 115
*Miles of Aisles*, 169
"Milestone in Pop, A," 9–10
Minella, Art, 54
*Minute by Minute*, 208
Miroff, Bruce, 120–23
*Mirror at the End of the Road, The* (Lyman),
     117
Mitchell, Bob, 60–62, 140
Mitchell, Joni, 12–13, 53, 87, 93, 97, 104–5,
     109, 116, 132, 143, 145, 169, 199, 245
Mitchell, Mitch, 83
Moby Grape, 64
Modern Jazz Quartet, 47
Mogull, Artie, 35
Mojo Men, 61, 74, 76–77
"Monday Morning," 182
Monkees, 2, 87, 103, 218
Monte, Lou, 47, 50
"Monterey," 82

*Monterey Pop!* (documentary), 67
Monterey Pop Festival, 67–69, 71–73,
   82–86
Montrose, 174
"Moonglow," 137
Morgado, Robert, 232, 235–43
Morris, Doug, 236–39, 242–43
Morris, Garrett, 201
Morrison, Jim, 87
Morrison, Sterling, 163
Morrison, Van, 12–13, 87, 93, 109, 132, 149,
   177, 223
Morrissey, 232
Morthland, John, 122
Mother Earth, 140–42
Mothers of Invention, 80–81, 153, 204
Motown Records, 123, 200
MTV, 217–19, 223–24, 231
*Mud Slide Slim and the Blue Horizon*, 151, 153
Muldaur, Geoff and Maria, 117
Mull, Martin, 172
Murdoch, Rupert, 222
Museum of Modern Art, 144
*Music for People with $3.98 Plus Tax (If Any)*,
   20, 25, 99
*Music from the Land of the Rising Sun*, 49
music videos, 142–43, 210, 217–20, 223–24
*My Fair Lady* (Broadway show), 33
*My Son, the Celebrity*, 34
*My Son, the Folk Singer*, 33–34
*My Son, the Nut*, 34

*Naked and the Dead, The* (Mailer), 79
Nash, Graham, 119, 193
*Nashville Skyline*, 122
National Academy of Recording Arts and
   Sciences (NARAS), 24
National Association of Recording
   Merchandisers (NARM), 146–48
"Nearer My God to Thee," 3
Nechenie, Amy (*later* Bansak), 104
Nelson, Ozzie and Harriet, 44
Nelson, Ricky, 44
NEMS Enterprises, 217
Nesmith, Mike, 218
Nevada Gaming Commission, 51
*Never Mind the Bollocks . . . Here's the Sex
   Pistols*, 202
Newhart, Bob, 13, 29–32, 56, 222
"New Kid in Town," 198

Newman, Irving, 75, 78
Newman, Randy, 3, 13, 74–79, 92, 101–6,
   109, 131, 137, 142, 153, 160–61, 172, 198,
   250
Newport Folk Festival, 80, 95, 110, 117
*Newsweek*, 68, 87
*New Yorker*, 9
*New York Magazine*, 9
*New York Post*, 131n
*New York Times Magazine*, 131
New Youth, 5
Next Exit, 109
Nice, The, 181
Nichols, Mike, 31
Nickelodeon (cable network), 218
Nicks, Stevie, 109, 182–84, 219
Nico, 164
Nikita the K, 109
*1969 Warner-Reprise Record Show*, 17
*1969 Warner-Reprise Songbook*, 114
Nirvana, 236
Nitzsche, Jack, 80
Nixon, Pat, 186
Nixon, Richard, 186, 204
"Nixon Now (More Than Ever)," 204
NLE Choppa, 245
Nonesuch Records, 154
Noone, Peter, 103
*Northern Review* (magazine), 101
"Not the Lovin' Kind," 59
NRBQ, 203
"Number Nine," 6

Ochs, Phil, 85, 149
"Ode to Billie Joe," 2
"Oh, Atlanta," 175
"Oh, Well," 181
*Ol' Blue Eyes Is Back*, 169
*Ol' Calliope Man at the Fair, The*, 47
*Ol' Calliope Man Visits a German Hofbrau,
   The*, 49
*Old Grey Whistle Test* (TV show), 175
Oldham, Andrew Loog, 86, 181
Olivier, Laurence, 48
Orbison, Roy, 226
Osmond family, 204
Ostin, Evelyn, 93–94, 129, 136, 138, 158–59,
   172, 177–78, 188, 249–50
Ostin, Kenny, 93–94, 249–50
Ostin, Michael, 93–94, 210, 239, 248–49

Ostin, Mo (*born* Morris Meyer Ostrofsky), 4, 8, 107
  ads, parties, and promotions and, 136, 138, 167, 177, 186
  artists signed by, 57–58, 69–72, 78–80, 109–10, 117–19, 176–78, 180–82, 185, 190–91, 201–3, 225–29, 232–33
  Atlantic and, 90–92
  audiovisual services and, 161, 163
  background of, 40–43
  Berson hired by, 94–95, 116–17
  *Car Wash* and, 200–201
  as chairman emeritus of Warner, 244
  as chairman of Warner-Reprise, with Smith as president, 196
  Chalet headquarters and, 180
  contracts and bonuses and, 126, 128, 170–73
  Cornyn and, 10, 12, 64, 99, 102, 106
  corporate culture and artistic (no hits) values of, 12, 14, 73–78, 81, 112–13, 131, 148, 169, 176, 214–15, 228–29
  cutbacks of 1979 and, 208, 210–11
  deals with smaller labels, 57–58, 203–6
  death of sons and, 249–50
  death of wife Evelyn and, 250
  Dream Works and, 243
  early career at Verve and, 42–44
  European package tour and, 174
  family life and, 93–94
  FM radio and, 98
  as general manager of Reprise, 39–40, 46–50, 56–57, 59, 69
  health problems of, 95
  in-house management and, 142
  interview of 2018 and, 247–49
  James Taylor poached away from, 187–90
  JFK and, 48–49
  "just go do" and, 16, 211–14
  Kinney purchase of Warner and, 128
  marriage to Evelyn Bardavid and, 42, 46, 172, 177–78
  Masked Marauders and, 122
  negotiations and, 160–61
  Parks and, 6, 9, 12, 142–43, 161–63, 250
  as president of Warner, 129–30
  Prince movie project and, 223
  resignation of, 235–43
  rock and roll and, 69, 72–73
  Ross and, 134, 168–73, 190, 195, 207–8
  Rudin and, 44–45, 49, 126
  Smith and, 53–54, 195–97
  Stein and, 248–49
  successes of, 125–26, 132–34, 152–53, 158–60, 185
  Verve sale to MGM and, 46
  vision and legacy of, 246
  Warner executives and, 168–69, 191–92, 194, 230–32
  Warner-Reprise merger and, 54–56
  Warner-Reprise merger with Seven Arts and, 88, 92–96
  Warner-Reprise united by, 157, 192
  Waronker promoted to president by, 15–16, 196–97, 211–14
  Wickham hired by, 83, 85–87
Ostin, Randy, 93–94, 250
Ostrofsky, Bertha, 40–41
Ostrofsky, Julius, 40–41, 152
"Our Love Is Here to Stay," 172
*Out of Time*, 228
"Over My Head," 182–83
Owens, Buck, 148
*Ozzie and Harriet* (TV sitcom), 44

Pacific Radio Store, 54
Page, Jimmy, 90–91, 120
Page, Patti, 26
Palmer, Bruce, 76
Parks, Carson, 6
Parks, Durrie, 5, 143
Parks, Van Dyke, 1–12, 17, 74, 77–78, 81, 92, 96, 100–101, 104, 109, 131, 142–45, 148–49, 161–64, 212, 227, 229, 250
*Parsley, Sage, Rosemary and Thyme*, 77
Parsons, Gram, 148
*Partridge Family* (TV sitcom), 205
*Pata Pata*, 81
Paul, Les, 42
Payne, Bill, 148, 175
"Peace Song," 199
Penn, Arthur, 131
Pennebaker, D. A., 67, 94
Pentangle, 114
Penthaus, Solomon (Pete Johnson), 123–24
"Pepino the Italian Mouse," 50
Perry, Linda, 91–92
Perry, Richard, 91–92, 132, 149
Peter, Paul and Mary, 9, 13, 35–38, 60, 154, 203
*Peter, Paul and Mary*, 37

*Pet Sounds*, 7
Petty, Tom, 12, 225–27
Phillips, John, 68
Picasso, Pablo, 45
Pickett, Wilson, 70, 88, 90, 119
Pigpen Look Alike contest, 103
Pink Floyd, 197
Pinza, Ezio, 5
Pittman, Bob, 218
Plant, Robert, 120, 175
Plaster Caster, Cynthia, 137
Pointer Sisters, 196
Polanski, Roman, 118
Polydor Records, 70
"Pomp and Circumstance," 137
Ponchielli, Amilcare, 34
*PopClips* (TV program), 218
Porter, Cole, 78
Presley, Elvis, 25, 47, 49
Pretenders, 221, 249
Prince, 12, 210, 215–17, 219–20, 223–24, 232, 245
*Prince*, 216
"Prisoner of Love," 120
Procol Harum, 84
Pryor, Richard, 13, 201
"Purple Haze," 70
*Purple Rain* (film and soundtrack), 223–24
Pye Records, 57–58, 95

Queen, 220
Quicksilver Messenger Service, 64, 72
Qwest Records, 232

Rabbit, Eddie, 196
*Radio & Records* (trade paper), 183
*Radio Unnameable* (radio show), 80
"Rainy Day Man," 110
Raitt, Bonnie, 172, 191, 220–23, 236
Ramones, 203, 220
*Randy Newman*, 101–2, 104–5
*Randy Newman—Live*, 153–54
Rascals, 90
RCA, 125
Reagan, Ronald, 247
*Rebel Without a Cause* (film), 87
Recording Industry Association of America (RIAA), 126, 170, 197–98
Record Plant, 184
*Record World*, 99, 123, 185, 242

Redding, Otis, 88, 90, 119
Red Hot Chili Peppers, 13, 232–33
Reed, Lou, 163, 232
Regehr, Bob, 133–39, 166–67, 173–75, 180, 201–2, 209–10, 215, 217, 219–20, 224
R.E.M., 12–13, 145, 227–29, 232, 245
Replacements, 13, 221, 229, 246
Reprise Records, 4, 39–40, 46–51, 55, 181, 242, 246
    Warner label absorbs, 157
    Warner merges with, 4, 38, 52, 54–56, 59
Rey, Alvino, 20
"Rhiannon," 182–83
*Rhythm of the Saints, The*, 13
Rhythm Orchids, 50
Rich, Buddy, 42
*Richard D. Herbruck Presents Jim Kweskin's America*, 118
Richman, Jonathan, 223
Riddle, Nelson, 56
"Ridgetop," 199
Rifkin, Danny, 65, 111
Righteous Brothers, 61
*Ring-a-Ding Ding*, 47
RKO radio, 107
Roberts, Elliott, 169
Rock and Roll Hall of Fame, 13
"Rock and Roll Music," 198
"Rock Around the Clock," 28
"Rock Morality, The" (Cornyn), 146–48
Rockwell, John, 162–63
Rodgers, Jimmie, 26
Rogers, Kenny, 74
*Rolling Stone*, 10, 96, 97, 98, 105, 120–24, 144, 162, 216–17
Rolling Stones, 70, 71, 80, 86, 91–92, 121, 192, 207, 217–18
Ronettes, 61
Ronstadt, Linda, 169, 207
Rosenblatt, Eddie, 153–54, 183, 196–97, 212–13
Rosenthal, Jerry, 44
Ross, Steve, 154–56, 169–73, 191–92, 194, 207–8, 221–22, 235–36
    death of, 233–36, 239, 246
    Ostin and, 130, 134, 158, 160, 168–69, 190, 195, 231
    Smith and, 195–96
    Time Warner merger and, 233
    Warner bought by, 127–30, 154

Rotten, Johnny, 202–3
Roulette Records, 50
RSO Records, 207
Rubin, Rick, 232
Ruby Tuesday column (Wickwire), 108
Rudin, Mickey, 39–40, 44–46, 49, 54–55, 126, 160
*Rumours*, 184, 190, 198, 207, 208n, 219
Rundgren, Todd, 203
Russell, Leon, 77–78, 199
*Rust Never Sleeps*, 232

*Safe as Milk*, 145
Salinger, Pierre, 48
Sandburg, Carl, 175
Sande and Greene Fun-Time Band, 47, 49
Sanders, Ed, 79
"San Francisco," 68
Sanicola, Hank, 39
Santana, 115
"Sarah Jackman," 33
"Sarah" (music video), 219
"Satisfaction," 59
*Saturday Night Fever* (soundtrack), 197, 207
"Say You Love Me," 183
"School's Out," 139
*School's Out*, 139
Scott, Carl, 112, 139–42, 159, 174, 180, 218
Scully, Rock, 65–66
Seals and Crofts, 169, 177
"Season of the Witch," 120
Sebastian, John, 116
"Second Hand News," 184
*Seduction Through Witchcraft*, 109
"See Ya Later, Alligator," 28
*September of My Years*, 99
Seven Arts Associated, 87–92, 154, 203
*77 Sunset Strip* (TV show and album), 27–28, 63
Sex Pistols, 12, 201–3
*Sgt. Pepper's Lonely Hearts Club Band*, 2, 7, 10
Sherman, Allan, 32–34
Sherman, Dick, 123
Shirelles, 47, 49
"Short People," 198
Siegel, Cliff, 215
Silvers, Phil, 39
Simmons, Patrick, 141
Simon, Carly, 149, 188–89

Simon, Paul, 12–13, 190–91, 213, 220, 222, 225, 232
Simon and Garfunkel, 5, 15, 77, 190, 220, 222
Sims, Judith, 106–7
Sinatra, Frank, 4, 6–7, 9, 12–13, 45–59, 62, 81–82, 85, 97, 99, 112, 126, 157, 160–61, 167, 169
  Reprise founded by, 38–40, 46–47
  rock and roll and, 49–50, 53, 72
  Warner-Reprise merger and, 51–52, 54–56, 59
Sinatra, Nancy, 51, 81, 148
*Sinatra at the Sands*, 62, 99
*Siren Song* (Stein), 249
Sire Records, 203, 220, 232, 234, 246, 248–49
"Sister," 216
"Sit Down, I Think I Love You," 76–77
*Sit Down Young Stranger*, 132
*16* (magazine), 103
Slash company, 232
Sledge, Percy, 88
Slick, Grace, 61
Sly and the Family Stone, 174
*Smile*, 2, 5, 164
Smith, Donnie, 64, 65, 82, 138
Smith, Joe, 4, 95
  ads parties, and promotions and, 36–38, 136, 138, 167, 176–77, 186
  artists signed by, 58, 81–83, 105, 109–10
  Autumn Records and, 61–62
  background of, 36–37, 195
  Capitol Records and, 239
  contracts and, 126, 128, 195–96
  Cornyn and, 10–11, 64, 99, 105–6
  corporate culture and, 112–13
  Elektra/Asylum taken over by, 196, 203
  Grateful Dead and, 64–66, 69, 72, 111, 149–51, 155, 235
  hired by Warner, 36–38, 74
  in-house management and tour support and, 135, 140–42, 174, 176
  Kinney purchase of Warner and, 128–30, 170
  manages Warner side, after Reprise merger, 56
  Ostin and, 53–54, 130, 195–97
  as president of Warner, 195–96, 211
  rock and roll and, 64, 72–73
  *Song Cycle* and, 7–9, 12

successes of, 125
Warner executives and, 170, 191–92, 194, 239
WCI corporate largesse and, 171–72
Smiths, 221, 232
"Soft and Wet," 216
*Sold for the Prevention of Disease Only*, 109–10
*Some of Our Best Friends*, 114
Somers, Adam, 167–68, 206
"Something in the Way She Moves," 110
"Somethin' Stupid," 51
"Somewhere My Love," 137
"Songbird," 184
*Song Cycle*, 1–12, 81, 104, 142, 162, 250
*Song for Juli*, 199
*Songs in the Key of Life*, 197
*Songs That Followed the Kids Home from Camp*, 21
Sonic Youth, 236
"Sonny Boy," 23
Sony/Epic Records, 233
Soul Clan, 119
"Sound of Silence," 190
Southern, Terry, 121
Spector, Phil, 149
Spencer, Jeremy, 149, 181
Spielberg, Steven, 243
Springer, Charlie, 132
Springsteen, Bruce, 224
Spungen, Nancy, 202–3
Stamp, Chris, 70
Starr, Herman, 27, 55
Starr, Ringo, 177
Steeltown Two, 6
Stein, Seymour, 203, 220–21, 224, 232, 248–49
Steppenwolf, 137
*Stereo Review*, 10, 130–31, 132
Steve Miller Blues Band, 72
Stevens, Connie, 23–24, 27
Stewart, Rod, 199, 207, 218, 220, 222, 232
*Still Crazy After All These Years*, 190
Stills, Stephen, 76, 87, 119–20, 193
Stone, Sly, 61
Stookey, Noel Paul, 35, 37–38, 154
*Stranger, The*, 197
"Strangers in the Night," 51
*Strangers in the Night*, 62
Streisand, Barbra, 250

Stromberg, Gary, 200–201
"Sugar Magnolia," 151
Summer, Donna, 204, 208
"Summer Breeze," 169
*Sunflower*, 154
*Super Session* albums, 120, 123
*Surf's Up*, 153–54, 156
*Swan, The* (film), 6
*Sweet Baby James*, 110–11, 132, 151

"Takin' It to the Streets," 198
*Takin' It to the Streets*, 198
Talese, Gay, 45, 160
Talking Heads, 13, 203, 221, 249
Tannen, Mike, 190–91
Tate, Sharon, 118n
Tausch, Eleanor, 186
Taylor, Derek, 84–85, 108
Taylor, Irving, 21
Taylor, James, 12–13, 53, 105–6, 109–11, 117, 132, 145, 151, 153, 171, 187–90
Taylor, Joan, 161, 167
"Teenager's Romance, A," 44
*Teen Beat* (magazine), 103
Tegan and Sara, 245
Television, 196, 203
Templeman, Ted, 74, 135, 149, 160, 164, 188
*Tempo* (tip sheet), 61
"Tennessee Waltz," 26
Tex, Joe, 119
"That's Life," 51–52
*Their Greatest Hits* (Eagles), 197n
Them, 87
*Themes from Great Foreign Films*, 47–48
*Then Play On*, 181
"Third Stone from the Sun," 71
"This Masquerade," 199
*This Was*, 101
Thrasher, Ed, 173–74, 179–80
*Thriller*, 197n
Thyret, Russ, 159–60, 168, 172, 178, 182, 210–11, 215, 242–45
Tikis (*later* Harper's Bizarre), 61, 74, 77–78, 140
*Time* (magazine), 10, 151, 188
"Times They Are A-Changin', The," 60
Time Warner, 233–36, 239, 244
Tiny Tim, 80, 97, 131, 149
"Tip-Toe Thru the Tulips with Me," 131
"Tired of Waiting for You," 58

Titelman, Russ, 148–49, 164–65, 188, 212–13, 216
Tommy Boy Records, 232
Toots and the Maytals, 204
*Tops of the Pops*, 25
Toscanini, Arturo, 5
"To Sir with Love," 2
*Toulouse Street*, 141
Tower of Power, 174, 177
Track Records, 70
Tracy, Spencer, 39
Traffic, 120
Traveling Wilburys, 226
Travers, Mary, 35, 37–38, 154
Trower, Robin, 203
*Tru Blue*, 225
"Truckin'," 151
Tucker, Ken, 216–17
Tucker, Marshall, Band, 203
Tucker, Moe, 163
Turner, Big Joe, 88
Turner, Ike and Tina, 217
*Tusk*, 208n, 219
"Tusk" (music video), 219
TV Mama, 136–38
"Twist, The," 49
*200 Motels* (film), 143
Twombly, Cy, 248

U2, 12, 210, 219, 228, 232
"Uncle John's Band," 149–51
"Under the Bridge," 233
Universal Pictures, 201
*Unplugged*, 231

Van Halen, 13, 207, 220, 225, 232
Vanilla Fudge, 90
*Variety*, 81, 99
Velvet Underground, 163, 164, 204
Verve Records (*formerly* Clef), 4, 40–46, 55, 73, 117, 126
Vicious, Sid, 202–3
"Video Killed the Radio Star," 219
Village People, 204
*Village Voice* (newspaper), 104
"Vine Street," 3, 250
Vitaphonic, 26
*Vogue*, 132
Vogue Records, 58
Voorheis, Brian, 121

Wadleigh, Michael, 116
*Wall, The*, 197
Walsh, Joe, 207
"Wanderer, The," 49
"Warm Ways," 182
Warner, Albert, 22
Warner, Harry, 22
Warner, Jack, 4, 22–25, 31–32, 51–52, 56–57, 65, 87–88, 90, 126, 128, 154, 207
Warner, Sam, 22
Warner Bros. Music Show, 174–76
Warner Bros. Pictures, 22–23, 31, 52, 62, 87, 88–89, 116, 126–27, 163, 223
Warner Bros. Television, 24, 26–27
Warner Bros. (Warner-Reprise) Records. *See also* Ostin, Mo; Reprise Records; *and specific albums; associated labels; groups; individuals; and songs*
   Kinney merger and, 127–28
   Reprise merger and, 4, 51–52, 54–56
   Seven Arts merger and, 88
Warner Cable, 218
Warner Communications Inc., 156, 217, 219, 221–23
Warner-Electra-Atlantic (WEA), 185
   distribution network, 156–57, 185–87, 203–4, 210
   International, 235–36
Warner Music Group, 211, 232, 234–38, 244
Warner Music–U.S., 238–39
Warner Record Group, 221
Waronker, Lenny, 2–3, 6–9, 11–12, 14–18, 74–80, 92, 101, 132–33, 140, 148–49, 164–65, 187–88, 210–16, 223–32, 237–44, 250
Waronker, Simon, 75
Warwick, Dionne, 61
Waters, Muddy, 162
Watts 103rd Street Rhythm Band, 109, 132
Watts, Alan, 74
Watts, Charlie, 86
*Wax Paper* (newsletter), 211
WBAI-FM, 80
Weaver, Ken, 79
Webb, Jack, 24–25
Weir, Bob, 150
Weiss, Nat, 189
Welch, Bob, 109, 181
Welch, Ken, 30
Welch, Mitzi, 30

Welk, Lawrence, 7
Wells, Cynthia Sue, 164
Wenner, Jann, 121, 124
West, Ed, 27–28
West Coast Pop Art Experimental Band, 109
"Wet Dream," 79
Wexler, Jerry, 70, 79, 89–91, 154, 191–94
Whalley, Tom, 244
Wham of Sam, The, 47
"What a Fool Believes," 208
What's Happening! (documentary), 56–57
What's Welsh for Zen (Cale), 163
"When Doves Cry" (music video), 223–24
White, Jack, 29
White Light/White Heat, 163
"Whiter Shade of Pale," 84
Whitfield, Norman, 200–201
Who, 70–71, 220
WIBG-AM, 139
Wickham, Andy, 83, 85–87, 105, 132, 148, 164
Wickwire, Alison, 108
Wiki Bird (WCI jet), 171–72, 189
Wild, David, 104
Wilderness Road, 109
Wildflowers, 226
Wilson, Brian, 2, 5, 7, 164
Wilson, Dennis, 118n
"Win a Fug Dream Date" contest, 103
"Windy," 2
Winner, Langdon, 121–24, 144
Winwood, Steve, 120
Witherspoon, Jimmy, 47
Wizard of Oz, The (film), 126
WMEX, 36

"Woe-Is-Uh-Me-Bop," 143
Wolfe, Murray, 49
Wonder, Stevie, 61, 197
"Woodstock," 116
Woodstock (documentary), 116
Woodstock Music and Art Fair, 115–16, 119
Workingman's Dead, 132, 149–51, 155
"Wreck of the Edmund Fitzgerald, The," 198
Wright, Charles, 109, 132
Wright, Wil, 94

X-15 and Other Sounds, The, 47

Yardbirds, 90, 119–20
Yarrow, Peter, 35, 37–38
"Yesterday," 69
Yetnikoff, Walter, 187–91
"YMCA," 204
York, Linda, 183
"You Light Up My Life," 205–6, 229
Young, Charles, 144
Young, Jesse Colin, 199
Young, Neil, 12–13, 76, 87, 96, 105, 109, 118n, 132, 157, 167, 199, 207, 232, 242
Youngbloods, 199
"Young Love," 24–25
"You Really Got Me," 57–58

Zabriskie Point (film), 118
Zanes, Warren, 151, 160
Zappa, Frank, 17, 80, 87, 93, 109, 113, 135, 143, 153, 204
Zevon, Warren, 196, 207
Zukor, 87
ZZ Top, 13, 225

## ABOUT THE AUTHOR

**Peter Ames Carlin** is a writer and the bestselling author of several books, including *Homeward Bound: The Life of Paul Simon* and *Bruce*, the biography of Bruce Springsteen. Carlin has also been a freelance journalist, a senior writer at *People* in New York City, and a television columnist at the *Oregonian* in Portland. A regular speaker on music, writing, and popular culture, Carlin lives in Portland, Oregon.